Crime and Control in Comparative Perspectives

Crime and Control in Comparative Perspectives

Editors
Hans-Günther Heiland · Louise I. Shelley ·
Hisao Katoh

Walter de Gruyter · Berlin · New York 1992

Dr. Hans-Günther Heiland
Akademischer Mitarbeiter, Fachbereich 8/Soziologie der Universität Bremen, Bremen, Germany

Louise I. Shelley
Professor and Chair, Department of Justice, Law and Society, The American University, Washington, D.C. 20016, U.S.A.

Dr. Hisao Katoh
Professor of Criminal Law and Criminology at Keio University, Tokyo, Japan

With 18 figures and 48 tables

⊛ Printed on acid-free paper which falls within the guidelines of the ANSI to ensure permanence and durability

Library of Congress Cataloging-in-Publication Data

Crime and control in comparative perspectives / editors, Hans-Günther Heiland, Louise I. Shelley. Hisao Katōh.
p. cm.
Includes bibliographical references and index.
ISBN 3-11-012614-1 (U.S.)
1. Criminology – Cross-cultural studies. I. Hans-Günther, Heiland, 1951– II. Shelley. Louise I. III. Katō, Hisao, 1942–
HV6028.C69 1991
364–dc20 91-32813
CIP

Die Deutsche Bibliothek – Cataloging-in-Publication Data

Crime and control in comparative perspectives / ed. Hans-Günther Heiland ... – Berlin ; New York : de Gruyter, 1991
ISBN 3-11-012614-1
NE: Heiland, Hans-Günther [Hrsg.]

Typesetting: Knipp Textverarbeitungen, Wetter –
Printing: Ratzlow Druck, Berlin. – Binding: D. Mikolai, Berlin. –
Cover Design: Johannes Rother, Berlin. – Printed in Germany.

Preface

Some of the contributions to this anthology were conceived in a working-group at the "Comparative Analysis of Development of Delinquency and Criminal Justice", which conferred, under the direction of Hans-Günther Heiland and Hisao Katoh, at the 10th International Congress on Criminology in September 1988 in Hamburg. The idea originated with Hans Haferkamp and Hans-Günther Heiland. Unfortunately, because of Haferkamp's sudden death in June 1987, he was not able to implement his plans or lead the working-group. Hans-Günther Heiland and Hisao Katoh took Hans Haferkamp's ideas and worked out an attractive programme. The contributions by Hyacinthe Ellis, Louise Shelley, Hisao Katoh, Matti Joutsen and Lothar Reuter are revised and expanded versions of their lectures at the Hamburg meeting.

Professor Reuter's presentation was the only one from a socialist country. Louise Shelley suggested that we collect further contributions from socialist countries in order to compare the development of crime and social control in different cultures and economic systems. The publishers would like to take this opportunity to thank Katalin Gönczöl, He Bingsong, Olufunmilayo Oloruntimehin, Christopher Birkbeck, and R.S. Shrivastava for contributing to this anthology at such short notice. These articles have been expanded upon by an essay by Hans-Günther Heiland and an article by Hans Haferkamp and Hyacinthe Ellis. Haferkamp and Ellis originally intended to present their paper to the XI World Congress on Sociology in India 1986.

It must not be forgotten that the publishing of this anthology coincides with far-reaching changes in Eastern European countries. The contribution by Lothar Reuter is concerned with the developments in crime and control before the fall of the "Iron Curtain". His article is an historical document. At the time of its writing, the failed development and contradictions in his country could not be discussed. Only the official State version which reflected a social reality which was only part of the real truth could be presented.

When choosing the contributions, we did not seek a unified theoretical explanation. Rather, we placed much more importance upon diversity in the explanatory perspectives and in obtaining an interdisciplinary outlook.

Obviously, it was not the aim of this book to develop a systematic theory of the development of crime and control in differing societies. The introduction by Hans-Günther Heiland and Louise Shelley and the team effort by Hans Haferkamp and Hyacinthe Ellis are, however, first steps in formulating a comprehensive declaration. This anthology can only point out the lack of a comprehensive description, and how difficult such an undertaking would be.

Striving for statements and explanations about the total dimension of crime and society's reaction to crime is part of the tradition of criminology. If this is to be one of the main aims of criminology, it will be impossible to achieve this objective without exploring the causes and reasons for the development of the phenomenon in different social, political and cultural contexts. Criminology must find answers to questions such as: What kinds of crime comprise the total crime picture and what affects the dynamics of the individual offenses? Can we say whether the total size of crime in a country is rising or falling, simply by taking registered crimes and the estimated number of unknown cases into account? How does society react to developments in delinquency? What can we say are the reasons and causes for the change in total crime phenomenon? Are penal sanctions expanding or are they shrinking? What are the special features of the modern forms of crime and modern forms of penal sanctions?

The focal point of our analysis has been the total level of a society's crime and society's reaction to delinquency. Special attention has been paid to an analysis of 'Crime and Penal Sanctions'. Each explanation can only be convincing when it is not designed only for certain countries (e.g. Japan or the USA) but drawn up comparatively. These comparisons reflect differences and changes in delinquency and punitive sanctions across societies attributable to different causes. The explanation gains in persuasiveness if it includes countries with different structures that are analyzed systematically. This is the reason why we deliberately selected a variety of different countries.

Even though a systematic theoretical analysis is not at the forefront of this anthology, we still want to lay the foundations for such an analysis. Above all we intend to give new impetus to the debate concerning the development of modern forms of delinquency and social reaction to them.

While making our preparation, we challenged the authors with two theses concerning the development of crime and forms of control. We also presented specially formulated questions. Some of these contributors have dealt with these questions implicitly, wheras others have addressed these questions explicitly. First, from the view of observers living in highly industrialized countries, the new delinquency can be described as a move away from general discipline, a denial of the standards of civilized behaviour, and of norms and aims based on consensus. Attacks on the property and capital of others normally concern individuals only indirectly. It is the large anonymous social units such as insurance companies, trading companies and department stores which are directly involved.

This first hypothesis is based on the dominance of offenses against property (such as larceny, burglary, fraud) in Western societies. It has been deliberately formulated in a provocative manner and from the view-point of Western societies. If we consider them individually, can we say that forms of delinquency can be interpretated as a decrease in dicipline and civilized behaviour? Do modern forms of criminality express a tendency towards an increase in free and uncontrolled acts? Is it a characteristic of modern society to move from the individual as a victim towards larger, anonymous victims, such as insurance companies, trading companies and department stores?

Second, modern forms of delinquency are set against a sentencing policy which in a catch phrase could be labelled mitigation of sanctions and the waiving of punishments. Characteristics of this policy are decriminalization, failure to report offenses, decline in offense clearance rates, an increase in dropping of prosecutions, the imposition of lightest possible sentences, and the institutionalization of diversion programs. The new forms of sanctions are no longer characterized by general re-internalization of norms and aims, but by personalized, restitutional sanctions which allow the parties involved greater freedom of activity. Are there tendencies which lead to the restraint of sanctions, and if so, how are these trends illustrated? Is the waiving of sanctions a change common to penal policies in modern society? Which are the cases where the omission of sanctioning is common? How is society affected by the omission of sanctioning, the imposition of milder sentences and the increase of restitution? On the whole, how can we judge the function of substitutes for prison sentences? How important is the death penalty for society today? Are there tendencies which lead to the restraint of sanctions, and if so, how are these trends illustrated? Is it possible to interpret the development in sanctioning as a tendency towards more tolerance/leniency or severity/repression? Does the interpretation change with time? What are the causes or reasons for this development? In which phases of social development (social/economical) do sanctions become more severe and when are they applied more leniently? Are lenient sentences or informal measures of social control less drastic measures of social repression? What significance does the personalisation of sanctions have for society? Do the efforts of probation officers, the addition of prison staff to treat and care for prisoners, treatment, the use of social workers and of personal mediators in agreements between the offender and the victim make a difference? How are these developments to be rated and how are they to be explained? In which fields do increased penalties occur? How does economic change contribute to the changes in criminality and sanctions? What correlation exists between the development of punishments and of crime rates? Can the concommitant rise of crime rates together with a fall in discipline be explained by the diminution of social control and more lenient sentencing practices or is there another meaning? Do the waiving of sanctions, lighter sentencing and restitution, have the same meaning as civilizing social control?

How is one to explain the increasing lack of discipline and the lack of civilized behaviour of the offenders, on the one hand, and the growing caution, personalization, and individualization of the bodies of social control? Are these tendencies common features exclusive to welfare societies or are there similar or totally different developments within other societies? It may even be that welfare societies do not show these tendencies at all. Are the numerous references to modernity or development sufficient as explanations? The rising crime rate is not a common feature of all modern societies, no more than the waiving of sanctions, mitigation of sentences, treatment and diversion are universal characteristics of societies.

We have raised many questions, only a few of which will be answered in the following articles. This is not a shortcoming but the beginning of a productive debate about modern forms of crime and social control.

We have to thank Britta Kurz and Andrea Stechel for typing the manuscript and Monika Snieges and Werner Schulte for their assistance in preparing tables and figures. Anja and Paul McCallion deserve more than a mention of their assistance with translations.

Finally, thanks are due to all the contributors for producing this material so efficiently and delivering it so promptly.

We dedicate this publication to the memory of Hans Haferkamp, whose idea it first was but who did not, alas, live to see it fulfilled.

Hans-Günther Heiland
Louise Shelley
Hisao Katoh

Contents

Civilization, Modernization and the Development of Crime and Control

Hans-Günther Heiland
Louise Shelley

1 Introduction

There have been very few explanatory models in criminology to describe and analyse the long term structural changes in crime and crime control. Whereas sociological theory has often been split between Durkheimian and Marxian explanations of social development, such larger theoretical explanations have rarely been part of criminology. The discipline has generally focused on smaller scale studies of the crime phenomenon rather than the historical and cross-cultural analyses that are necessary for the construction and application of theory.

The book evaluates the evolution of criminal behaviour and social control in the last three decades in a diverse group of countries. It analyses these developments in terms of two competing paradigms: those of modernization and civilization. Both of these perspectives attempt to analyse the evolution of crime in response to larger social processes and to examine the way in which the state has chosen to officially respond to violations of law. The analysis, therefore, examines the crime phenomenon in terms of external forces as well as the policy choices made by governments.

Modernization theory has been applied to the analysis of crime by several scholars including one of the editors of this collection. Tobias (1967) described the effects of early industrialization and showed its long lasting influence on the development of crime and social control. Shelley (1981) examined the impact of urbanization and industrialization using a modernization perspective. Although she did not take a uni-dimensional perspective and indicated the complexity of the connections between social change processes and patterns of crime (p. xvi), she was criticized for overestimating the influence of industrialization and urbanization. But this analytical perspective has many limitations which Shelley acknowledged (1986) when she reconsidered the weaknesses of a modernization perspective. One of the main weaknesses is the fact that many countries in the world have industrialized and urbanized but have not really modernized. The applicability of the modernization perspective has been considered in this collection but each essay has also focused on a competing explanation – the concept of civilization.

The applicability of the civilization concept was raised by van Dijk (1989) at the criminological debates at the 10th International Congress on Criminology. Using the Elias concept of civilization, he tried to coordinate discussions of the crisis in punishment with the abolitionist debate presently raging primarily in Europe. The application of this concept permits us to understand whether there is a common process of legal development which leads to processes of humanization and liberalization. It suggests that state policy has changed in the post-World War II period as a result of direct state decisions. In this respect, crime and the criminal reactions are not some unavoidable process but a transformation that the society can help direct or influence.

2 Civilization and Modernization – Two Paradigms to Describe Long Term Changes in Crime and Control

2.1 The Civilization Concept

The subject of N. Elias' Civilization Theory (1982) is the link between the long-term structural change and the alteration of personality structures. He sees this process of change occurring at different levels, all of which are interdependent. Two central arguments of Elias' theory are most useful to the analysis of crime and social control.

The first micro-sociological argument posited by Elias deals with changes in the personality structure from pre-modern to modern society. By analyzing changes in standards of conduct among the aristocracy from the 9th to the 18th century, Elias ascertained that there was an ever increasing refinement of customs and manners, an obvious pacification of the conditions of daily life and an intensification of instinctive and affected inhibitions. According to Kuzmics (1988, p. 152f), the civilization process covers the "Psychologization and Rationalization of the Affection".

These social changes are not explicable without considering the macro structural framework. The second Elias argument focuses on the institutions (i.e., the emergent state monopoly of power, the capitalist production system), which during the civilization process became increasingly dominant and influential in the the formation of social structures. Elias cites three larger societal factors crucial to the development of greater individual control. They are: the monopolization of the instruments of power, the centralization of state power, and the creation of a power monopoly. Modern society is not characterized by unrestrained instincts, moods and behaviours, but rather the taming of these forms of conduct. Only control of behaviour opens the possibility for the different deployment of opportunities in relatively peaceful situations. Wherever freedom of the individual does not circumscribe freedom for others, real possibilities for individual creative action arise.

Limitations on individual behaviour can only find equilibrium when they are part of a relatively stable and easily comprehensible arrangement of actions by the broader society. Such a situation occurs when there is a monopoly of social institutions. This provides a guarantee for fields of social activity, free from acts of violence, thereby permitting individual activity to develop and flourish.

Elias not only fuses the civilization of societies with a central accumulation of power, but he also posits that the change in the process of social control is closely connected to the monopolization of social opportunities. The extent to which individual action is transformed is determined by how successfully outside compulsion is transformed into personal self-constraint.

According to Elias' key hypothesis, in the pre-modern age sanctions controlled individual actions by external controls. But with the development of civilization, controls are slowly shifting inward. Therefore, the impact of sanctions is increasingly not the result of external pressures but the consequence of self-control of individual members of society.

"Whatever particular differences there might be among different societies, the overall direction of the change is the same, towards a more or less automatic self-control, to the subordination of short term impulses to the commands of an ingrained long term view, and to the formation of a more complex and secure "Superego Agency" (see von Krieken 1989, p. 200; Elias 1982, p. 248 f).

The process of civilizing is evident in the transformation of law and legal institutions. This should be apparent in the legislative process and the system of administration of justice. Along with the development of civilization in the western context, comes the decriminalization of the penal law, greater tolerance of deviant behaviour, the reduction of lengthy periods of imprisonment, fewer sanctions and the creation of prison alternatives.

The internalization of controls changes individuals' relations to themselves, a point emphasized by von Ferber (1984, p. 110). Individuals who are highly capable of self-restraint in the public sphere are those who know how to anticipate the expected, and fear external sanctions. Anticipating the behaviour of others leads to enhanced sensitivity in specific situations. To link changes in interpersonal relations and individual conduct with the differentiation of social institutions and the process of the state monopolization of violence provides a completely new explanatory perspective on criminology. This analytical perspective makes it possible to examine the types and levels of sanctions imposed by a society as a measure of civilization. As van Dijk explains, "the basic idea, however, that the nature of a society's policy on crime reflects its level of civilization is not dated at all" (p. 201).

We believe there is another noteworthy point central to the assessment of the changes in social control and patterns of crime control. Kuzmics (1990, p. 228f) points out correctly, that during the process of change from external to internal constraints, individuals still experience self-restraint and expect similar conduct from other members of society. The external, formal methods of control recede in importance and there is reduced differentiation in sanctioning. But this diminution in the severity of punishment opens the possibility for greater alternative sanctions that rely less on physical force and more on self-discipline and technology. "In this perspective", writes van Dijk (p. 199), "the criminal justice system and forms of informal social control between citizens are two sides of the same coin: both are civilized alternatives to the use of physical force by individuals".

Civilized societies are those which can create a variety of penal sanctions that encompass a range of possibilities from punitive to therapeutic, reactive to preventive, direct to indirect, general to differentiated. This range of strategies reflects a civilized society that enjoys a concentration of power and the control of technology enjoyed by a modern society. In this political context, repression is no longer emphasized. Rather, the focus is on treatment and preventive social, education and health policies. But such societies are placing ever increasing demands on their citizens to be responsible, self-disciplined individuals. The focus must be on developing the internal norms needed to ensure self-restraint rather than on the development of negative sanctions. Individual deviation is held in check by the individual rather than through societal proscriptions and external constraints.

The civilization process is not the only way in which societal objectives and controls are changed, but it appears to be a very important factor in explaining the development of criminality and of penal sanctions, particularly in Western European society. If Elias' hypothesis is correct that interpersonal relations change with the civilization of society, then so should the nature of interpersonal violence and crime. Important indicators of this process of civilization would be a decline in violent crimes and an increase in self-inflicted harm (i.e., drugs) on individuals.

Processes of civilizing by no means only mean the way in which control and aims are changed. Important changes in the patterns of crime should also be made apparent. If it is correct that the relations towards violence among people, within the development of the civilizing process, change, then this changed relationship should also be identifiable within the patterns of action. A fall in violent cases and an increase in damages concerning individuals (as e.g., through drugs) would be indicators of effective civilizing processes.

2.2 The Modernization Concept

The modernization concept, like the civilization concept, analyses the process of societal transformation. This process, which has occurred in many societies, runs in phases and many sectors of society pay a high price for its occurrence. The modernization process occurs as a progression of demographic, economic, and technological changes. To many observers, it seems to solve or reduce seemingly unsolvable social and political problems of the pre-modern, or traditional society (see Flora 1974). But modernization not only has a problem - solving effect, but also deepens many existing social problems and creates many in newly overcrowded cities. The enormous increase in crime for example, and its high level of importance in current analyses, could also be seen as proof of this (see Durkheim 1977).

The phenomenon of modernization has occured not only in Europe, but in many societies where the forces associated with modernization, industrialization and urbanization have not resulted in more modern societies. Instead, they have produced countries in which some sectors of society are living in an advanced, modern country while the majority of the population is left behind in this development process. This is the case in many of the so-called developing countries.

Even if there is no generally valid definition of modernization, there is a generally shared view that modernization stands for the processes of cultural, political and economic development. Modernization is a continually developing process of structural differentiation, combined with an increase in the complexity of the norms of social organisation. A decisive stimulus for the modernization of societies (their structures, their legal and political institutions, their cultural basis, and their forms of awareness) is ecologically technological progress (Levy 1966). Other social scientific approaches place more emphasis upon social and cultural development in economic or religious areas (e.g., Weber 1920). Besides these more global descriptions and analyses of momentous modernizing processes, it is also possible to analyse single elements of this societal change separately, as well as in the interdependent relationship among the elements. The ecological and social processes of modernization have received disproportionate attention. It has been graphically shown the modernization does not always lead to more contentment and harmony. Rather, enhanced social tensions, conflicts, and societal disharmony are the results of social differentiation, the growing number of life choices, and the relative deprivation that accompanies the modernization process.

The influence of urbanization and industrialization processes on social behaviour has aroused considerable interest among those concerned with crime. The books by Shelley, Tobias and Zehr are particularly noteworthy examples of theoretical analyses of modernization.

The modernization concept has great explanatory powers because it permits a multi-dimensional model. To analyse the process of modernization, it is possible to combine empirically verifiable data along with historical and ethnographic description. Shelley attempts to make this point in the epilogue of her book.

Examining crime and crime-control from the modernization perspective does not focus on societal transformation as a consistent process. Rather, it focuses on the confusion, the relapses, and the regional differences in modernization. It suggests that modernization proceeds at different rates and in some areas or subcultures, it many be only a very partial process. Many societies do not completely modernize but retain elements of traditional and pre-modern societies. In former colonies, the traditions of the pre-colonial past merge with those of the colonial power. The norms that emerge may reflect the adaptation of those of the colonial power rather than the modernization of the legal system.

With modernization, a shift occurs in the relationship among forms of criminal behaviour. Violent offenses become relatively less important as property offenses achieve pre-eminence. In modernized societies, crimes against property become the dominant form of crime.

Modernization leads not only to changes in forms and patterns of crime but also to changed rates of crime. A general characteristic of the modernizing process is the increase in the total rate of crime and, in particular, an increase in the frequency of crimes against property. The causes of crime also change.

Taking an historical perspective, we find at the beginning of the modernization process a close link between poverty and crime. As the population becomes more satisfied and their existence becomes more secure, a marked evolution in crime patterns occurs. As modernization proceeds, inequality still exists (e.g., income, distribution of wealth), the crime pattern begins to change from crimes typical of poverty to crimes common to the affluent society. Many property crimes are not caused by societal or individual crises such as unemployment or illness, but by wealth and the abundance of goods. Theft, fraud and robbery take place no matter what the economic and social conditions of society. But an important change occurs in the object of criminal acts in modern affluent societies. No longer are single persons and groups of people the only victims of criminal acts; instead, we find that large organizations such as insurance companies are victims of criminal activity. But these large corporations, which are often economic monopolies, are themselves perpetrators of offenses (e.g., environmental crimes). The most decisive factor here is the change in the status of the offenders. No longer are offenders exclusively lower class, but members of the middle and upper classes. As a result of this expanding criminal population, a rise in crime can continually be observed.

3 Civilizing and Modernizing: Concerning the Exploratory Power of Two Paradigms

Examining the complementary and sometimes contradictory concepts of civilization and modernization led us to important assumptions concerning the development of crime and social control. In the following section, we will analyse these hypotheses by examining the insights provided by the case studies contained in this anthology.

3.1 Civilizing and Modernizing and Their Impact on Crime and Control in Developed Societies

The paradigm of civilization claims that two substantial change processes have occurred. First, civilizing has altered interpersonal relations and individual standards of conduct. It has altered the attitude towards the use of violence against others. The theory of civilization as well as the concept of modernization, both expect a structural change in the forms and patterns of crime, as well as an increase in the level of crime. Examining the contributions to this volume confirms the validity of the expectations of these theories.

A quick look at the contributions by Heiland, Joutsen, Katoh and Shelley[1], is sufficient to show that since World War II, crime in Western Europe, the USA and Japan has developed very differently. Crime has

1 The contributions to this anthology by the authors named are meant, unless otherwise stated.

increased in frequency in the Nordic countries (Denmark, Norway, Sweden and Finland) and in the Federal Republic of Germany. But in comparison to the above countries, the rise in the USA has been much stronger. A high degree of stability, however, is shown in the frequency of registered crime in Japan.

If one examines individual forms of crime, the picture remains consistent. Taking a long-term perspective, crime against property has become the dominant crime pattern. This is true for all the countries analysed, even including Japan. Joutsen, Katoh, and Shelley see this development as closely related to the urbanization and industrialization of societies. The long-term assessment of crime trends also reveals that the proportionate contribution of violent cases has declined. The only exception among these is the United States.

In the Federal Republic of Germany, the proportion of violent cases lies between 6 and 7 percent, a much lower share than in the USA. A contrasting trend can, however, be observed within the index of violence. While the total index of fatalities is almost stable, cases against personal freedom and self-determination are on the rise.

Of all the Nordic countries, Finland has the highest level of violence. In the 1960's, the assault rate made a tremendous upward leap. In the 1970's, an increase in the homicide rate was observed. The level of violence in Norway and Denmark is distinctly lower than in Finland. Sweden on the other hand lies in the middle. The proportional contribution of violent crime in these countries lies well under that of the USA.

In the 1980's, violent crime declined in Japan. In 1984, the homicide rate was 1.5 and in 1987 1.3, compared to the USA (1984: 7.9; 1987: 8.3) and the Federal Republic of Germany (1984: 4.5; 1987: 4.3). "The 5-year average for the years 1981-1985 was 4.0 homicides per 100,000 inhabitants (15-67 years) in Finland, compared to 1.7-1.8 in Denmark, Norway and Sweden" (see von Hofer 1988, p. 13).

Let us turn once more to the subject of crimes against property. This category of criminality causes all countries their problems. Since World War II, crimes against property have increased drastically in all the developed nations (including Japan).

Cases of crimes against property are the dominant crime pattern in developed societies. They amount to more than 60 percent of all registered criminal acts. All the contributors are in agreement concerning the increasing importance of larceny crimes. A disproportionate rate of growth is recorded in two categories of theft: thefts of or from motor vehicles or bicycles; thefts from shops/department stores.

While Shelley and Joutsen see the expansion of opportunities for crime as being the main reason for the increase of these offenses in their countries, Heiland was able to show that typical cases (of automobile or motor-cycle theft) in the Federal Republic of Germany are not neccessarily connected with an expansion of opportunities. His interpretation for increased frequency of larceny cases, lies in existing or newly formed inequalities, which have not been removed by the process of modernization. They are, therefore, unintended consequences of the modernization process.

Two other important developments need to be emphasized. They are the increase in armed robberies and in crimes involving narcotics.

Narcotics cases do not only play an important role in the way society views them, but rather we can assume that since the 1960's the observed rise in narcotics cases is due to the increase in the use of narcotics. According to Shelley, the rise in the consumption of narcotics is closely linked to the almost parallel increase in armed robberies. Narcotics use leads to an accumulation of problems. The need to find money to purchase drugs leads to robberies, break-ins, and thefts.

Similar problems can be found in western European countries, although the situation is not as dramatic as that described in the United States. Japan is not exempt from narcotics problems, although there are distinctive interesting cultural variations. Because of Japan's insularity, the narcotics market is less accessible. In place of hard drugs like heroin, amphetamines and "sniff" products are consumed. These are largely manufactured inside the country and distributed by the local Mafia.

There is less uniformity in the development of punishment than of crime. For many years of the post World War II period, the Federal Republic of Germany followed a process consistent with the civilization theory. For many years, the criminal law became less restrictive as there were limits placed on the State's power monopoly in order to preserve a high level of freedom and rights for the individual. But the present development contradicts the civilization theory because penalties have increased and criminal law proceedings have been tightened to fight terrorism. Haferkamp/Ellis present this finding in their comprehensive contribution, "Trends towards leniency", which not only refers to law reform, but also to trends in sanctioning. Indicative of these developments was the abolition of the death penalty and the closing penitentiaries, the reduction in the length of prison sentences, the expansion of suspended sentences, and fines.

In the Nordic countries we also observe a trend of greater tolerance towards criminal offenders and greater leniency in sanctions and their application. As evidence of this, Joutsen notes the application of minimal prison sentences and a reduction in the average length of prison sentences. Accompanying this trend is the growing use of noncustodial sanctions, e.g., suspended sentences, fine or day-fine, or community services. These are all clear examples of the increasing use of civilizing alternatives.

Such clear-cut tendencies cannot be found in the USA. Haferkamp/Ellis call the pattern of development in the USA a wave-movement. It oscillates around a long-term trend. The following trends are evidence of a substantial deviation from a reduction in penalties: 1) the reintroduction of the death penalty, 2) a rise in the prison population, 3) the introduction of retaliatory punishments, and 4) the renewed threat of penal punishment for certain forms of behaviour.

In addition, Shelley refers to the rise since 1971 in the number of prison inmates, of criminal justice employees, and of more punitive criminal policies. Another important factor in the level of social control is the rise in the number of security staff employed by private companies. It would be presumptuous to suggest that the tendency towards civilization is absent in the USA. The developments which have been described here, however, show that it is possible to have serious deviations from this trend. This makes it evident how difficult it is to maintain the standards of a civilized society.

It is still surprising that in the USA, in spite of the society's high level of violence, short prison sentences are sometimes applied for offences of a serious nature. Suspended sentences and probation are widespread on a level which would be inconceivable for Western Europe. Shelley also refers to the improved legal position of detainees as a result of court actions. In Japan, as in the USA, the death penalty has not been abolished, though it is imposed and enforced with great restraint.

In comparison to Western European nations and the USA, Japan has a very low rate of imprisonment, but the punishments imposed are hard and degrading for the prisoners. Their rights are limited to a high degree and the observation of these rights is left to the discretion of the prison administration. In contrast to the total control inside institutions, there are less strong formal controls in day-to-day Japanese life. As Katoh writes, the Japanese criminal justice system including the police, is not harsh. Its punishments are mild and it is reasonably respectful of the procedural rights of the accused. The reason that the development of crime in Japan has remained almost stable over a long period of time, says Katoh, can be ascribed to the effectiveness of informal controls. The social organization of every day life in the domestic, neighbourhood and work settings, constitutes an extraordinarily powerful system of social control. They do much of the work which in Western European nations and the USA, is considered to be the work of the police. The second reason for the constant crime rates is that the criminal justice system, although not harsh, is nonetheless extremely effective. It is effective largely because Japanese citizens willingly cooperate with the system. In comparison, the Nordic countries, the Federal Republic of Germany and the USA show numerous forms of social control which are either operated by the state or closely connected to the centralized state power. In most of these societies there is a religious outlook that lets its members forgive and tolerate. But Japan, long a hierarchical society which valued subordinance to authority, has adopted more of the penal methods associated with the civilization process than either the United States or Western Europe.

3.2 Civilizing and Modernizing and Their Impact on Crime and Control in Developing Societies

Almost all the developing countries studies are of newly independent countries emerging from a period of colonialism. Jamaica, India, and Nigeria are all suffering from problems of political authority, a direct consequence of long-term colonial rule, which makes it difficult for them to maintain order and control crime. In many of these countries, there has not been consistent development. Nigeria and Venezuela benefitted from oil wealth in the early 1980's which ultimately did not last and proved very disruptive to these societies. There has not been development in several of these countries, but an active decline in living standards in recent years.

As in the developed societies, we find in developing societies a drift towards a higher rate of crime. The levels, forms and patterns differ notably from those of developed societies.

The individual country analyses included do not reveal disproportionately higher crime rates than in developed societies. But these societies perceive that they are facing a worsening crime problem. As Birkbeck's analysis of Venezuela shows, the representatives of the business world and politics feel threatened by such spectacular crimes as murder, kidnapping, and armed robbery. Although there are no precise data that supports a dramatic increase in crime in Venezuela, the spectacular crime cases are used as justification for expanding statutory definitions and strengthening controls over the population.

Jamaica is also identified as a country with a high level of crime. In this analysis, Ellis also shows that the crime level in Jamaica does not lie above that of developed societies. Jamaica's crime problem lies uniquely in its high level of violence. Ellis sees this high level as being a direct consequence of Jamaican independence and the problems of implementing a policy to create an egalitarian society. After independence, there was a problem of rising expectations. Political problems were presented by the failure to fulfill promises and to realize expectations.

In Jamaica, the disappointment of the citizenry occurred simultaneously with losses of authority by the government and the political parties. The continued existence of social problems and social differences, combined with loss of authority by the national elite, lead to growing deviant behaviour. The central themes of the Haferkamp/Ellis analysis were the connections among the waiving of sanctions, the reacquisition of power, and the loss of power by the ruling elite. Ellis stresses the fact that the development of violent crime in Jamaica is not connected with the process of modernization. This is correct in so far as Jamaica generally does not show the structural characteristics of a modern, developed society. The development of crime in Jamaica, as described here, however, is not contradictory to the conclusions of modernization theory. The hypothesis of modernization theory concerns structural change. These change processes must naturally be taken into consideration within the analyses.

Developing countries, like Jamaica, even though they have based their newly independent society on a philosophy of egalitarianism, do not have the financial resources needed to institutionalize a welfare state system. In this context, modernization is identified with the process of cultivating a national identity, defending the frontiers against outside attack, and the protection of the members of society against the deviant behaviour of others. But these structural features of modernization do not seem to be sufficiently anchored in society. This is especially clear in the introduction and application of liberalized penal legislation. They have only a symbolical status and a low lewel of relevance. This is why they could be not only changed at will but also depending on the situation, reversed. This experience also, occurred when the now developed societies started off on the road to modernizing.

India's situation is similar to Jamaica because they also had to deal with the legacy of colonial power. Modernistic elements were interlinked with Indian tradition. Under British rule, political unit was encouraged and this colonial legacy had an impact on independent India. The power conflict between the political centre and patrimonial rulers increases regional conflicts and raises the complexity of problem solving. Shrivastava sees the relatively high level of violence in Indian society as a result of the conditions introduced by the British. In its search for democratic structures, Indian society, which is neither oriented primarily towards western models nor founded entirely upon Indian tradition, is exposed to an increasing erosion of its moral and ethical standards. Unrestrained corruption and violence are indicators of this crisis. One might also make the point that India is only at the beginning of the modernization process. Traditional and modern elements are not yet free from conflict and do not harmonize with each other.

As in Jamaica, we can also observe decriminalization processes in India. Leading members of the business world and of Indian politics are themselves involved in criminal activity, and hence are highly ineffective in dealing with crime. The pervasive corruption and other forms of economic crime are sure signs of the modernization process.

Oloruntimehin directly links the modernization processes with the rise in crime. Industrialization and urbanization, linked with the population shift from rural to urban centres is characteristic of modernization in Nigeria, in which large areas of industry, trade, and administration have concentrated. These urban centres have become focal points for those parts of the population who live in either less industrialized or rural areas.

This leads to a mass population movement from rural to urban areas. The relative shortage of living-space, work and infrastructure in turn, leads to a significant deprivation for large groups of society. They can only survive in urban centers by means of criminal activity. Because of these discrepancies between wealth in the economic centres on the one hand, and the less industrialized agriculturally structured environment on the other, crime continues to grow.

Oloruntimehin sees the increase in crimes against property to be closely connected to the rapid industrialization of the state of Nigeria after the oil boom. The continuing industrialization of society leads furthermore to all manners and varieties of crime. Along with such traditional areas of criminal activity as the smuggling of goods and currencies, robbery and theft, there has been an increase in crimes against insurance companies. Fraud and banking frauds, coupled with many kinds of computer crimes, are also the result of modernization. Nigeria shows the distinctive crime patterns of modern, developing societies. Despite the similarities with developed societies, it should not be suggested that modernization in Nigeria has become a main structural characteristic of this society. The riches gained through wealth have not yet been invested extensively in social security systems, in education, or other parts of the infrastructure necessary for the creation of a modern society.

The development of crime as well as the development of control is part and parcel of these social processes. Societies whose economic and political elite are entangled in crime processes take only minor initiatives towards the creation of a legal order equally binding on all members of society.

In Venezuala, the increase in predatory crimes leads to extremely strong control of the poor neighbourhoods. In addition to this, by tightening the application of the vagrancy laws, persons considered potentially dangerous are held in prison without the chance of courtroom proceedings.

In India, the system of justice is so tightly linked with the economic and political elite that proceedings can be stopped or cancelled completely. The problems of criminal corruption in society exist as prominently in the law enforcement apparatus.

In Nigeria, long periods of detention prior to trial can be used for example, to force involuntary confessions or to keep undesirable persons in prison. Certain criminal cases can be hushed up and others can be resolved outside the formal justice system.

The developing societies studied maintain the death penalty. The death penalty has been retained as a deterrent punishment, especially for drug trafficking and armed robbery in Nigeria and Jamaica and for repeated violations of narcotic drugs and psychotropic drug offences in India. In Nigeria, lynch-law is applied for armed robbery, child stealing, and manslaughter. All of the above mentioned examples are in sharp contrast to the civilizing process.

These societies would, however, be perceived incorrectly if their attempts at civilizing their justice systems were not taken into consideration. Even though the death penalty has been retained, it is practiced in a more restrained manner. In India, for example, murder is no longer always punished by the death penalty. Also, in cases where the accused has been detained in prison awaiting trial for longer than two years, life sentences are given in place of the death penalty. In Nigeria, the death penalty for drug trafficking was abolished in 1986.

Even though the introduction of probation in Venezuela, the application of less severe punishments for cases of bodily harm in Jamaica and an increase in the application of fines have taken place in India and Nigeria. The picture remains that in developing societies civilizing alternatives are being used less. The strong punitive character of criminal policies, the continuing lack of rights of the accused during criminal proceedings, the long periods of imprisonment prior to trial and the sometimes inhumane conditions in prisons, are by far too pervasive. Apart from the above differences, there are, however, some surprising similarities between developed and developing societies. The debate concerning the responsibility of the multi-national company, Union Carbide, in Bhopal, India, shows clearly how modernizing processes produce similar normative concepts in differing cultures. Similarities in the conceptions of "morals", "morality" and "law" can be detected. Normative behavioural expectations are increasingly directed towards organisations and not individuals. With the process of modernization, individual welfare increasingly depends on large organizations than individuals. This means that individuals are placing greater pressure on collective bodies to abide by legal norms.

3.3 Civilizing and Modernizing and Their Impact on Crime and Control in Socialist Nations

Socialist societies have claimed a low crime rate. But these claims to lower criminality have become increasingly difficult to make in recent years as the political authority of these countries has declined and social disorder has grown. All this has occurred despite highly structured apparati of social control.

The ideological commitment to Marxism which stated that crime would wither away under communism has forced socialist societies to claim that their crime has been disappearing. According to their ideology, crime is extricably linked to capitalist society.

The socialist countries examined come from two different cultures: European and Asian. It is important to note that the discussions of the crime problem in Hungary, the GDR, and China are dominated by the ideological perspective of the societies rather than the cultural differences. Scholars from both China and the GDR noted the decline in crime after the consolidation of the socialist system. In Hungary too, after World War II, the level of crime was also well below what it was before the war broke out. During the 1960's, crime rates were at a level of 119,000 cases per year. But a drastic and continual increase in crime occurred from 1979 onwards. This growth may possibly explained by Haferkamp's theory on declining political authority and increased criminality. Because the waning authority of the Socialist system was evident earlier in Hungary than elsewhere in Eastern Europe. These drastic increases did not occur in the GDR. Reuter explains that the 1987 amnesty is the sole reason for the increases in that year.

Even if the level of crime in Socialist countries does not reach that of developed countries, it is clear that crime patterns are very similar. In Socialist countries, property crimes represent over 50 percent of all crime. The level of violence is low in the GDR. Many violent offences, such as armed robbery and other similar serious crimes, are virtually unknown. Narcotics crimes, as well as economic crimes, do not constitute grave social problems. Crime in the GDR is based on minor thefts and frauds. Sex offences, cases of bodily injury, crimes against public order and general security, planned and organized serious crimes against state-owned national property are, however, all of importance.

Bingsong was able to observe a drastic increase in the level of violence in China, only after the open-door policy was introduced. He also makes reference in his investigation to the patterns of smuggling, gambling, black marketeering and illegal speculation. These crimes are all evidence of the serious economic problems of Chinese society, mainly linked to the socialist economy. Furthermore, public servants at the local, provincial, and central levels are involved in large-scale embezzlement schemes. Such forms of crimes, as organized prostitution and the use of drugs, long thought to have been overcome, are returning. With the end of the 1970's we can observe increases in serious crime in Hungary, too. Economic crimes (e.g., bribery, fraud, corruption) appear frequently. These increases are evidence of the burgeoning second economy which became increasingly dominant in Hungarian society. In Hungary, as in China, the black market has undermined the foundations of the socialist economy. Bingsong and Gönczöl see the increases and changes in the forms and patterns of crime as being closely associated with the urbanization and industrialization of their societies. The transition towards the modernized society led to instability and to inequalities between rural and urban areas, discrepancies between supply and demand, and pretensions and reality. One of the main reasons for the continuing rise of crime in China and Hungary is poverty, something which modernization has not been able to eradicate. Bingsong's assertions show clearly that China has developed into a sharply stratified class society.

According to Reuter the low level of GDR crime and the reduction in some of the more severe forms of crime is a consequence of the reduced social inequality and the increased security of the population. But since the collapse of the GDR, it has become clear that much of the change in crime was attributable to the system of social controls rather than to internal changes within the society.

Socialist countries do not pardon criminal offenders who have impaired the system's ability to function, damaged public security or order, or used socialist property to increase their individual wealth. Such forms of behaviour are punished severely. In Hungary, people who are reluctant to work are treated harshly. In 1984, the law on "Public Danger, Reluctance to Work" was amended and the sanction of aggravated correctional work was introduced. Individuals considered reluctant to work are those who withdraw from work defined as socially beneficial and whose life-style often leads to crime. This law not only added one new form of sanctioning but strengthened the "voluntary" duty to work. This heightened external control on the individual. Furthermore, we find important decriminalization in certain categories of crimes against property. Theft, embezzlement, and fraud, formerly acts punishable by the criminal law, now were classified as infringements of the law if they do not exceed a certain level of damages. New punitive measures, such as the introduction of community service or release on probation, have helped reduce the burden on prisons by limiting the number of short sentences. Even though the introduction of these measures, in Hungary, is economically justified, the effect of these changes cannot be overlooked. Many convicted persons, therefore, were not deprived of their liberty. The Hungarian reforms of the 1980's lead to a great number of civilizing alternatives to prison.

In 1987, an important step was undertaken in the GDR that further developed the civilizing process. With the abolition of the death penalty, the state went beyond the earlier elimination in the 1970's of the death penalty for murder. The GDR, as opposed to other Socialist societies, showed a much greater tradition of liberalizing sanctions. In the 1950's short sentences were mostly not imposed, but changed in favour of probation. Reuter characterizes the post-1945 development in the GDR as a tendency towards leniency, although not towards clemency.

In the socialist societies of Eastern Europe, we find definite tendencies towards reducing external constraints and towards strengthening internal controls. The change is without doubt a key indicator of the civilizing process, which we outlined earlier.

4 Remarks Concerning the Rewards of the Concepts of Civilizing and Modernizing

The concepts of civilizing and modernizing identified common developmental tendencies in cultures with differing levels, patterns, and forms of crime and criminalization.

One can state that both conceptions can be applied to describe the different tendencies within societies. Trends common to development can be detected in the evaluation of general patterns of crime. These developments occur completely independently of the characteristics of the respective cultures. All the countries included in the analysis have their own crime problems. Over the last 20-30 years, crime has risen in all countries examined with the exception of Japan and the GDR. Furthermore, the differences in the patterns of crime are not that great. Regardless of whether one talks of socialist, developed, or developing societies, there is always the dominance or the developing dominance of crime against property. The differences are, however, much starker concerning the level of violence in these societies. The United States is a developed society with a distinctively high level of violence. The high level of violence is explained by the disproportionate criminality of the poor urban population. Individuals left behind in the development process do not respond to the general conditions of society. This result seems to indicate that modernization and civilization do not necessarily correspond with each other. A high degree of modernization of a total society can, however, correspond with a low level of civilization. Further combinations are possible. Added to which, in all these cases, the most important thing would be to illustrate the processes which led to both the discrepancies and the correlations. This we could not and did not want to do. Instead, we merely wished to sketch a general framework. Detailed studies to probe these relationships remain the concern of future work.

Both concepts let us focus on certain characteristics of particular societies. One can examine the difference in levels of external and internal controls within societies. Collective definitions of violence and the use of violence differ among societies. Japan, for example, appears to be a developed society which has succeeded in both developing and civilizing. Because of this, Japan has produced on the one hand low crime rates, and on the other, maintains liberal criminal policies. India, too, shows a high adaptability in dealing with tradition and modernity. The distribution of power and the possibility of realizing interests within a group may be the reason for the completely different picture of criminality.

These are examples of possible perspectives for closer comparative analyses. Even though only a few generalizations are possible, it is our opinion that having examined the two conceptions, they contribute to an analysis of post World War II crime and criminal policy. But these concepts do not answer all questions and they need further development. The Haferkamp/Ellis contribution, without specific references to the modernization and civilization concepts, provide many points worthy of further examination. Among the most important is the concept of the centralization of power structures and processes that could well be integrated with the conceptions of civilization and modernization. The centralization of power is evident not only in the government manner, but also in the corporate world or in the centralized economic structures of socialist societies. Corporate crimes are committed by members of national elites and economic offenses by the party elite in socialist economies. Crime very often is a function of the power structure and influences struggles among dominant national elites and among the powerless seeking to regain or expand their power. The explanatory value of the power dimension, added to the historical and developmental dimension suggested by us enhences our understanding of the changing patterns, forms, and levels of crime and social control.

We can suggest that the triad of modernization, power and civilization leads to a comprehensive macro-structural explanatory framework, which may be able to explain different criminological developments in diverse societies. This could possibly prove to be a starting point from which may come a new conceptual orientation in criminology.

References

van Dijk, Jan J.M. (1989) "Penal Sanctions and the Process of Civilization", in: Annales internationales de Criminologie, vol. 27, pp. 191-204.
Durkheim, E. (1977) Über die Teilung der sozialen Arbeit, Frankfurt/M.
Elias, N. (1982) The Civilizing Process, Vol. 2: Power and Civility, New York: Pantheon.
Elias, N. (1988) "Violence and Civilization: the State Monopoly of Physical Violence and its Infringement", in: Civil Society and the State, John Keane ed., London and New York, pp. 177-198.
von Ferber, Christian (1984) "Zur Zivilisationstheorie von Norbert Elias – heute", in: Macht und Zivilisation, P. Gleichmann, J. Goudsblom and H. Korte eds.,Frankfurt/M., pp. 105-128.
Flora, Peter (1974) Modernisierungsforschung, Düsseldorf.
von Hofer, H. (1988) Nordic Criminal Statistics 1950-1980(86). Summary of a Report, 4th revised edition, Stockholm.
van Krieken, Robert (1989) "Violence, self-discipline and modernity, beyond the 'civilizing process'", in: Theory, Culture and Society, vol. 6, pp. 193-218.
Kuzmics, Helmut (1988) "The Civilizing Process", in: John Keane (ed.), Civil Society and the State, London and New York, pp. 149-176.
Kuzmics, Helmut (1990) "Das 'moderne Selbst' und der langfristige Prozeß der Zivilisation", in: Gesellschaftliche Prozesse und individuelle Praxis, H. Korte ed., Frankfurt/M., pp. 216-255.
Levy, M.J. Jr. (1966) Modernization and the Structure of Societies, vol. 1, Princeton.
Shelley, L. I.(1981) Crime and Modernization, Carbondale, Illinois.
Shelley, L. I. (1986) "Crime and Modernization reexamined", in: Annales internationales de Criminologie, vol. 24, pp. 7-21.
Tobias, J.J. (1967) Crime and Industrial Society in the 19th century, London.
Weber, Alfred (1920) "Prinzipielles zur Kultursoziologie: Gesellschaftsprozess, Zivilisationsprozess und Kulturbewegung", in: Archiv für Sozialwissenschaft und Sozialpolitik, vol. 47, pp. 1-49.
Zehr, H. (1976) Crime and the Development of Modern Society. Pattern of Criminality in 19th century Germany and France, Rowman and Littlefield.

Part I
Crime and Control in Developed Nations

Developments in Delinquency and Criminal Justice: A Nordic Perspective

Matti Joutsen

1 Background

The general hypotheses presented by the editors of this anthology can be summarised as follows:

(1) to an increasing degree, crime is being directed at anonymous social units and not directly at individuals;
(2) there has been a general relaxing of the operation of the criminal justice system. This can be seen in a move towards decriminalization, a lowering of the reporting and clearance rates, an increase in the waiving of measures, and the use of lighter sentences and diversion; and
(3) The new sanctions do not involve reinternalization of norms but instead restitution, with greater freedom of activity (i.e. less restraint on the offender).

These hypotheses provide a framework for the following report, which seeks to see what evidence there is for such hypotheses in the Nordic perspective. The time-frame is the post-war period.

2 The Development of Crime in the Nordic Countries

According to the first main hypothesis, crime is becoming increasingly directed more at anonymous social units than private individuals. This could be understood in one of two ways. It could imply that crimes that were formerly directed at private individuals (in particular, property offences), are now directed more and more at "anonymous social units" such as corporate bodies or, for example, the State. It could also mean that the number of crimes directed against these anonymous social units is increasing more rapidly than those against private individuals.

Table 1: Offences registered by the police

a) Completed murder

	Number of offences				per 100,000 inhabitants aged 15 - 67 (Norway 14 - 67)			
Year	**DK**	**SF**	**N**	**S**	**DK**	**SF**	**N**	**S**
1950	-	136	-	53	-	5.2	-	1.1
1955	-	109	-	64	-	4.0	-	1.0
1960	18	109	14	46	0.6	3.8	0.6	0.9
1965	23	79	5	87	0.7	2.5	0.2	1.6
1970	26	56	6	64	0.8	1.8	0.2	1.2
1975	26	145	211	22	0.8	4.4	0.8	2.2
1980	76	111	311	35	2.2	3.3	1.1	2.4
1981	81	107	271	46	2.3	3.2	1.0	2.6
1982	66	107	471	25	1.9	3.1	1.7	2.2
1983	71	114	381	21	2.0	3.3	1.3	2.1
1984	60	107	411	16	1.7	3.1	1.4	2.1
1985	78	117	371	26	2.2	3.4	1.3	2.2
1986	64	143	371	47	1.8	4.1	1.3	2.6

b) Assault

	Number of offences				per 100,000 inhabitants aged 15 - 67 (Norway 14 - 67)			
Year	**DK**	**SF**	**N**	**S**	**DK**	**SF**	**N**	**S**
1950	1613	5937	....	7395	57	226	...	153
1955	1600	5637	....	8615	55	206	...	174
1960	1632	5571	1802	8711	53	193	75	169
1965	1944	5823	1965	11803	60	187	78	219
1970	2401	11230	3092	18385	72	355	119	332
1975	3121	13138	3495	21509	92	397	130	389
1980	4854	13964	4041	24668	140	414	146	440
1981	5326	14730	4492	24314	152	434	161	432
1982	5169	15723	4459	28200	147	461	160	500
1983	5256	15248	5070	29220	149	444	180	517
1984	5390	16442	4975	30785	153	477	174	544
1985	5865	16425	5325	31996	166	475	189	564
1986	6071	16707	5340	32805	171	482	187	577

Table 1 (continued): Offences registered by the police

c) Rape

	Number of offences				per 100,000 inhabitants aged 15 - 67 (Norway 14 - 67)			
Year	**DK**	**SF**	**N**	**S**	**DK**	**SF**	**N**	**S**
1950	-	-	-	350	-	-	-	7.2
1955	-	137	-	375	-	5.0	-	7.6
1960	200	222	66	512	6.5	7.7	2.7	9.9
1965	162	320	93	587	6.0	10.3	3.7	10.9
1970	215	325	109	692	6.5	10.3	4.2	12.5
1975	252	375	119	769	7.4	11.3	4.4	13.9
1980	422	367	129	885	12.1	10.9	4.6	15.8
1981	442	417	114	865	12.6	12.3	4 1	15.4
1982	396	370	136	941	11.3	10.8	4.9	16.7
1983	527	296	175	923	15.0	8.6	6.2	16.3
1984	424	317	201	995	12.0	9.2	7.0	17.6
1985	541	300	241	1035	15.3	8.7	8.6	18.3
1986	587	292	255	1046	16.5	8.4	8.9	18.4

d) Robbery

	Number of offences				per 100,000 inhabitants aged 15 - 67 (Norway 14 - 67)			
Year	**DK**	**SF**	**N**	**S**	**DK**	**SF**	**N**	**S**
1950	189	210	-	190	6.6	8.0	-	3.9
1955	116	146	-	316	4.0	5.3	-	6.4
1960	344	294	65	469	11.2	10.2	2.7	9.1
1965	222	334	132	963	6.9	10.7	5.2	17.9
1970	396	947	262	1511	11.9	29.9	10 1	27.3
1975	787	1968	306	2336	23.2	59.4	11.4	42.2
1980	1461	1869	317	3427	42.0	55.5	11.4	61.1
1981	1651	1828	395	3228	47.2	53.9	14.1	57.4
1982	1410	1763	408	3530	40.2	51.7	14.6	62.6
1983	1529	1604	530	3473	43.4	46.7	18.8	61.5
1984	1819	1509	568	3681	51.6	43.8	19.9	65.1
1985	1834	1532	657	3851	51 9	44.3	23.4	67.9
1986	1812	1584	604	3806	51.0	45.7	21.2	66.9

Table 1 (continued): Offences registered by the police

e) Theft (excl. robbery)

	Number of offences				per 100,000 inhabitants aged 15 - 67 (Norway 14 - 67)			
Year	**DK**	**SF**	**N**	**S**	**DK**	**SF**	**N**	**S**
1950	82,664	20,328	-	110,470	2,901	775	-	2,282
1955	88,675	18,406	-	163,407	3,035	673	-	3,307
1960	103,430	31,020	26,796	203,675	3,361	1,072	1,110	3,955
1965	125,109	44,922	34,410	284,728	3,881	1,441	1,367	5,293
1970	220,276	61,934	47,331	390,523	6,617	1,957	1,816	7,058
1975	245,213	109,244	76,148	465,396	7,232	3,299	2,830	8,410
1980	340,891	108,963	95,011	514,130	9,809	3,234	3,424	9,165
1981	334,149	117,088	101,197	511,898	9,559	3,454	3,621	9,101
1982	336,079	122,927	115,366	541,096	9,571	3,603	4,128	9,597
1983	331,607	121,097	121,403	539,754	9,408	3,527	4,312	9,557
1984	361,668	121,071	114,172	574,533	10,261	3,510	4,001	10,157
1985	379,151	133,609	122,941	615,189	10,721	3,861	4,372	10,854
1986	409,844	137,928	124,074	667,057	11,535	3,982	4,352	11,727

e) Fraud

	Number of offences				per 100,000 inhabitants aged 15 - 67 (Norway 14 - 67)			
Year	**DK**	**SF**	**N**	**S**	**DK**	**SF**	**N**	**S**
1950	14156	7167	-	18820	497	273	-	389
1955	13768	6883	-	21378	471	252	-	433
1960	8590	8686	3282	23969	279	300	136	465
1965	9072	7240	3318	36091	281	232	132	671
1970	14376	12464	4376	71029	432	395	168	1284
1975	11146	10376	4478	47539	329	313	166	859
1980	10580	12511	3746	96701	304	371	135	1724
1981	11643	16752	3933	92539	333	494	141	1645
1982	13828	22634	4441	89789	394	663	159	1593
1983	15756	22077	5725	84494	447	643	203	1496
1984	14105	27835	6025	88814	400	807	211	1570
1985	15290	35890	7227	94899	432	1037	257	1674
1986	16296	43687	6665	97634	459	1261	234	1716

Table 1 (continued): Offences registered by the police

f) Total Penal Code

	Number of offences				per 100,000 inhabitants aged 15 - 67 (Norway 14 - 67)			
Year	**DK**	**SF**	**N**	**S**	**DK**	**SF**	**N**	**S**
1950	109117	51273	-	161778	3829	1954	-	3342
1955	115928	48240	-	225231	3967	1764	-	4559
1960	126367	65201	38584	276314	4106	2254	1599	5365
1965	155238	81427	47532	393660	4816	2612	1886	7317
1970	260072	122849	64866	563138	7812	3882	2489	10177
1975	290450	191704	96754	643405	8566	5789	3596	11627
1980	408177	198105	119042	760911	11745	5880	4240	13564
1981	407517	216851	127842	760614	11657	6396	4574	13523
1982	414800	235156	144920	805569	11812	6892	5185	14286
1983	416636	229861	155524	799457	11821	6694	5524	14155
1984	451069	240072	147145	845706	12798	6960	5167	14951
1985	478919	267125	159994	894396	13542	7719	5689	15780
1986	514599	281877	161670	960080	14484	8138	5670	16879

Source: Yearbook of Nordic Statistics 1987 (NORD 1987: 73), Table 230.

Notes: With the exception of murder the offence categories include attempt and various forms of participation. Concerning the definition of offences see the publication "Nordic Criminal Statistics 1950-1980."
Norway: The statistics only cover offences where the investigation has been finished.

The hypothesis cannot be assessed, however, unless the term "crime" is made much more specific. To the layman, "crime" brings an image of murder, rape and robbery. To the criminologist, it involves not only these traditional crimes but also modern crimes (narcotics offences, environmental offences, computer crime, white-collar crime) as well as such less seriously regarded acts as traffic and alcohol offences. There is very little worthwhile that can be said in general about such a heterogeneous category. Some restrictions must be made in order to focus the discussion.

The hypothesis can be examined most appropriately in respect to those categories of crime that can be committed against either private individuals or anonymous social units; it would be trite to compare, for example, the development of violent offences with the development of, for example, traffic or narcotics offences. Thus, we should look at the development of certain types of property offences.

Table 2: All Theft. Reported Offences.

	absolute figures				per 100 000			
Year	**DK**	**N**	**S**	**SF**	**DK**	**N**	**S**	**SF**
1950	82664	-	110470	20328	2901	-	2282	775
1951	97521	-	134110	[a]20143	3409	-	2757	765
1952	92215	-	131332	18719	3210	-	2690	705
1953	89265	-	138104	20923	3093	-	2821	780
1954	84640	-	142632	18857	2913	-	2902	696
1955	88675	-	163407	18406	3035	-	3307	673
1956	87192	17610	172445	21483	2970	766	3472	774
1957	91970	22147	193608	25362	3122	944	3864	909
1958	92719	24718	212943	28302	3126	1055	4210	1005
1959	97049	25835	207543	29125	3198	1082	4066	1045
1960	[a]103430	26796	203675	31020	3361	1110	3955	1072
1961	108520	30830	208935	33106	3485	1263	4015	1134
1962	114338	31257	219246	35217	3629	1268	4177	1184
1963	119255	33551	232528	39927	3752	1350	4396	1319
1964	125928	34068	255021	45369	3934	1372	4781	1475
1965	125109	34410	[ac]284728	44922	3881	1367	5293	1441
1966	127470	34865	290632	42657	3933	1377	5368	1354
1967	145125	37107	300911	50932	4450	1450	5683	1599
1968	162379	38158	[a]334277	56864	4956	1487	6129	1769
1969	176958	44386	328762	55955	5370	1718	5986	1761
1970	220276	47331	390523	61934	6617	1816	7058	1957
1971	256234	54310	453032	[a]74988	7669	2077	8176	2340
1972	255411	[b]59471	447540	86997	7602	2265	8089	2685
1973	268817	65928	394699	95116	7959	2495	7143	2908
1974	280724	69005	403139	96625	8288	2578	7291	2932
1975	245213	76148	[a]465396	109244	7232	2830	8410	3299
1976	234983	68710	501467	105477	6906	2538	9049	3176
1977	260936	69460	520583	107938	7637	2551	9374	3240
1978	288111	79892	493367	104760	8384	2915	8862	3133
1979	[a]295710	82892	487033	105838	8553	3006	8712	3154
1980	340891	95011	[d]514130	108963	9809	3424	9165	3234

Our main source of data is the statistics on reported crime.[1]

1 Ideally, the arguments could be analyzed on the basis of longitudinal research showing the victimization risk of both private persons and corporate bodies. However, although major national victimization surveys have been carried out in Denmark, Finland, Norway and Sweden, these surveys have focused on offences committed directly against individuals. Furthermore, these studies deal primarily with violent offences. Property offences were dealt with in, for example, the Finnish studies in 1974 and 1980, and the Swedish 1978 study (see e.g.

Table 2 (continued): All Theft. Reported Offences.

	Population Index 1970=100			
Year	**DK**	**N**	**S**	**SF**
1950	44	-	32	40
1951	52	-	39	39
1952	49	-	38	36
1953	47	-	40	40
1954	44	-	41	36
1955	46	-	47	34
1956	45	42	49	40
1957	47	52	55	46
1958	47	58	60	51
1959	48	60	58	53
1960	51	61	56	55
1961	53	70	57	58
1962	55	70	59	61
1963	57	74	62	67
1964	59	76	68	75
1965	59	75	75	74
1966	59	76	76	69
1967	67	80	81	82
1968	75	82	87	90
1969	81	95	85	90
1970	100	100	100	100
1971	116	114	116	120
1972	115	125	115	137
1973	120	137	101	149
1974	125	142	103	150
1975	109	156	119	169
1976	104	140	128	162
1977	115	140	133	166
1978	127	160	126	160
1979	129	166	123	161
1980	148	188	130	165

Source: Nordic Criminal Statistics 1950-1980. Hanns von Hofer (ed.), Table 2.8.1.
Notes:
a) Change of statistical practices.
b) Change in the law.
c) New Penal Code.
d) Change in statistical reporting.

Table 3: All Theft. Clearance Rate.

Year	DK	N	S	SF
1950	32	-	34	52
1951	32	-	25	53
1952	32	-	27	51
1953	32	-	26	53
1954	33	-	25	55
1955	30	-	25	56
1956	31	-	26	56
1957	32	28	24	54
1958	31	29	25	53
1959	29	35	25	55
1960	23	32	26	54
1961	26	30	26	53
1962	25	32	26	53
1963	26	30	25	51
1964	23	31	24	55
1965	24	30	[a] --	51
1966	25	31	26	50
1967	24	31	27	48
1968	23	31	[a] 25	45
1969	21	28	23	44
1970	20	28	21	43
1971	19	28	16	40
1972	18	[b] 26	16	38
1973	19	24	21	37
1974	19	21	20	37
1975	20	20	[a] 19	38
1976	19	22	17	37
1977	18	20	15	40
1978	17	18	17	41
1979	13	18	16	38
1980	-	-	17	42

Source : Nordic Criminal Statistics 1950-1980 (Hanns von Hofer, ed.), Table 2.8.2.
Notes:
a) Change of statistical practices.
b) Excl. petty theft.

Risto Lättilä and Tuomo Niskanen (1983) Hidden Criminality. A Survey on Reported and Unreported Offences Against the Person, Central Statistical Office of Finland, Studies no. 93, Helsinki, and Levnadsförhallanden. Rapport 24. Offer för valds- och egendomsbrott 1978, Sveriges officiella statistik, Stockholm 1981).

Table 4: All Theft. Number Of Persons Found Guilty.

Year	Absolute Figures				Per 100 000 Pop 15(14)-67			
	DK	N	[b]S	SF	DK	N	S	SF
1950	6871	2214	7365	4162	241	98	152	159
1951	8346	2189	8732	[a] 3993	292	96	179	152
1952	7739	2374	9536	3807	269	104	195	143
1953	6909	2235	9515	3720	239	98	194	139
1954	6125	2135	10684	3230	211	92	217	119
1955	5985	2291	11618	3095	205	100	235	113
1956	6409	2775	13056	2995	218	121	263	108
1957	6290	3174	14762	3578	214	135	295	128
1958	6146	3305	16557	3959	207	141	327	141
1959	6190	3505	18289	-	204	147	358	-
1960	[a] 8309	3721	18309	4068	270	154	355	141
1961	8851	4136	[a] 18571	3978	284	169	357	136
1962	8734	4357	19267	4192	277	177	367	141
1963	8255	4463	20265	4778	260	180	383	158
1964	7958	4962	21921	5931	249	198	411	193
1965	7850	4986	[ac] 20913	6076	244	199	389	195
1966	8065	5284	25022	6012	249	209	462	191
1967	8195	5639	27450	6803	251	220	505	214
1968	9499	5749	28573	7595	290	224	524	236
1969	8857	6065	26268	7793	269	235	478	241
1970	9998	6070	28566	7909	300	233	516	250
1971	11584	6211	30263	11415	347	238	546	356
1972	11885	[c] 6392	[a] 31614	-	354	243	571	-
1973	12114	5635	30521	15303	359	213	552	468
1974	13419	5615	26616	-	396	210	481	-
1975	13586	5299	29333	19623	401	197	530	593
1976	11839	5712	28537	-	348	211	515	-
1977	12854	5333	29990	[a] 23012	376	196	540	691
1978	13216	[a] 5557	31371	23424	385	203	563	701
1979	-	5980	30100	21833	-	217	538	651
1980	-	-	29578	22841	-	-	527	678

Although we are all aware of the many shortcomings of statistics as a source of data on the amount of crime in society, the general statistical trend would appear to match reality: recorded property crime has increased considerably during the post-war period.[2]

The Finnish and Swedish police statistics, moreover, provide at least

2 See the statistics in the annex and esp. Hanns von Hofer, Nordic Criminal Statistics 1950 -1980, pp. 135-240

Table 4 (continued): All Theft. Number Of Persons Found Guilty

Index 1970=100

Year	**DK**	**N**	**S**	**SF**
1950	80	42	29	63
1951	97	41	35	61
1952	90	45	38	57
1953	80	42	38	55
1954	70	40	42	48
1955	68	43	46	45
1956	73	52	51	43
1957	71	58	57	51
1958	69	61	63	56
1959	68	63	69	-
1960	90	66	69	56
1961	95	73	69	55
1962	92	76	71	56
1963	86	77	74	63
1964	83	85	80	77
1965	81	85	75	78
1966	83	90	90	76
1967	84	95	98	85
1968	97	96	101	95
1969	90	101	93	96
1970	100	100	100	100
1971	115	102	106	142
1972	118	105	111	-
1973	119	92	107	187
1974	132	90	93	-
1975	133	85	103	237
1976	116	91	100	-
1977	125	84	105	276
1978	128	87	109	280
1979	-	93	104	260
1980	-	-	102	271

Source: Nordic Criminal Statistics 1950-1980 (Hanns von Hofer, ed.), Table 2.8.3.
Notes:
a) Change of statistical practices.
b) 1950-1960: Original data, no summations.
c) Change in the law.

Table 5: All Theft. Number Of Persons Found Guilty, By Sanction

Year	Imprisonment				Fines				Suspended Sentence			
	DK	N	S	SF	DK	N	S	SF	DK	N	S	SF
Absolute Figures												
1950	-	842	-	2332	-	47	-	806	-	576	-	1022
1955	-	735	-	1521	-	90	-	669	-	519	-	904
1960	1721	817	4401	1800	2015	134	4292	824	1009	841	5162	1443
1965	2292	1370	4004	2487	1011	243	6151	1445	1389	1609	4731	2143
1970	2848	1564	4136	2912	1027	516	7892	2760	2008	1858	6838	2236
1975	2989	1730	3025	5719	3867	24	7692	11284	3141	1829	7508	2620
1980	2616	2346	3197	4464	4310	23	9569	14890	2889	2192	7275	3487

Table 5 (continued): All Theft. Number Of Persons Found Guilty, By Sanction

Year	Waivers Of Prosecution				Other Sanctions				Sum			
	DK	N	S	SF	DK	N	S	SF	DK	N	S	SF
Absolute Figures												
1950	-	722	-	-	-	2	-	2	-	2189	-	4162
1955	-	946	-	-	-	1	-	1	-	2291	-	3095
1960	2727	1813	5345	-	-	116	67	1	7472	3721	19257	4068
1965	2447	1764	5996	-	-	-	31	1	7139	4986	20913	6076
1970	3021	2132	9689	-	11	-	11	1	8915	6070	28566	7909
1975	2257	1716	11096	-	6	-	12	-	12260	5299	29333	19623
1980	1871	1419	9508	-	17	-	29	-	11703	5980	29578	22841

Table 5 (continued): All Theft. Number Of Persons Found Guilty, By Sanction

Year	Imprisonment				Fines				Suspended Sentence			
	DK	N	S	SF	DK	N	S	SF	DK	N	S	SF
Percentage												
1950	-	38	-	56	-	2	-	19	-	26	-	25
1955	-	32	-	49	-	4	-	22	-	23	-	29
1960	23	22	23	44	27	4	22	20	14	23	27	35
1965	32	27	19	41	14	5	29	24	20	32	23	35
1970	32	26	14	37	12	9	28	35	22	31	24	28
1975	24	33	10	29	32	0	26	58	26	35	26	13
1980	22	39	11	20	37	0	32	65	25	37	25	15

Table 5 (continued): All Theft. Number Of Persons Found Guilty, By Sanction

Year	Waivers Of Prosecution				Other Sanctions				Sum			
	DK	N	S	SF	DK	N	S	SF	DK	N	S	SF
Percentage												
1950	33	-	-	-	0	-	0	-	99	-	100	
1955	-	41	-	-	-	0	-	0	-	100	-	100
1960	36	49	28	-	-	3	0	0	100	101	100	99
1965	34	35	29	-	-	-	0	0	100	99	100	100
1970	34	35	34	-	0	-	0	0	100	101	100	100
1975	18	32	38	-	0	-	0	-	100	100	100	100
1980	16	24	32	-	0	-	0	-	100	100	100	100

Source: Nordic Statistics 1950-1980 (Hanns von Hofer, ed.), Table 2.8.4.

some hints of the identity of the victims of thefts. The Swedish statistics note, for example, how many of the thefts were classified as shoplifting, and how many burglaries were made in homes as opposed to e.g. shops. (However, the victims of the great majority of the offences are not specified.) An analysis of the most recent police statistics has led both the Swedish National Council of Crime Prevention and the Finnish National Research Institute of Legal Policy to conclude that the risk of corporate bodies being victimized by a property offence (in particular, a burglary) has increased over the past decade, while the risk of private individuals being victimized has remained somewhat the same.[3]

As for another property offence, fraud, both the Swedish and the Finnish research institutes emphasize that the amount of fraud is due largely to the opportunity structure; in this case, to the wider use of cheques and credit cards.[4] Such forms of fraud are generally committed against a corporate body.

The example of fraud illustrates the point that the development of property crime can generally be explained to a large extent by referring to the structure of opportunities as well as the structure of ownership. Since the end of the Second World War, several factors have combined to increase the opportunities for property offences. These factors are, in particular, the greater availability of goods, the decrease in the supervision of goods and social control in general, and the greater mobility of potential offenders.

During the same period, the structure of ownership has also changed. The increase in opportunities is offered primarily by corporate bodies: self-service shops provide opportunities for shoplifting; motor vehicles are to an increasing degree owned by corporate bodies (either as "company cars" or as objects of trade by rental or leasing companies); offices are becoming equipped with goods that have a significant re-sale value; the introduction of e.g. credit cards, cash cards and computers provides entirely new opportunities for crime. Although the wealth of private individuals has also increased, the opportunity they offer for crime has not increased at all as rapidly. In addition, it may be conjectured that private individuals pay more attention to the protection of their property.[5]

---

3 Brottsutveckling 1987, pp. 69 – 70 in re burglary; Rikollisuustilanne 1986, p. 22 in re thefts in general.

4 Brottsutveckling 1987, p. 88; Rikollisuustilanne 1986, pp. 27-28

5 The Finnish National Research Institute of Legal Policy suggests that "the increase in the number of thefts from private houses and other theft of private property may have been checked for example by the more widespread use of locks and the advice given by the police and insurance companies on the protection of property." (Rikollisuustilanne 1986, p. 22)

What, then, could we say of the first argument? The evidence would appear to show that proportionately, more (property) crime is indeed being directed against anonymous social units (i e., corporate bodies) than directly against private individuals. However, what little we know of victimization would indicate that the absolute risk that private individuals have of being victimized has not decreased. There would not appear to have been any shift from private individuals to corporate bodies as victims. At the most, we might suggest that the increase in victimization risk is directed at corporate bodies.

3 Changes in the Development of Crime Control in the Nordic Countries.

According to the second and third hypotheses, there has been a general relaxing of the operation of the criminal justice system (decriminalization, a lowering of the reporting and clearance rates, an increase in the waiving of measures, and the use of lighter sentences and diversion) and a move to new sanctions (such as restitution) that involve less restraint on the offender.[6]

It is difficult to answer in general the question of how society has reacted to the change in delinquency. The answer must specify which segment of society is reacting (the politicians, the police or the courts, the criminologists, the press or the "man in the street") as well as the nature of the reaction to be considered (for example, whether the changes should be assessed in terms of tolerance, attitudes, fear or the use of protective measures).

The easy changes to document are those made by the politicians: the amendment of law. In particular in Finland, there has been a clear tendency towards more open-ended definitions of crime (e.g. theft, assault) as opposed to explicitly detailed essential elements. Furthermore, some modern crimes have required amendment of the law, as the legalistic tradition in the Nordic country would not permit the extension of the

6 One of the sanctions referred to by the organizers – the death penalty – is not an issue in any of the Nordic countries. All of the Nordic countries have eliminated capital punishment. It was outlawed even in time of war in Finland in 1973, and in Sweden one year later. What is even more important is that, in times of peace, capital punishment has not been enforced for a very long time. The last peace-time execution in Sweden was in 1910, in Finland over 160 years ago – 1826.

existing law to them. A good example of this is hacking, unauthorized entry into a computer system. The old law on unauthorized use of property or on vandalism is inappropriate, and so amendments are required.[7]

Some of these amendments have been made in order to extend the protection of law to objects not previously protected, as in the case of hacking. Usually, however, the amendments are made in order to adjust the scale of punishment of certain behaviour. One example of this is the unauthorized use of motor vehicles. Unauthorized use of property in an agriculturally oriented society was not considered to be a very serious matter. With the rapid increase in the unauthorised use of motor vehicles, the attitude changed – and the penal latitudes were raised.

The possible changes in informal reactions – the reactions of the man in the street – are more difficult to assess. One indicator of public attitudes is the reporting rate. Involving the official criminal justice system in the resolution of one's personal difficulties (including cases where one has been victimized by an offence) is not at all a self-evident matter. In the historical perspective, it has only been relatively recently that the public has formally reported victimisation to the police to any appreciable extent. Even today, the reporting rate for property offences remains relatively low (in Finland and Sweden, it is around 20% of property offences with private persons as victims).[8] Reporting of property offences is connected, e.g., with the value of the goods, and with whether or not the property in question is insured. One question has so far remained unanswered: is the increase in reported property crime attributable in part to the fact that the public is becoming more willing to report crimes to the police – in other words, has their reaction to crime and to the use of official control changed?

The statistics on clearance rates are easier to follow, although also here there is room for conjecture.[9] These rates have decreased in all of the

---

7 Hanns von Hofer, op.cit., provides a detailed review of amendments of criminal law in four Nordic countries from 1950 to 1980.

8 See e.g. Rikollisuustilanne 1986, p. 23 and Brottsutveckling 1986, p. 92; the former source notes no significant change in this rate during the 1970s.

9 Statistics on clearance rates serve most appropriately as a measure of police effectiveness in connection with those offences that require some work, and not with those offences (such as drunken driving or assault of an official) which are, in practice, "cleared" at the same time as the report is made. Even if the clearance statistics are "cleansed" of such offences, however, caution should be maintained. It is possible that, for example, a lowering of the clearance rate of property offences in general is due to an increase in the reporting of offences that are difficult to clear (e.g. damage to property) and not to the reduced effectiveness of the police.

Nordic countries during the post-war period. For example in Finland, the clearance rate for all theft offences in 1950 was 52% while in 1980 it was 42%. The corresponding decrease in Denmark was from 32% (1950) to 13% (1979) and in Sweden from 34% (1950) to 17% (1980).[10]

Yet another "reaction" of society to crime that can be followed in the statistics is sentencing. Although the courts are very meticulous about following statutory law as to essential elements and sentences, there is considerable leeway for discretion in sentencing. For example, the penal latitudes stipulated by law are rather wide, and the courts often have a choice between sanctions (e g., between imprisonment and a suspended sentence).

There have been fundamental changes in sentencing in the Nordic countries, usually in the direction of increased leniency. The most important such change is the decrease in the use of imprisonment. Not only is imprisonment being used less frequently (relatively speaking), but also the average length of the sentences is decreasing.[11] This is perhaps clearest in Finland, where the median length of all sentences of imprisonment has sunk from 7.6 months in 1950 to 3.3 months in 1985. At the same time, the median length of sentences of imprisonment for theft offences has decreased from 9.8 to 3.5 months.[12]

Despite the decrease in the use of imprisonment, the Nordic countries have not made significant use of any "new" non-custodial sanctions. The basic alternatives continue to be suspended sentences and the fine or, in Finland and Sweden, the day-fine. At the moment, Denmark and Norway are experimenting with community service, and Sweden and Finland appear to be about to follow this lead.[13]

Most of these changes have not required any amendments, as they have taken place within the range of permissible penal sanctions. At present, for example the Finnish courts are sentencing almost at the bottom of the permissible sanctions. However, in addition there have been some legal amendments designed specifically to lower the general level of punishment. The expansion of the legal possibilities for the use of suspended sentences is one such example. Another is the lowering of the minimum

10 See von Hofer, op.cit., p. 201

11 See the tables in the text

12 In connection with the increase in officially recorded crime, however, more and more cases are coming to the courts. Therefore, the increased leniency in sentencing could also be due to an influx of less serious offences, which in themselves would lead (all other things being equal) to less severe sentences on the average.

13 See the reports on these countries in Norman Bishop, Non-Custodial Sanctions in Europe, Helsinki 1988

and/or maximum punishments stipulated by the law. A third is the rewriting of the essential elements of an offence, or a redefinition of the borderline between "petty" and "ordinary", or "ordinary" and "aggravated" forms of an offence (as was the case with drunken driving in Finland).

Restitution has so far had very little significance in the Nordic countries as a penal sanction. Although the increased focus on the victim (a development which is also to be found throughout Scandinavia) has raised suggestions that restitution be used more widely as a sanction, little has been done in practice.

The importance of the victim movement can be seen in another direction, that of greater use of mediation as an alternative to criminal justice. Norway has already experimented with a relatively wide-spread network of "conflict councils", and the other countries have made more limited experiments. Their over-all effect on official crime control and sentencing, however, so far has remained slight.

The trend in sentencing is not all in one direction. Sanctions are becoming more severe for so-called modern offences, in particular economic offences. Certain serious narcotics offences are also leading to greater punishment.[14]

One of the central hypotheses put forward by the editors of this anthology – that the new sanctions "do not involve reinternalization of norms but instead restitution, with greater freedom of activity" (i.e. less restraint on the offender) is, perhaps, impossible to prove or disprove on the basis of statistics and the available research results. The assumption behind the assumption appears to be that imprisonment serves to reinternalize norms while the "new alternatives" do not.

The penal policy of all of the Nordic countries rests on general prevention, on the view that the punishment of an offender serves to remind the public of the readiness of society to enforce its penal norms. This general prevention is not based on deterrence through fear, but on a

14 In this reassessment of penal values – with more lenient sentences suggested for some offences, and more severe sentences for others – a distinction should be made between long-term and short-term swings, and between statutory amendment of tariffs and shifts within these tariffs (sentencing). The movement towards more lenient sentences would indeed appear to be a long term development that is taking place in respect of both statutory tariffs and sentencing practice. However, in the short run it may be offset by sudden increases of severity for specific offences, often in reaction to "public demand". Drunken driving is an example of such an offence; sexual offences, domestic violence and vandalism are other examples. The success of such efforts depends on the susceptibleness of politicians and the courts to such pressure. So far, the Nordic countries have (with some notable exceptions) defused such efforts.

combination of a high risk of detection and apprehension and of the strengthening of internal norms. From this point of view, a small fine for a traffic offence serves the "reinternalization of norms" just as well as a lengthy sentence of imprisonment for robbery or theft. Mention might be made of the motivation for a proposal to adopt a new sanction in Finland, a "penal warning"; it was argued that, although the essence would be the same as a waiving of measures entirely, the terminology used would strengthen the reinternalization of norms.

As for imprisonment itself, the official policy of the Nordic countries has abandoned the conception that the purpose of imprisonment is rehabilitation (a highly developed form of the reinternalization of norms). Imprisonment should only consist of the deprivation of liberty. Although the prisoners are to be provided with all possible social welfare and health services as well as vocational training, this is on a voluntary basis. Release from prison does not depend on any assessment of whether or not the offender has been "cured of his criminality".

4 The Connection between Crime and Crime Control: Conclusions

To summarize the two main observations that have been made above regarding changes in crime and crime control in the Nordic countries over the past forty years:

– there has been a significant increase in crime (this was illustrated with the example of property crime); and

- the measures used by the criminal justice system are, on the average, increasingly lenient.

What further hypotheses – if any – are we permitted to draw from such very general observations?

One possible hypothesis is that the increase in crime is overburdening our criminal justice system, and the increased leniency is a way to cut down on the costs of sanctions. Society is not prepared to pay the costs of a harsh criminal policy. For this reason, many argue for the reduction of the use of imprisonment on purely economic considerations. They point out the costs of constructing prisons, staffing them, developing penological programmes, arranging for after-care, and so on, and counterbalance this with attractive cost breakdowns for community service or probation programmes.[15]

Although this hypothesis has obvious merit – our criminal justice system is becoming overburdened, and the self-regulatory mechanisms of the system are leading to efforts to simplify and speed up the criminal process as well as avoid costly sanctions – it can not be considered decisive. Even the most expensive sanction, imprisonment, remains in wide use. There appears to be a strong reluctance to make criminal policy decisions on the basis of economic factors alone, at least explicitly.

A second possible hypothesis – a very idealistic one – is that we are becoming more enlightened about the drawbacks of certain forms of punishment (in particular, imprisonment). We are also becoming aware that crime is not (always) due to a deliberate decision of the offender to break the law, and that indeed, many crimes are committed in excusable or at least understandable circumstances. Although crime is increasing, we would, therefore, be reluctant to use such abhorrent punishments as imprisonment unless this is absolutely necessary.

Also this hypothesis seems shaky. Although it would be nice to imagine that our decision-makers are constantly working to spread sweetness and light, the hypothesis assumes that all those in the criminal justice system – in particular the police, the prosecutors, the judges and the prison officials – are agreed on this general view of human nature and of punishment. This would not seem to match what we know about the operation of the criminal justice system.

A third possible hypothesis is more Macchiavellian: our decisionmakers in criminal policy have realized that explicitly punitive measures are not successful, and are turning to a hidden agenda of more lenient sentences with a simultaneous expansion of social control (the net-widening effect) and the replacement of penal measures with, for example, medical and other treatment measures.

Although it appears clear that official social control has, indeed, expanded – the citizen of today runs a far larger risk of being punished for some infraction than was the case a few decades ago – this hypothesis has the same weaknesses as the second. It assumes that the decisionmakers and practitioners are working in harmony for the same goal.

Yet a fourth possible hypothesis is that the two basic observations of an increase in recorded crime and an increase in the leniency of punishments are a reflection of the general improvement of the standard of living in Nordic societies. It was already noted that the increase in (property) crime

---

15 On the appositeness of cost-reduction as a factor arguing for increased use of non-custodial sanctions, see e.g. Norman Bishop (1988) Non-Custodial Alternatives in Europe, Helsinki, pp. 130 ff.

is connected with the increase in opportunities, which in turn is due to the increased wealth of the Nordic countries: simply put, there is more to steal, and it is easier to steal. The improvement in the standard of living, in turn, affects for example our attitude towards deprivation of freedom as a sanction. Because we value our freedom more, and are more prepared to use money as a measure, the use of fines is increasing, while prison sentences are becoming shorter. The penal value of imprisonment has changed.[16]

All four of these hypotheses can be combined together. Our image of the amount and seriousness of crime in society – and of the proper response to this crime – is not based on any absolutes. Even those of us who have been involved in criminal justice throughout the entire post-war period cannot state with any certainty that, for example, there is X amount more crime today than in 1950, or that punishment is Y units less severe. We take our frame of reference from fleeting factors, the net result of which – to apply Habermas's terminology – is our world-picture.

Our world-picture is a result of our way of structuring the world – our attitudes towards ourself and others, our expectations about how we and other people should behave, and our concept of justice. If I were to assault the chairman – or challenge him to a duel, which is ritualized assault – it would make all the difference to how my behaviour is judged by my friends and by the law if we were living in Hamburg in 1788, 1888 or 1988. To take another, more general, example of assault, it is possible that the increase in reported assault over the past decades is not due to an increase in the phenomenon itself, but instead to our attitude towards assault. During the last century, the master still had the right to chastise his servants and the teacher his students; today, this would be assault. It was not too long ago that we took it for granted that husbands could beat their wives, and parents could spank their children. Here, too, our attitudes have changed. Although some people speak of an increase in the brutality of assault (without comparing the level of violence in modern society with previous centuries), the fact that more and more violent behaviour is becoming condemned by society could be taken as a sign that there is in fact less violence.

Thus, the over-arching hypothesis would be that there has been a change in the world-picture, in our penal values. There are many developments that have changed our attitudes towards crime and crime control since the Second World War. First of all, there is more crime, and it is increasingly expensive to control it (the first hypothesis). Second, we are becoming more enlightened about the causes of crime and the effects of

---

16 See Nils Christie (1966) Changes in Penal Values, Scandinavian Studies in Criminology, vol. 2.

punishment (the second hypothesis). Third, we are growing more and more aware that criminal behaviour can be and in fact is controlled through non-penal means (the third hypothesis). And fourth, our standard of living has indeed improved considerably (the fourth hypothesis).

It follows from this that the question of whether there has been a change in crime and in the severity of punishment is perhaps impossible to answer. Furthermore, if the hypothesis of a change in the world picture is accepted, the question might even be considered immaterial: the measures and values of one world picture are not valid in another. Although there might be some general interest in knowing whether crime at the end of the 1940s was in some sense different from crime at the end of the 1980s – or whether today the thief or robber is sentenced to more or less severe punishment than his counterpart was forty years ago – it is more important to examine crime and crime control against the background of the society in question.

Modern Patterns of Crime and Control in the Federal Republic of Germany[1]

Hans-Günther Heiland

1 The Welfare-State-Thesis

The Federal Republic of Germany (FRG) has been in a phase of radical change since the beginning of the 1970's. The economic crisis of the years 1966/67, has left deep scars in its economic and socio-political development. The crisis brought the period of the "economic miracle" to an end. This phase had begun with a relatively fast and strong stimulation of economical activity. The continuous growth of the economy was and still helps guarantee the fullfilling of economic aims, e.g. full employment and price stability. The West German variant of the welfare state (Zapf 1986) with its growth period surplus and its socio-political apparatus, seemed to offer the best conditions for the following:

a)The redistribution of resources, goods and profits in order to eradicate inequality.

b)The founding and establishment of public welfare systems in order to eliminate serious uncertainties.

c)The institution of insurance systems and transfer payments in order to gurantee income in cases of unemployment, handicapped, and retirees.

However, high growth rates are also considered to be a yardstick for the success and productivity of a society. They provide chances for individuals to become socially integrated when chances of participating fully in social life are lessened, due to individual (e.g. handicaps) or social (e.g. unemployment) risk factors. It was thought that the foundations had been laid for integration by satisfying the most urgent wishes for more consumption, more attractive offers of jobs, the widening of social security and the enhancement of offers of social services. Economic, currency and energy crises, destroyed the "dream of everlasting prosperity" (Lutz 1984). The FRG is being confronted more and more with structural problems and an increasing willingness to engage in conflicts. The socio-politically created expectations of the members of society are continuously being disappointed. Reports about the limits of economic growth do nothing to

1 This paper makes no reference to the reunification of Germany and what this might hold for the state, the economy, crime and social control.

strengthen the trust in the power of economics. Since the beginning of the 1970's fear and insecurity have topped public opinion polls, followed in second place by the feeling of security. Instead of social integration and participation, clear signs of social desintegration and social instability have arisen.

In view of these manifest tendencies towards crises in the FRG, the rapid increase in crime appears to be an inevitable result of social destabilization. The German sociologist H. Klages (1975) summarized the noticeable, contradictory tendencies within the Welfare-State-Thesis as follows: while welfare state benefits have expanded and while the wish for a life without risk factors has almost been satisfied, the deviation from law and order is growing. Deviations are put down to the development of the welfare state and its inability to achieve a balance between the state-generated demands and expectations, on the one hand, that are perceived and intensified by its citizens on the other. The population and the political-administrative elite diverge and disagree in their perceptions and judgements concerning the capabilities of the state. According to Klages, the result of this development is various forms of anomie (e.g. delinquency, alcoholism, the use of drugs and suicide).[2]

Penal legislation is the reaction of the personnel of state-run institutions to the incompatibility of the decreasing capability of the state to provide national security and the growing demand by the populace for this condition. This penal legislation can be characterized by an increase in mitigation and an enhanced toleration of anomic behaviour. I want to call this dual explanation the Welfare-State-Thesis. It is able to unravel muddled, habitual ways of thinking in criminology as well as criminal sociology.

In this article I want to examine the extent of explanatory power of this thesis. We shall now concentrate on the development of crime and control in the FRG since the end of the 2nd World War.

---

2 See also: Janowitz (1976) claims that the growth of the welfare state has led to deficiencies in legitimation and weak governments. In contrast to Klages, Janowitz considers the further expansion of the welfare state to be at risk, due to fiscal limits. He also realises the necessity to create new institutions to, e. g. institutionalize social control, to achieve social integration through an intensification of the density of control. Authoritarian alternatives however, are not popular.

2 Development of Crime and Control in the FRG from 1950 to 1987

2.1 Development of Crime

The Welfare-State-Thesis claims that anomic behaviour is spreading in industrialized countries. We therefore, want to analyze the development of crime as one form of anomie in the FRG. Examining the general direction of the development of crime, we observe an increase in criminality. Between 1963 and 1985, the registered crime rate[3] increased 2.5 times (from 1963: 2914 to 1987: 7269; see table 1).

Each report concerning the total size and the changes in criminality does not provide sufficient specifics about the dynamics of crime. It is well known that registered crime[4] represents only a small portion of the total number of criminal acts. However, statements can be made about the dark figures of FRG crime only for specific periods of time. If one adds the limited available data on the dark figure of crime, there still is an increase in the total rate of crime (Schwind 1988). This is a remarkable fact. Even though it is possible to consider dark figures from different periods of time, it can still be concluded that delinquency has increased and obviously will increase still further.

Let us now turn to the second statement that determines our overall examination of criminality. By examining only the total size of registered crime, it does not permit one to make specific statements because the growth in crime may be based on a disproportionate increase in a certain group of criminal acts, while other groups of offences are decreasing or stagnating. Therefore, we will try to be more precise about the general statements concerning the increase in the total size of crime.

---

3 The offence rate is the number of cases known altogether or of various kinds of offences, calculated on the basis of 100,000 inhabitants. The offence rate expressed the risk of being a victim of one of these offences. See Bundeskriminalamt, Polizeiliche Kriminalstatistik 1987, Wiesbaden, 1988, p. 223

4 The felonies and misdemeanours handled by the police, inclusive of punishable attempts, are recorded in the Criminal Statistics of the Police.

Table 1: Crimes known to the Police 1963 - 1987

Year	**1963**	**1965**	**1970**	**1975**	**1980**	**1985**	**1987**
All Non-Traffic Crimes							
- Absolute	16,788,840	1,789,319	2,413,586	2,919,390	3,815,774	4,215,451	4,444,108
- Rate	2,914	3,031	3,924	4,722	6,198	6,909	7,269
Crimes of Violence							
- Absolute	45,218	45,889	60,701	80,699	99,554	102,967	100,003
- Rate	79	78	99	131	162	169	164
Burglaries							
- Absolute	268,135	336,988	646,325	1,044,569	1,273,507	1,539,546	1,729,892
- Rate	466	571	1,051	1,689	2,069	2,523	2,829
Fraud							
- Absolute	180,914	177,343	170,702	209,841	247,133	372,196	358,493
- Rate	314	300	278	339	401	610	586
Embezzlement							
- Absolute	46,490	41,689	36,121	33,169	35,881	48,085	49,846
- Rate	81	71	59	54	58	79	82
Drug Offences							
- Absolute	820	1,003	16,104	29,805	62,395	60,941	74,894
- Rate	1	2	26	48	101	100	123

Definition: Crimes of Violence: Murder and Manslaughter, Aggravated Assault, Rape, Robbery etc.
Burglary: Theft under aggravating circumstances
Drug offences: Possession and/or selling of illegal drugs
Notes: In 1971: Change in registration practise. Change from input to output statistics
- : Figures are not available
Source: Bundeskriminalamt (Ed.), Polizeiliche Kriminalstatistik 1987, Wiesbaden, 1988

2.1.1 Development of Violent Crime

Let us, therefore, first of all look at violent crime.[5] This category includes offences such as murder, manslaughter, robbery, predatory extortion and

---

5 The total number of cases reported in each of the following categories includes both attempts and cases with death resulting. Attempts are listed in a separate column in the Police Crime Statistics (Teske/Arnold 1982)

predatory assault upon a motorist, dangerous assault and assault with serious bodily injury and also forcible rape.

When examining the statistics we find a well known development: From 1953 to 1987 the total figures for murder and manslaughter have trebled, for dangerous assault have risen by 2.5 times, and the figures for robbery have risen almost eight times. Within the group of violent offences, the figures for dangerous assault with serious bodily harm and for dangerous assault have risen drastically (see table 2). Since 1955 all these offences have shown a rising trend. Furthermore, examining the results of the first parallel study about the dark figures of crime, we can state that there has been no serious change in these figures. The ratio of bodily assault within the dark figure was 1:6 (1975 it was 1:7). We can, therefore, assume a consistent tendency to report cases of bodily assault. Thus, we have to note a considerable increase of cases of dangerous assault and assault with serious bodily injury.

The registered number of forcible rape offences shows a stagnating development with some variations. However, here, the dark figure is very high, so that the stagnant picture is probably not representative and probably needs some correction. One can see from the statistics that the absolute figures show a decline. However, the absolute figures for robbery as well as the offence rate for robbery is an exception. If we do not group violent crime using the legal definitions, but use instead a sum index, including all cases where a death was involved, our analysis provides the following picture: Since 1963, the rate of cases where a death took place, would not have risen in the FRG (Kerner 1986). Now if we assume that the attitude of reporting cases of murder, manslaughter, dangerous assault, assault with serious bodily injury, as well as cases of robbery, predatory extortion, predatory assault upon a motorist, has not changed considerably either, we are able to say that violent crime in the FRG is on the increase.

Within this picture of rising crime, we can also see an extraordinary increase in offences against personal liberty, such as kidnapping, abduction, wrongful deprivation of personal liberty, coercion and threat. The dark figure concerning these criminal offences, is very high and the attitude towards reporting such cases is not constant. A clear statement is, therefore, not possible.

2.1.2 Development of Drug Offences

Drastic changes can not only be seen in the field of violent crime, but also in other criminal acts. From 1963 when there were 820 cases, the figure of registered drug offences has risen by 91 times (see table 2). As the dark figure here has been, and still is, extremely high (1:10), it cannot be said

Table 2: Offences against Life and Personal Liberty

Year	1955	1960	1965	1970	1975	1980	1985	1987
Murder and Manslaughter; Attempts included	927	1,116	1,556	2,403	2,908	2,705	2,778	2,632
Forcible Rape	4,574	6,436	5,923	6,889	6,850	6,904	5,919	5,281
Sexual Coercion	–	–	–	2,051	2,496	3,565	3,847	3,411
Sexual Misuse of Children	16,634	17,908	17,630	16,468	14,546	13,165	10,417	10,085
Robbery, Predatory Extortion and Predatory Assault upon a Motorist	3,685	5,790	7,655	9,830	15,831	17,031	19,504	18,331
Assault (with death resulting)	–	–	274	210	188	158	123	108
Dangerous Assault and Assault with Serious Bodily Injury	26,824	29,072	30,403	37,895	50,274	65,479	64,314	63,711
Ill-treatment of Children	–	–	–	–	–	**1,507**	**1,424**	**1,120**
Slight Bodily Injury with Intent	–	47,919	58,096	70,704	65,674	112,021	118,130	121,132
Felonies and Misdemeanours against Personal Liberty	–	–	11,694	18,671	34,169	44,944	52,598	54,060
Kidnapping with Extortion	–	–	–	–	37	43	69	66
Keeping a Person as Hostage	–	–	–	–	30	38	59	62
Total	–	–	–	165,121	193,003	267,560	279,182	279,990
Percentage of all Crimes known to the Police	–	–	–	6.8	6.6	7.0	6.6	6.3
Drug Offences	1,295	916	1,003	16,104	29,805	62,395	60,941	74,894

Note: See Table 1

for sure whether the statistically registered number of crimes, really reflects the actual development, or whether the drastic increase in these cases is due to increasing controls by the police and customs. The huge rise in drug offences since the end of the 2nd World War is verified and supported by further information concerning the number of drug addicts (Haferkamp 1975; Kreutzer 1987) and the attitude of the population towards reporting such cases.

It is a very serious problem that consumers of hard drugs, who need ever-increasing doses, are forced to traffic in drugs or become involved in other crimes (e.g. larceny, robbery) in order to obtain money lost through unemployment or the loss of financial support from either parents or the state. There is no exact information about whether the criminal acts resulting from drug consumption have found expression in the statistics of violent crime or larceny; however, there is much speculation concerning this subject.

2.1.3 Development of Larceny Cases

I would like to single out from the group of property offences, those offences, which are particularly interesting because of their development and their frequency.

About 2,8 million offences against property were registered in the FRG in 1987 (see table 3). Compared with 1955, this number is about five times higher. Offences against property total nearly two thirds of all registered cases, and this characterizes criminality as a whole.

The rate of larcenies in department stores, shops and self-service stores in 1987, was 10 times higher than in 1963 (43,3245) and up to 428,688 in 1987. A similar increase for the same period can also be seen in larceny of cars (8 times higher). Other mass crimes which increased considerably up to 1983, have since declined especially the cases of larceny of mopeds, motorcycles, bicycles and the theft of the attachments of motor vehicles, (aerials, tyres etc). One reason for this decline is probably that insurance conditions have changed.[6] Moreover, this development is also part of a trend, which is not directly noticeable from the statistics and which had already started before the insurance companies changed their conditions.

It is taken for granted that the absolute figures and the number of offenders are applied to the population as a whole. If we do not regard the offence rates, but include other control variables in the analysis, instructive developments can be seen. We intend to do this by seeing the offence rate in terms of the development of opportunity structures. We create

6 Damages caused through larceny, of up to DM 300,- must be borne by the vehicle owner.

Table 3: Offences against Organisations

Year	1955	1960	1965	1971	1975	1980	1985	1987
Robbery of Banks, Saving Institutions, Post Offices, etc.	-	-	-	1,099	1,349	2,145	4,544	4,386
Bag - Snatcher	-	-	-	2,301	3,182	5,017	5,637	5,405
Larceny of Motor Vehicles and Unauthorized use of a Vehicle	-	-	53,270	78,782	62,607	64,131	69,659	74,109
Larceny of Mopeds and Motorcycles	-	-	43,004	52,343	104,587	153,153	73,442	46,212
Larceny of Bicycles	78,652	125,361	104,383	133,459	220,643	358,865	337,337	325,603
Larceny in/out of Automaton	-	-	41,517	51,773	54,080	73,333	103,889	115,211
Larceny in Department Stores, Shops and Self-Service Stores	-	-	55,344	147,315	238,807	357,893	437,035	438,688
Larceny in/out of Motor Vehicles	-	-	131,818	212,726	300,494	317,328	594,891	776,140
Larceny of Motor Vehicles	-	-	83,945	146,981	163,586	297,131	165,296	147,846
Pocket Picking	7,597	7,699	9,763	11,229	12,394	13,574	16,324	26,239
Fraud	211,464	205,826	177,343	170,702	209,841	247,133	372,196	358,493
Embezzlement	65,960	54,776	41,689	36,121	33,169	35,881	48,085	49,846
Forgery of Documents	14,224	16,298	18,321	17,178	25,698	34,845	37,420	40,052
Acts of Fraudulent	-	-	502	543	960	1,208	2,241	2,485
Arson with intent	1,261	2,132	2,415	4,966	6,282	8,468	9,037	9,778
Damage to Property	-	-	107,236	178,081	213,746	330,811	342,309	386,309
Total	-	-	870,550	1,245,599	1,651,425	2,300,916	2,619,342	2,806,802
Percentage of Offences against Organisations	-	-	48.7	51.6	56.6	60.3	62.1	63.2

Notes: see Table 1

Figure 1:
Stock of Motor-Vehicles and Theft of Motor-Vehicles
(1970 = 100)

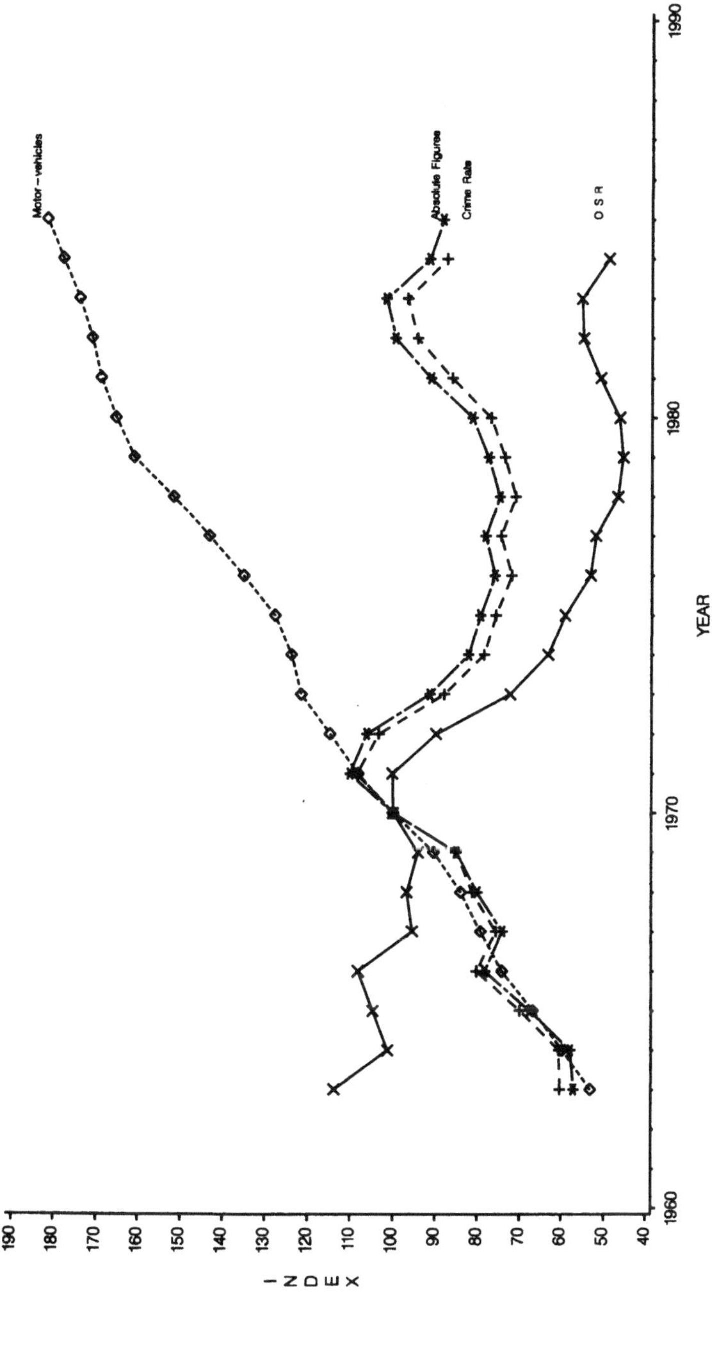

then a so-called Opportunity-Standardized-Rate (OSR), which takes the size of the population at a given time, and the number of opportunities into consideration[7]. Thus, cars, bicycles and motor-cycles become the objects of criminal acts, if they are common in society. Let us therefore, take the stock of cars and motor-cycles in the FRG as opportunity indicators and calculate the so-called OSR. From figure 1 we can see that during the first years after the war, there were very few opportunities for larcenies of cars, because the pre-war stock of cars had been drastically reduced. Owning a car was regarded as a privilege in those days. Therefore, the OSR is very high. After 1970, the reverse development is true. The OSRs not only do keep up with the increase in opportunities but also follow a negative trend. With the increased number of cars in daily life and the increased acquisition of motor vehicles by households, the probability of cars being stolen decreased. In the year 1972, every second household in the FRG had a car.

Larcenies of motor-cycles show a different development. People who did not own a car in the post-war and "economic miracle" periods, at least had a motor-cycle or bicycle. For many citizens the motor-cycle was a substitute for the car they wished to own, but could not afford. We can see this development from figure 2: the stock of motor-cycles decreased and the crime rate stagnated.

With the decrease of stocks of motor-cycles and bicycles, the crime rate began to climb. From 1973 until 1983, it passes over a parallel course with the number of opportunities. Since 1980, the figures have been sinking, while the opportunities have been increasing enormously. The course of the OSR shows this development even clearer. The decreasing stock of motor-cycles led to an increase of the OSR until 1972. After 1972, the stock of motor-cycles grew again, while the OSR took a negative course.

A different development can be seen in shoplifting. The figures clearly show that during the 70's this kind of offence increased drastically. The OSR is much higher than the number of opportunities (=sales areas of self-service stores). The change towards a considerable increase is obvious, especially in this kind of criminal act.

---

7 "It is important to note, however, that standardization for variations in opportunities for crime is not an alternative to standardization for the size of the population available to commit crimes. Instead, both the population of potential offenders, and the stock of available opportunities for crime, should be reflected in the denominator of crime rate" (Sparks 1975, p. 22). The opportunity standardized-rate (OSR) is a function of 1) the number of crimes comitted, 2) the number of persons available to commit crimes, 3) opportunities for the type of crime in question, 4) a constant chosen to give a convenient base or rate.

Figure 2:
Stock of Motor-Cycles and Theft of Motor-Cycles
(1970 = 100)

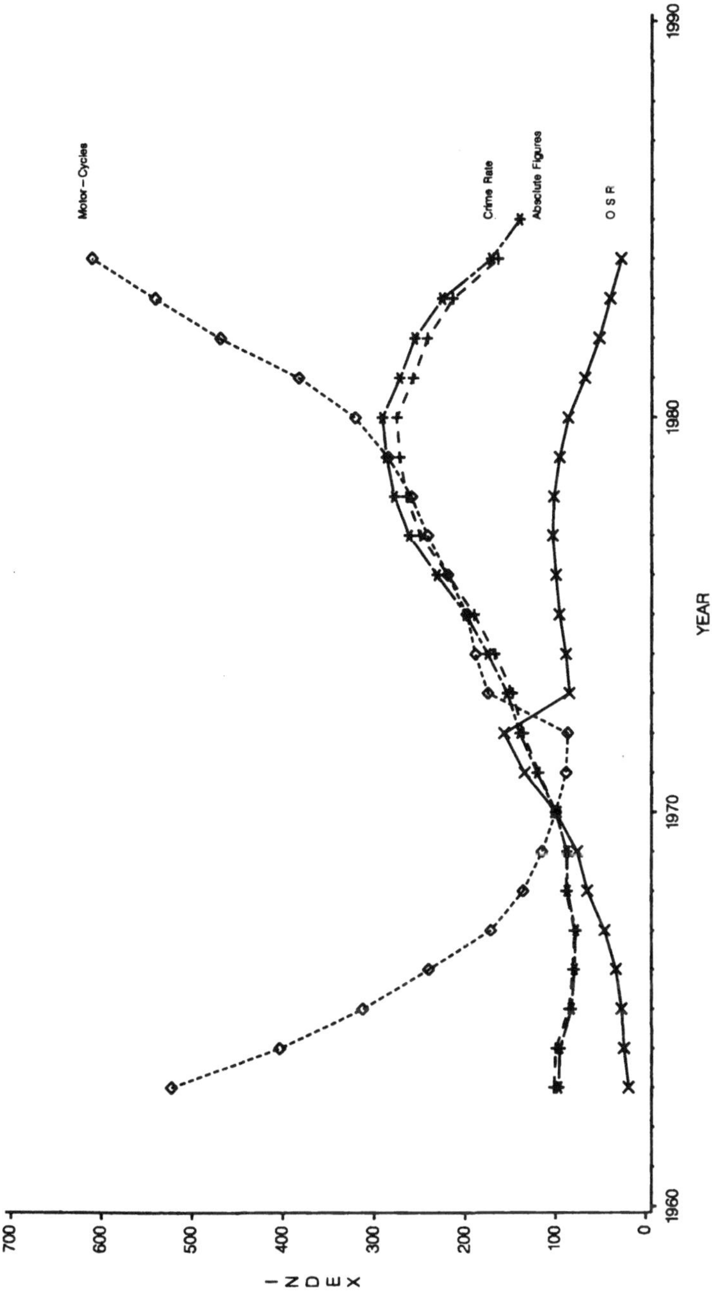

Figure 3:
Sales Areas of Self-Service Stores and Shoplifting
(1970 = 100)

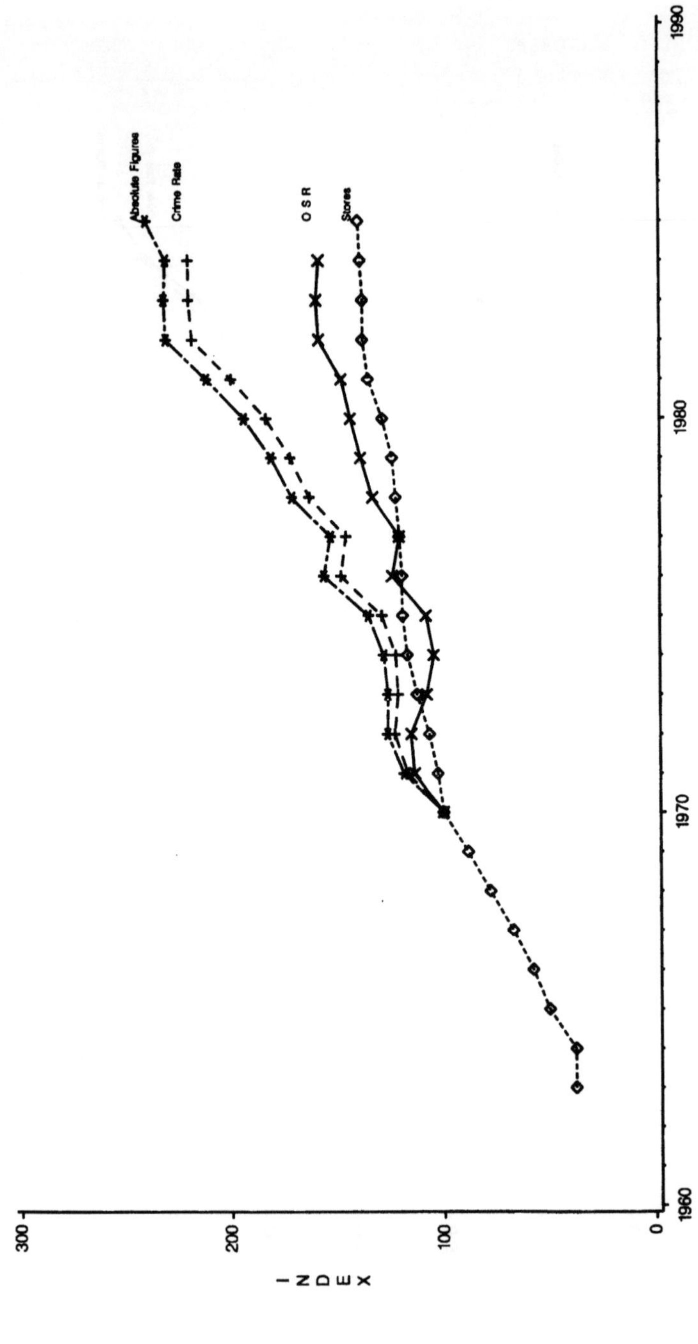

2.1.4 Development of Other Important Criminal Offences

Significant increases are also to be noted, concerning environmental offences. The rate for these offences in 1985 was 7 times higher than in 1973. During the last few years the public has been paying more attention to this kind of criminal offence, so that we can assume that this figure is the expression of an increasing tendency to report these cases. Further indicators of an increased registration of this type of criminal act, are the intensified controls by the police and also the forming of Special Investigation Squads (Meinberg 1988).

A disproportionate growth in the following offences has taken place: The rate of burglary in a dwelling[8] in 1987 was 6,5 times higher than the rate in 1957; the figure for offences related to bankruptcy was 5 times higher in 1987 than in 1963; the number of cases of damage to property was 4.5 times higher in 1987 than in 1963; the rate of cases of arson and intentional arson was 7 times higher in 1987 than in 1953.

2.1.5 Summary

Let us sum up the results so far. The most important fact is that within the development of FRG delinquency those criminal acts which do the most damage or create losses for big anonymous organisations (such as department stores, insurance companies, the state, the general public) have grown disproportionately. Even though individuals and their property are still affected, the damage done is borne and re-imbursed by insurance companies.

Let us now group the data into two large sections, by separating the offences aimed at organizations, from those aimed directly at the individual (see table 2 and 3). The data then shows the above described development: While the offences aimed at organizations are growing steadily and while the percentage contribution of these offences is increasing continuously, the percentage of offences aimed at the individual, doing damage to life and limb, has decreased in the 80's.

In addition, a pattern typical for industrialized societies is developing – the tendency towards individualization.[9] This behaviour is shown particularly in the use of narcotics and in the misuse of personal trust, e.g. in the offence of shoplifting.

At first sight, these results seem to confirm the Welfare-State-Thesis. However, we also have to consider that not all kinds of offences have

---

8 Theft under aggravating circumstances (entry may be by force through an insecure or secure connecting door or window etc).

9 See Hans Haferkamp and Hyacinthe Ellis in this volume

grown disproportionally. The decline of registered larceny crimes and the low increase of sex crimes and crimes against personal freedom, mark developments which are obstacles to the Welfare-State-Thesis. This is shown especially in the negative development of crimes concerning cars and motor-cycles, which indicates a trend aparently caused by the increase in households equipped with cars and motor-cycles. The increase of material wealth in households leads, obviously, to the assumption of the Welfare-State-Thesis, which is, social integration. It would furthermore be a problem if, simultaneously with an increase in deviant behaviour, conformity increased as well. There are, in the FRG, certain signs, which indicate that more conformity in behaviour has developed, while at the same time, prosperity has increased. We thus had to face the paradoxical development of both conformity and deviation, which the Welfare-State-Thesis cannot explain.

2.2 The Development of Social Control

Let us now concentrate on the second part of the Welfare-State-Thesis. It claims, that those responsible, react to anomic tendencies by tolerating these forms of behaviour and showing more leniency in the application of sanctions. As an example, we will examine the development of Criminal Law and its application.

2.2.1 Criminal Justice Process: Sentences

With the abolition of death penalty and penal servitude in the FRG, the first signs pointing to a humanization of Criminal Law were to be seen.

If we look at the remaining, most severe sanction in the FRG, life imprisonment, we see that the absolute figure for this kind of conviction shows sharp fluctuations. There was a continual increase in the number of life imprisonment sentences from 781 convictions in 1963 to 1084 in 1969. In 1974, we find the lowest number with only 936 convictions. In 1986, 1088 were convicted to life imprisonment; with this number, the levels of the 60's had once again been reached. In 1987, judges imposed life imprisonment in 83 cases. The 4,4 million offences reported to the police in 1986 resulted in 591,321 people being sentenced (see table 4). This was a decrease of 2.3% compared with 1986. If we analyse the trend in sentences there are considerable variations in the absolute figures. A large number of variations can be explained by the various reforms in the 1960s and 1970s. A number of offences were removed from the Criminal Code. Since 1963, the majority of traffic and vagrancy type offences are dealt with as administrative violations, punishable by administrative fines only.

Table 4: Different Criminal Sanctions in the FRG

Year	1963	1965	1970	1975	1980	1985	1987
Total Number of Sentenced Offenders - Absolute	499,117	505,441	553,692	567,605	599,832	600,798	591,321
Sentenced Offenders	159,547	174,100	88,248	94,019	104,850	111,876	108,528
Percentage of Sentenced Offenders	32	35	16	17	18	19	18
Suspended Prison Offences	56,450	58,617	46,972	57,924	68,878	74,147	74,239
Percentage of Suspended Prison Offences	11	12	9	10	12	12	13
Fines	338,637	330,610	464,818	472,577	494,114	488,414	482,347
Percentage of Fines	68	65	84	83	82	81	82

Notes: Main sanctions only; excluding juveniles
Source: Statistisches Bundesamt (Ed.), Fachserie 10: Rechtspflege, Reihe 3: Strafverfolgung, Mainz und Wiesbaden

Administrative fines cannot be transformed into a prison term in case of non-payment. Additionally the penalties for pornography, procuring and prostitution have been liberalized and non-violent sex and other moral offences, like homosexual acts between consenting adults, were removed from the Criminal Code.

Of the total number of sentences in 1986, burglary is the most widespread offence (8.5% compared with 4.9% in 1961). The list continues with intentional injury 3.7% (3.7% in 1961) and robbery 1.4% compared with 0.5% in 1961.

The absolute figures for limited prison sentences of more than one year were 75% higher in 1987 than in 1971. The average number, per month, of people in prison in the FRG in 1980 was almost 56,000. If one compares the prison population of 1961 (47,391 on 31. March) with that of 1986 (45,342) a progressive decline over the years is noticeable, with only temporary increases as compared with previous years. Compared with its highest level in 1965 (49,573), the prison population has declined by 8.5%. In the 1970s the prison population settled around an average level of

36,000 (up to 1977). Towards the end of the 1970s this figure increased. In 1987, however, the figures were still markedly below the figures for 1961. The decline can be attributed to a 1969 reform in criminal law legislation which had the following effects:

a) many traffic offences were removed from the Criminal Code and became mere administrative violations; punishable only by fines;

b) many non-violent sex-related offences were decriminalized;

c) prison sentences of up to one year became suspendable;

d) fines became an important alternative to sentencing for most criminal offences.

The high percentage of prisoners awaiting trial is especially remarkable; it is more than 25%. Thus, the rate of imprisonments in the FRG is 99 per 100,000 population, a high rate compared to other countries. Examining the development of the penal system, a trend towards more order and control is obvious. After the Criminal Law reforms, which aimed to stem shorter term imprisonment, (i.e. imprisonment for less than 6 months) the percentage of short-term imprisonment dropped from 25% (1969) to 8.4% (1987) between 1969 and 1987. The number of convicts who have to stay in prison for more than 1 year is 75% higher in 1987 than in 1971 (abs.=7,651). The number of those sentenced to more than 2 years imprisonment first sank after the Criminal Law reforms of 1970/71, when only approximately 3% of all convicts sentenced to imprisonment had sentences longer than 2 years. Between 1971 and 1976 the number rose to 4.7% and in 1987 it was 5.8%. The criminal sentencing practices of the courts certainly play an important role in this development. While prison sentences of more than 2 years for grand larceny have steadily dropped, the criminal sentencing practice regarding robbery and predatory extortion has become more severe since 1973. Prison sentences of more than 2 years and up to 5 years for forcible rape, have also increased enormously. Of all prison sentences for rape, this length of sanction had been imposed on 20% of offenders in 1968, 23% in 1973 and 47% in 1982.

If we relate the number of convictions carrying imprisonment to the number of criminal acts, we see that the risk, per criminal act, of being sentenced to imprisonment has dropped. We need only refer to offences with a low dark figure to substantiate this statement: robbery and predatory extortion and predatory assault upon a motorist have nearly doubled. Theft under aggravating circumstances has almost doubled.

From the total amount of convictions, prison sentences dropped by more than 166% (1960=91,437 and 1987=34,289). The number of fines increased to over 80% of all sanctions and the number of suspended sentences rose from 11.8% in 1960, to 12.6% (1987). Thus, fines are quantatively the most important form of sanctioning in the FRG. In 1987, 81.6% of the total of 591,000 sentences, were fines. Thus, compared to the

Table 5: Prison Population and Persons Sentenced in Court

Year	1961	1965	1970	1975	1980	1985	1986
Prison Population Number of Prisoners on 31. March							
- Prison, Borstal and Remand Homes	47,391	49,572	35,927	32,608	42,235	48,402	45,342
- Psychiatric or Drug Clinics	–	5,281	4,401	3,677	3,225	3,462	3,423
Capacity of Prisons (remand and sentenced)	60,805	63,261	60,949	57,723	57,705	63,230	62,766
Persons Sentenced in Court							
- Burglary	16,080	14,778	27,495	37,641	34,967	40,156	37,433
- Robbery	1,674	1,754	2,819	4,226	4,939	6,218	5,979
- Intentional Injury	12,281	11,234	12,260	12,462	15,132	16,012	16,240

Definitions: Burglary: Theft under aggravating circumstances
Robbery: This term includes the following offence categories: Robbery (249); aggravated robbery (250, without Part 1); robbery with torture, causing grievious bodily harm or death or robbery in connection with death (251); use of violence or threat in flagrant theft (252); robbery-like extortion (255); robbery of drivers of vehicles (316a)
Intentional (bodily) Injury: Includes all cases in which persons were either physically assaulted or suffered permanent physical injury (223)
Sources: Statistisches Bundesamt (ed.): Fachserie 10: Rechtspflege, Reihe 3: Strafverfolgung, Mainz und Wiesbaden
Statistisches Bundesamt (ed.): Fachserie 10: Rechtspflege, Reihe 4: Strafvollzug, Mainz und Wiesbaden

1960 figure of 69.2%, there is an increase of 144%. This increase in use of fines is mainly due to the decrease in imposing short-term prison sentences (up to 3 months).

2.2.2 The Development of How the Prosecuting Attorney's Offices and the Courts Deal with Cases

Punishment and the execution of sentences are the final links in the chain of events dealing with a criminal case. We, therefore, want to return to the level of the courts and the prosecuting attorney's offices. The judicial system in the FRG consists of County or Regional Courts (AG), District or Local Courts (LG), Higher Land or Local Courts (OLG) and the Federal Court of Justice (BGH). The County or Regional Court ist the court of first instance, the Federal Court of Justice is the court of appeal and the highest instance. At all levels the judges make decisions about convictions, aquittals or the dismissal of a proceeding.

At the lowest level of the judicial system, cleared criminal actions have increased from 897,000 in 1975 to 975,204 in 1987. This increase is caused by a disproportional growth in indictment proceedings, compared to penal order proceedings[10]. Whereas in 1976, both types of criminal proceedings almost balanced each other out. The situation in 1980 had changed. About 500,000 proceedings (1987=456,404)that started with an indictment, resulted in 436,000 penal order proceedings (1987=452,896). Of the total of 452,896 penal orders, about 300,000 were accepted by the accused. In almost 152,000 cases the accused appealed against the sentence, or the judge ordered a main hearing.

It is remarkable, that since 1975 the acceptance of the written proceedings has declined and that a main hearing during the proceedings has been preferred. This result should, however, not be allowed to hide the fact that the number of cases cleared by dismissal, involving conditions and special rulings, has fallen continuously. By collating the data of conditional dismissals pronounced by the prosecution and the courts, Heinz estimated that the number of such proceedings was approximately more than 150,000 cases (Heinz 1982, p. 644).

Thus, prosecution and courts, in spite of the rising crime rate, through dismissals of proceedings and through lenient sentencing, have constibuted greatly to the waiving of sanctions and the general mitigation of sentences. Considering that the number of suspects has grown more than the number of convicts, and considering that the number of people imprisoned has not really increased, we could claim that the waiving of sanctions is the most important change in penal sanctioning in the FRG.

Apart from the waiving of sanctions, the mitigation of sentences should also be mentioned. Mitigation includes diversion projects, which are not aimed at changing the penal definition of offences, but at a change in

10 The 'penal order' (Strafbefehl) is an important way for the prosecutor to avoid a full-scale trial. This document describes the wrongful behaviour of the defendant and the evidence gathered and specifies the punishment imposed. It is prepared by the prosecutor and routinely signed by a judge. If the offender objects, the case will go on trial; if the offender does not object within one week, the penal order becomes the equivalent of a court sentence. Penal orders can be used for a wide variety of misdemeanors ranging from shoplifting and speeding, to car theft, fraud and embezzlement.

reaction to the criminal acts, especially those acts committed by juveniles. The aim is to help alternatives to traditional forms of sanctioning and to implement these alternatives, which have already been incorporated in the Penal Law. This form of diversion is intended to keep juvenile criminals in their social surroundings. They are to be encouraged to behave according to social norms by doing such activities as community work. Another promising alternative to traditional sanctioning is that offenders must compensate their victims for any damages done. Attempts to reconcile the offender with the victim, through compensation, are on the increase.

Suspended prison sentences are second only to the dominating sanction of fines. However, milder sentencing has not been a continual characteristic of the post-World War II development. The percentage of prison sentences which are not suspended, for example, has remained constant. This is no doubt the main reason for the constancy of the prison population. However, the data clearly shows that the change in the application of sentences from severe to more lenient sentences has taken place. Even though the scope of action for criminals has, in many cases, not changed, it is obvious that the extent of control does not necessarily have to decline. Although fewer individuals are imprisoned, the social control net is spreading. Individuals whose cases have been dismissed are being sanctioned. Law violators are not only repulsed by specialized forms of social control, (police, prison, homes and clinics) but also by welfare institutions and schools, which are becoming more and more sources of control.

2.2.3 The Definition of New Penal Case Facts

The results, which have so far been reported, can probably be considered to confirm the Welfare-State-Thesis: The reaction of the social elites to the spread of deviance is to tolerate this deviant behaviour. The most important key phrases are: the waiving of sanctions, the mitigation of sentences, diversion and restitution.

The criminal-political development is not only characterized by mitigation and toleration. Increases in the severity of penalties are also registered. The spread and expansion of social control is to be regarded as the opposite tendency to mitigation. Not only has the number of employees in the coercive authorities increased, but communications and the methods of investigation have improved due to new information systems. Increases in the severity of sentences for forcible rape, as well as the extensive application of the laws are characteristic of this trend.

Social behaviour is being partly decriminalized, but in other areas such as drugs, political penal law and terrorism, criminalization is expanding. These changes are taking place within the traditional field of penal law, whereas the definition of new criminal acts (e.g. crimes within the field of commerce, environmental and computer delinquency) has a new quality. With this new criminalization, penal law intervention is expanding into new spheres of action which are difficult to control. Thus, new groups in society are being criminalized. The main characteristic of newly criminalized social groups is that their members belong to the middle and the upper class. For example, the rules concerning the field of commercial crimes mainly threaten protagonists of a high status who work in industry. The statutory definitions dealing with environmental delinquency threaten those responsible in industry (managers, technicians) (Bussmann 1989). This new field of criminalization is leading to a change in penal law, which clearly shows altered expectations in industrialized societies. The normative expectations are not to be directed at individuals, but at organisations which are able to suppress, disguise and hush-up their deviant actions. The widening of statutory definitions in penal law can be regarded as an attempt to bind collective protagonists, normatively, because industrialized societies are dependent on the good conduct of their major organisations. Despite partial decriminalization, it must still be considered that the sphere of social control has by no means diminished.

The image of a self-accusing, tolerant State, can be matched with widespread tolerance, part apologetic, part lenient sentencing of deviant behaviour. Continuous or rather increasing control and repression, can not be fitted into this image. Tolerance, as well as control, characterize the welfare state development in the FRG. We can, therefore, safely speak of a toleration-control paradox.

3 Development Trends

Two noticeable paradoxes characterize the development of crime and control in the FRG. We have described them as the deviancy-conformity paradox and the toleration-control paradox. The Welfare-State-Thesis can explain deviant behaviour and tolerance but not conformity and control.

To sum up, we come to the conclusion, that apart from some trends which substantiate the Welfare-State-Thesis, there are numerous developments in the FRG, which can not be explained by this thesis.

Summarizing the results of our analysis, we must emphasize that obviously, an increasing number of protagonists commit actions which can be seen as undisciplined and uncivilized behaviour. In the field of crimes of drug abuse, tendencies towards individualism come together with actions which are not calculable. The offences of larceny and fraud are often characterized by the misuse of trust. Offences against property are increasingly aimed at big, anonymous victims, although at first sight the criminal act does damage to the individual. In the FRG we can clearly see a fall in disciplined and civilized behaviour, and the orientation of these anti-social acts towards abstract, anonymous social units (Haferkamp 1987).

Criminal acts in the field of middle and lower (mass-) delinquency, victimless offences, and offences where only minor damage is done are tolerated more than serious offences. The altered moral conceptions of the population often correspond with decriminalizing legislation. In cases where the State considers the main principles of the welfare state to be in danger, punishment is strengthened. Violent crimes and delinquency in the area of drug abuse are prosecuted intensively and are punished with severe sentences, whether or not they are committed in connection with terrorist activities. More lenient punishment can only be expected by drug users if they are willing to undergo therapy.

The change in the aims and the methods of control is very conspicuous. In the FRG there is a great willingness to react informally to criminal acts. Alternatives to traditional forms of sanctioning for minor and medium offences are preferred. These alternatives do not put punishment and deprivation of freedom in the foreground. It is, however, disturbing that, despite a great willingness to reduce short-term imprisonment, there is a move towards medium-length terms of imprisonment. During different periods of their development, criminalization and decriminalization overlap to such an extent, that clear trends are hardly recognizable. There is no clear trend towards tolerance or towards repression.

Social control no longer occurs directly, but works increasingly indirectly, in less visible ways. Rehabilitation, treatment and self-responsibility are the appropriate key words of a social control which is more preventive and less repressive. Even though methods to compensate the damage caused by offences are becoming more evident, this does not mean that social control is retrogressing appropriately. Conformist behaviour can not so much be achieved by repressive intervention, extensive control and severe sentencing, but more by restraint and "positive sentencing", such as restitution or regulation, according to the rules of Civil Law. Lenient sentencing and the waiving of intervention are by no means consistent characteristics of a "new" social control. The tightening of control and the intensification of punishment can mainly be seen in the criminalization of problematic and socially unwanted actions (drug offences, crimes in the field of commerce and computer crimes).

"New" social control is characterized on the one hand by enhanced and refined powers of State intervention and on the other hand by enhanced individual responsibility. The spectacular informal control which is less public has taken the place of the open, repressive policy of control.

References

Bussmann, Kai D. (1989)"Das moderne Experiment Strafrecht-Vom Strafrecht der Lebenswelt zum Strafrecht sozialer Systeme", in: Kriminalsoziologische Bibliografie, vol. 16.

Feest, Johannes B. (1982) Imprisonment and the Criminal Justice System in the Federal Republic of Germany, Bremen: Arbeitspapiere des Forschungsschwerpunktes Soziale Probleme: Kontrolle und Kompensation, Heft 8.

Haferkamp, Hans (1975) Kriminelle Karrieren, Reinbek bei Hamburg.

Haferkamp, Hans (1987) "Zur zukünftigen Neuorientierung der kriminologischen Forschung", in: Kriminologisches Journal, vol. 19, pp. 171 – 192.

Heinz, Wolfgang (1982) "Strafrechtsreform und Sanktionsentwicklung – Auswirkungen der sanktionenrechtlichen Regelungen des 1. und 2. StrRG 1969 sowie des EGStGB 1974 auf die Sanktionspraxis", in: Zeitschrift für die gesamte Strafrechtswissenschaft, vol. 94.

Janowitz, Morris (1976) The Social Control of the Welfare State, New York.

Kerner, Hans-Jürgen (1986) "Tötungsdelikte und lebenslange Freiheitsstrafe", in: Zeitschrift für die gesamte Strafrechtswissenschaft, vol. 98, 1986, pp. 874 – 918.

Klages, Helmut (1975) Die unruhige Gesellschaft. Untersuchungen über Grenzen und Probleme sozialer Stabilität, München.

Kreutzer, Arthur (1987) Jugend, Drogen, Kriminalität, Neuwied und Darmstadt, (3rd edition).

Lutz, Burkhart (1984) Der kurze Traum immerwährender Prosperität, Frankfurt/New York.

Meinberg, Volker (1988) "Empirische Erkenntnisse zum Vollzug des Umweltstrafrechts", in: Zeitschrift für die gesamte Strafrechtswissenschaft, vol. 100, pp. 112 – 157.

Schwind, Hans-Dieter (1988) "Dunkelfeldforschung in Bochum: 1975 und 1986. Die erste deutsche Replikationsstudie, in: Kriminologische Forschungen in den 80er Jahren, G. Kaiser, H. Kury, H.-J. Albrecht eds., Freiburg, pp. 943 – 959.

Sparks, Richard F. (1975) "Criminal opportunities and crime rates", in: Indicators of Crime and Criminal Justice: Quantitative Studies, Stephen

E. Fienberg and Albert J. Reiss, Jr. eds., Washington, D.C.: U.S. Government Printing Office.

Teske, Jr. Raymond H.C. and Harald R. Arnold (1982) "Comparison of the Criminal Statistics of the United States and the Federal Republic of Germany" Journal of Criminal Justice, vol. 10, pp. 359 – 374.

Zapf, Wolfgang (1986) "Die deutsche Version des Wohlfahrtstaates",in: Wirtschafts- und Sozialstatistik. Empirische Grundlagen politischer Entscheidungen, K. Hanau, R. Hujer und W. Neubauer eds., Göttingen, pp. 379 – 403.

The Development of Delinquency and Criminal Justice in Japan

Hisao Katoh

1 Criminal Trends in Japan

Not only we as criminologists, but also other people are very interested in whether a close relation exists between economic development and an increase in criminality. As far as I know, there is no scientific explanation. Many people have tried to explain this, but it is very difficult to establish the relationship, because the causes of crime are very uncertain and diversified.

First, I would like to describe the general situation of crime in Japan, and then to refer to the relationship between crime and the Japanese economic situation.

1.1 Penal Code Offences

In 1987, the total number of Penal Code Offences[1] reported to the police was 2,132,592, an increase of 8,353 (0.4%) over the previous year. But the number of Penal Code Offences recorded, excluding traffic and professional negligence offences, was 1,577,929, which represented a decrease of 3,449 (0.2%) compared with the previous year.

The total number of Penal Code Offences cleared by the police was 983,891 (of which 248,383 or 25.2% were juveniles), an increase of 15,919 (1.6%) over the previous year. The number of Penal Code Offences cleared, excluding traffic and professional negligence offences, was 404,722 (of which 187,165 or 46.2% were committed by juveniles). This represented an increase of 4,861 (1.2%) compared with the previous year. Trends since 1946 in the number of Penal Code Offences reported to the police and Penal Code Offenders cleared by the police are shown in figure 1.

As figure 1 shows, the number of Penal Code Offences (excluding traffic and professional negligence offences) reported to the police peaked

1 See Summary of the White Paper on Crime 1987, ed. by Research and Training Institute, Ministry of Justice.

Figure 1:
Trend in the Number of Penal Code Offences Reported
1950 – 1987

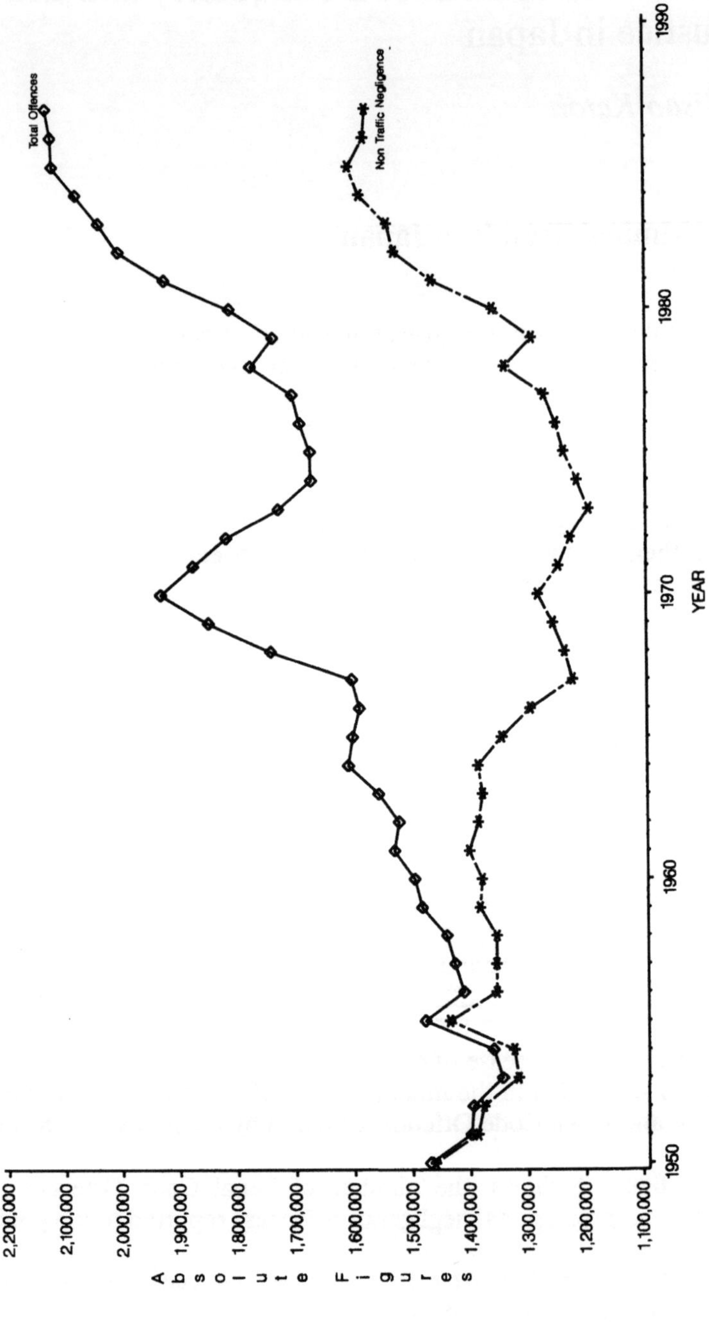

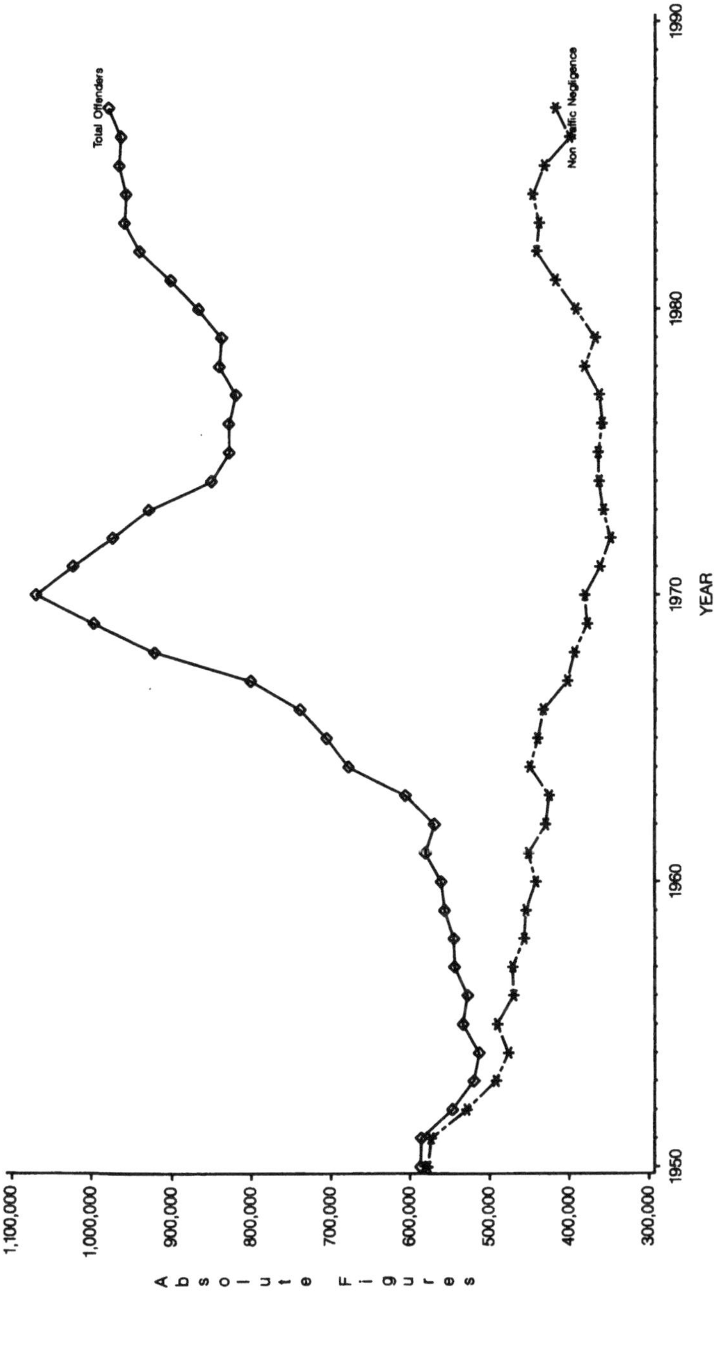

Figure 2:
Trends in the Number of Offenders Cleared
1950 – 1987

at 1,599,968 in 1948, and then declined to its post World War II low in 1974, when 1,190,534 were recorded. However, it has been showing an upward trend since 1974. In 1985, it reached 1,607,663, a number greater than that of 1949. In 1987 it decreased a little to 1,577,929.

In Japan, the high economic growth rate has been continuing since the end of the 1960s and at the same time our lifestyle and sense of values has been changing. But as figure 1 shows, during these 20 years there were no problems with the crime rate. There seems to be no relation between the crime rate and the economic growth rate in Japan. If no such relationship exists, we must analyse the reasons.

Among reported Penal Code Offences (excluding traffic and professional negligence offences) in 1987, larceny contributed the overwhelming majority of crimes (86.5%), followed by fraud which accounted for 4.4% and embezzlement which accounted for 2.7%. These property offences accounted for 93.6% of the total.

1.2 Major Penal Code Offences

Comparisons of 1987 crime data for the major penal code offences with those of the previous year reveals the following: total larceny cases 1,364,796: -0.7% decline); homicide(1,584:-5.5%), robbery(1,874: -3.8%) bodily injury(21,046: -0.6%), extortion (11,855: -8.1%). Increases were noted in the following categories: embezzlement (42,580: 13.7%) rape (1,823: 4,2%), indecent assault (2,404: 4.9%), arson(1,814: 2.1%) and traffic and professional negligence (554,663: 2.2%).

1.3 Offences against Special Laws

In 1987, the public prosecutors registered a total of 1,635,566 Special Law offenders which represented a decline of 687,536 (29,6%) from 1986. Comparing the dynamics of particular offences reveals that the number of suspects for the Public Election Law showed an increase of 6,118 (40.8%) because of the local elections. In most other categories of offences, however, sharp decreases were observed; i.e. the number of traffic offences declined by 685,394 (31.3%), those charged under the Poisonous Substances Control Law declined by 628 (2,6%), offenders against public morals declined by 1,711 (13.6%), and violators of laws regarding preservation of public peace went down by 1,926 (15,6%). Drug offences declined by 2,171 (4.0%), especially those charged under the Stimulant Drugs Control Law which decreased by 1,485 (5.2%) to 27,214.

2 Trends in certain Offences and Offenders

The following section focuses on particular crime problems in Japan. These are: 1) Crimes involving narcotics; 2) Organized crime (Bo-ryo-ku-dan, Yakuza); 3) Crimes committed by mentally disturbed criminals; 4) Terrorism; 5) Crimes committed by the elderly; 6) Crimes committed by females; 7) Crimes committed by juveniles

2.1 Drug Offences

While in most industrialized societies, the majority of narcotics cases concern drugs such as hashish and heroin, in Japan the drug problem mainly concerns the misuse of amphetamines, (e.g. wakemine) or other stimulants. The number of stimulant drug cases has shown a marked and remarkable increase since 1970 and has not as yet peaked, after more than ten years. Although in 1987 there were 31,301 stimulant drug cases identified, a decrease of 1,363 (4.2%) over the previous year, it should be estimated that these offences are continuing at a rather high level.

Among other drug offences, it is remarkable that the number of suspects for cannabis offences was 1,395 in 1987, an increase of 58 compared with the previous year. The punishment for drug abuse is long prison sentences.

2.2 Bo-ryo-ku-dan Offenders (Offenders composing or associated with Bo-ryo-ku-dan)

The organized crime groups, the so-called Bo-ryo-ku-dan[2] have a 400 year old tradition. The Bo-ryo-ku-dan deal mainly in illegal gambling, black-mail in order to receive protection money, the organisation of prostitution (in Japan still illegal) and also with the manufacture and handling of hard-core pornography.

Prostitution and pornography are by law strictly forbidden, but with the payment of enough money they can be attained without much problem at any time. Prostitution and pornography are part of every day life. In order to combat this problem, the decriminalization of this group of offenders

---

2 Bo-ryo-ku means violence and dan-gang. Bo-ryo-ku-dan are organized groups prone to committing violent, unlawful acts.

has been tried but so far this has not been successfully carried out within Japanese society.

The Japanese criminal organizations try to avoid involving people from outside their organizations, in crime, especially crimes of a violent nature. If for example a day-light shoot-out takes place, this can usually be put down to rivalry, revenge and reprisals between gangs. Organized crime is responsible for only 6.6% of reported offences. The dark area of this criminality is very large, as offences between criminals do not usually come to the attention of the police.

There were an estimated 3,201 Bo-ryo-ku-dan groups and their membership totalled 86,287 as of the end of 1987. However, this number does not include collaborating family members. In the same year, the number of Bo-ryo-ku-dan offenders cleared amounted to 40,257, a decrease of 4,808 (10.7%) from the previous year (excluding traffic professional and negligence offenders). Among Penal Code offenders cleared, the percentages of Bo-ryo-ku-dan offenders were noticeably high in special classes of offences. They represented 65% of those charged with intimidation, 40.6% of those charged with extortion, 35.4% of gamblers and 29.9% for those charged with homicide. Out of Special Law offenders cleared, the percentages were 45.1% for the violation of the Stimulant Drug Control Law, 52.7% for that of the Horse Race Law and 64.6% for the Bicycle Race Law.

In recent years, there has been an upward trend in violent cases backed by the menace of Bo-ryo-ku-dan threats. These have occurred in civil disputes concerned with the collection of money involving traffic accidents, loans or accounts due.

In 1986, 46,038 prisoners were put into penal institutions, 30.2% of whom were members of organized crime groups. Forty three percent of imprisoned organized crime members were put into "B-Class" institutions, which under our classification system are for recidivist offenders.

2.3 Mentally Disordered Offenders

In 1987, the number of either mentally disordered or in inadequate mental order, represented a total of 2,266 (adults, 2,140; juveniles. 126) Penal Code offenders cleared[3] or 0.6% (adults, 1.0%; juveniles, 0.07%) of all penal offenders. In certain categories of offences, the percentages were remarkably high, e.g., 19.7% for arson and 10.2% for homicide. In the same year, at the prosecution stage of the proceedings, 393 could not be

3 Excluding traffic professional negligence offenders.

prosecuted due to their mental disorders, and in the courts of the first instance five were acquitted for the same reason.

2.4 Offences by Terrorist Groups

In 1987, terroristic groups committed guerrilla-attack offences by utilizing delayed-action explosives or shooting devices to demonstrate their opposition to the national ceremony for the 60th anniversary of the reign of the Emperor, and to the 7th Summit Conference convened in Tokyo in the first half of that year. Terrorist offences were also committed to express opposition to the privatization and division of the Japan National Railways, and to try to block the implementation of the second phase of construction of the New Tokyo International Airport.

In 1987, 37 guerrilla-attack cases (a decrease of 52 over the previous year) and 4 violent struggles among the groups (a decrease of 5 over the previous year) were reported.

2.5 Aged Offenders

In 1987, the number of offenders over offences 60 years charged with totalled 19,031. Of these the largest percentage of age for larceny (74.8%) followed by 12.4% for embezzlement and 3.8% for fraud.

Aged offenders represented 4.7% of total Penal Code offenders cleared, well below their proportional share of the overall population (15.8%). However, it should be noted that the percentage of aged offenders is rising year by year.

2.6 Female Offenders

In 1987, the number of female Penal Code offenders cleared amounted to 78,062, of which 83.1% were charged with larceny, followed in frequency by 6.5% for embezzlement, 2.1% for bodily injury and 2.1% for fraud. Females represented 19.3% of all cleared Penal Code offenders. In certain categories of offences, the percentages were remarkably high, e.g., in larceny (24.8%) and in homicide (19.0%), and especially infanticide (94.3%).

2.7 Juvenile Delinquency

Juvenile crime and juvenile delinquency has taken a slightly different course in Japan than in other industrialized nations. In 1951 and 1964 the numbers peaked and have been on the increase again since 1972. The juvenile offenders are mainly from the middle-class. Their most frequent offences are shoplifting and bicycle larceny, violent attacks on teachers and parents (especially mothers) and also glue-sniffing.

In 1986, there were 1,376 cases of the use of violence in Japanese schools, of which 627 (45.6%) were against teachers.

Young people in Japan, compared with other countries, are better integrated into the society, although too much is sometimes asked of them. Japan is an education oriented society. It allows for the equality of all its citizens. The path to the best positions in society and business is through the best schools and universities which are open for all. The entrance examinations for the limited number of places in these schools and universities are very stiff, so that Japanese children and juveniles find themselves in relentless, hard competition from an early age. Children and juveniles who do not reach the high standards asked of them by their parents, lose their self-respect and fall into juvenile crime. As mothers in Japan bear the full weight of the work of bringing up their children, they are the ones who become the targets of attack from their children. Violence in schools is also, naturally, on the increase in Japan. Teachers and fellow pupils are attacked daily, school property is destroyed through vandalism. Offenders are mainly pupils who cannot or do not want to meet the demands of school.

The Japanese school system of today, no longer provides an education, but also is the means to attain a higher status. Activities in schools are oriented to the entrance examination for the next highest grade. All are targeted to this aim. On working days, lessons usually finish at 16.00 or 17.00, and on Saturdays at midday. The summer holidays are only one month long. After school, one learns further with a review teacher, or visits a prep-school, to prepare for the entry examination. School in Japan is a field of competition. Nowadays, this chain of events begins so early, that for many children compulsory school attendance begins with kindergarten. In 1983, about 2,5 million children (more than 60% of the appropriate age group) attended a kindergarten.

Aggression, not defined as juvenile delinquency, is also on the increase. Bullying and cruelty towards weaker juveniles are also on the increase. Sometimes these only lead to retaliatory attacks by the bullied victims, though it has been reported that suicide has been the result of such ill-treatment. There are certainly many reasons for bullying in schools.

The strong pressures of competition though, must surely play a leading role, as they are obstacle to, and a strain on friendship.

The number of juvenile and child offenders involved in the Penal Code offences cleared by the police in 1987 was 289,169, a decrease of 3,117 (1.1%) over the previous year. The percentage of juvenile and child offenders among the total number of offenders involved in offences cleared by the police was 28.2%.

The number of juvenile and child offenders involved in non-traffic Penal Code offences cleared by the police in 1987 was 227,978, a decrease of 7,198 (3.1%) from the previous year. Among them, males contributed 80.9% and females, 19.1%. Examining the individual offences, larceny accounted for an overwhelming 75.9% of them, followed by embezzlement at 10.1% and bodily injury at 4.4%. Almost all (99.9%) of embezzlement cases were conversions of lost articles and most of them involved the unauthorized use of unattended bicycles.

The number of juvenile and child offenders involved in traffic and professional negligence cases cleared by the police in 1987 was 61,218, an increase of 4,104 (7.2%) over the previous year. The number of juvenile and child offenders referred by the police to the Public Presecutor for Special Law offences (excluding traffic offences) was 31,174 in 1987, a decrease of 359 from the previous year. Examining the dynamics of particular offences, violations of the Poisonous and Hazardous Substances Control Law were the most frequently committed (71.8%), followed in frequency by violations of the Stimulant Drugs Control Law (4.8%).

3 The Penal System and Prison as a "Crime Control" in Japan

Most Japanese laws, i.e. The Civil Code, The Code of Commercial Law, The Penal Code, The Code of Prison Practices, The Code of Criminal Procedure were passed at the turn of the century and were based on German Law and its dominant dogma.

The Penal Code and the Code of Prison Practices came into force in 1908. Although different reform bills and alternatives to both laws were suggested by the Justice Ministry, criminal law specialists or criminal-political practitioners after the 2nd World War, they have not yet been implemented. This means that Japanese criminal law and politics and policies are old fashioned.

For this reason there is no point in discussing the Penal System and the

Code of Prison Practices in this essay. The Japanese Criminal Code still contains the same sanctions as did the German Criminal Code of 1871. These include the death penalty, three different types of prison sentences (prison sentence with or without enforced labour and imprisonment of up to 30 days) and fines. With six different sanctions, the present system of punishment is in a rut.

In 1985, 65,359 sentences were imposed by District Courts, of which nine individuals were sentenced to the death penalty, 39 to life imprisonment, 64,504 were given limited prison sentences (56% of which were suspended sentences) and 544 received fines. We have no imprisonment system to substitute fines. In 1986, 32,827 convicts were committed to penal institutions. 95.8% of all the convicts were male, 4.2% were female.

The average total of sentenced prisoners and prisoners awaiting trial reached an absolute peak of 103,170 in Japan after the 2nd World War (1950). It had sunk again by 1975 to 45,690 and began to rise again until 1986 when the number reached 55,348. The average total of sentenced prisoners went down from 85,254 in 1950 to 37,850 in 1970. It rose steadily once more to 46,107 by 1986. The number of sentenced female prisoners newly committed to penal institutions rose in the years 1972 to 1986 from 2.1% to 4.2%.

4 The Objectives and the Reality of Treatment in Penal Institutions

In 1986, there were a total of 74 prisons and jails for those awaiting trial. Of these, 58 were penitentiaries, 9 juvenile detention centres and 7 were jails for those awaiting trial. In addition, there were 9 branch penal institutions and 108 branch jails for those awaiting trial. All of these were directly linked to, and under the authority of the main penal institutions. Five penal institutions and branches served female prisoners and four additional ones housed the sick as well as the mentally and physically handicapped convicts.

In 1985, the total prisoner capacity of all the penal institutions was for 63,263 convicted and remanded prisoners but the actual number of convicted prisoners was 97.6% of the appropriate total capacity.

By law, the aim of imprisonment is identical in both Japan and West Germany. In both countries the objective is to enable the convict to lead a socially responsible life without crime, after his/her release. However, the term "resocialisation" has different meanings in Japan and West Germany. The reason for this can be found in the different social structures of the two countries. While Japanese society is still very much a strict hierarchy, in Germany these strict structures no longer exist. The once "closed" society has been replaced by an "open" society. Consequently, the contents of the term "resocialisation" result in different objectives. The aim in Japan is that the prisoner should be helped to voluntarily take the place reserved for him/her in society, once he/she has served the sentence. In Germany the aim is that the prisoner should be aided to become responsible enough to find his/her own place in the "open" society. In Japanese prison practise there is no meaningful treatment, or real therapeutic activity. Work is forced labour and at the same time serves the security of the institution. In 1972, 16,915 people were employed in Japanese prisons. In 1985, the number had only risen to 16,932. Meaningful work, and career supportive measures should be the prime objective. Wages are only seen as rewards for work done.

5 Reasons for a Low Incidence of Crime in Japan

We can think about the reasons for a low incidence of crime in Japan.

(1) Generally speaking, we no longer have crimes caused by familial poverty. According to the traditional criminological theories about the causes of crime, crime was thought to be closely connected to poverty. However as of recently we can not find evidence of this being a cause of crime in Japan, because the Japanese economic situation in the last 20 years has developed well. Surveys reveal that 85% of the Japanese people think that they belong to the middle class of our society.

The so-called "oil-crisis" also took place in Japan, but our Government succeeded in providing us with a very adequate economic policy. We therefore overcame the "oil-crisis".

We have a comparatively low incidence of unemployment. I think this fact has played an important role in the decrease in crime. In our society it is not difficult to find a job. Therefore, the young generation can live a comparatively good life and most of them are also given good economic support by their parents. Most of them have, therefore, no economic frustration.

(2) We have a homogeneous social structure. The informal control systems of society, those of family, school, neighbourhood, work place (office) and also mass media, are functioning comparatively well in our community. Regardless of the urbanisation and anonymity of life in the big city, we always have to consider that such informal social controls

affect our everyday life. The lifestyle and life-feelings of our young generation have drastically changed, especially since the end of the 2nd World War. But thought patterns and behavioural patterns have not fundamentally changed. For example, most people like to take the decisions or lifestyle of their neighbours and acquaintances into consideration and their decisions depend on another's.

(3) In Japan, family relations are still intact. But if these relations are damaged, it will manifest itself in the form of so-called family violence. Recently, in Japan, it has been reported that children are hitting their parents and that fathers hit their wives and children because of their own frustrations. I think the relationship in families changes with the changes in social structures. New ideal models for families are required in Japan too.

(4) We cannot overlook the education system as an informal social control. Generally speaking, there is a high standard of education in Japan. Of course, we have considered and analysed fully, the contents of our education. Most children want to be part of the present education system, but some children drop out of it, which is illustrated by violence in schools. Three thousand cases of school violence are reported annually.

(5) Our police system is functioning comparatively well as a formal social control system. In 1987, the average number of the Japanese population per police officer was 555. The ratio of the Japanese police to the local population is by far greater than those of our European and American counterparts. The Japanese police are organized on a prefectual basis. Prefectural police are placed in each prefecture to perform various tasks under the supervision of the prefectural public safety commission.

The "Police Box" and "Residential Police Box" function as a base for patrol police activities and as a police window to which citizens may bring their problems. At present, there are about 15,000 of them across Japan.

(6) Recently, an increase in the numbers of foreign workers coming into Japan, especially from Southeast Asia, has become a social issue. These people find jobs in the amusement business or are engaged in simple and unskilled work in the construction and manufacturing industries. In 1986, a total of 9,095 people were expelled from Japan for activities outside the terms of their visa-granted status, or for overstaying, in accordance with the provisions of the Immigration Control and Refugee Recognition Act. This figure represents an increase of 7,279 persons or 400.8% over the previous five years. Of these foreigners, 6,738 or 74.1% were Filipinos and 1,052 or 11,6% were Thais. This means that 85,7% of the foreign nationals expelled were from either of these two countries.

West Germany and France who have both accepted foreign workers are now afflicted by the unemployment of these labourers and other related social problems. At present there are not many crimes committed by foreign workers in Japan. For instance, in 1987 the total number of Penal Code offences by foreigners reported to the police was 8,575. Of these 46 were cases of homicide, 399 were bodily injury, 289 were fraud, and 7,110 were larceny.

For the moment there is no big problem concerning foreign offenders, though for the future it is feared that Japan will also be confronted with a variety of social issues arising from the foreign labour force, which might undermine the high level of public safety in Japan.

(7) I think that the strict firearms controls are also a reason for a low incidence of crime in Japan. In Japan there are strict controls on the possession of handguns and other firearms. This means that the illegal possession of firearms threatens the very foundation of public safety. In Japan, the Swords & Firearms Control Law prohibits people from owning handguns except where police hold them by law. As rivalries and conflicts among organized crime groups have recently become more serious, the illegal possession of handguns is becoming more widespread among this fraternity. There is thus the need to strengthen crackdowns on handgun ownership.

In 1987 the total number of handguns seized was 1,592 (1,335 genuine handguns), an increase of 142 (9.8%) compared with the previous year. Most of the genuine handguns are made in other countries and so are thought to have been smuggled into Japan. Control of handguns is very strict in Japan, while in foreign countries, handguns are less rigorously controlled and thus easily obtained. Japanese organized crime groups rely on these nations for the procurement of handguns.

(8) In Japan, especially in big cities there are a lot of places for the relief of sexual frustration. By law, prostitution and pornography are strictly prohibited. But as mentioned previously, there are always ways and means of obtaining access to such things, for example bars, clubs and cabaret bars.

The Development of American Crime: A Comparative Perspective

Louise I. Shelley

The United States is known worldwide for its serious crime problem and not just because Americans like to talk about crime or pride themselves on showing violence in movies and on television. The United States actually has much higher rates of criminality for the traditional violent and property offenses than other industrialized countries. Crime patterns do not differ in many other respects from that of other societies of comparable level of development. The difference in criminality between the United States and other industrialized countries is one of quantity rather than of quality. There is a similar level of female participation in crime, a serious problem of juvenile delinquency and a highly similar distribution of criminality among the various offenses. Homicide and theft assume a similar share of total American crime commission as in other industrialized societies. The aggregate figures for all violent and property crimes are also highly similar. Yet total crime rates in the United States are significantly higher.

Violent offenses contribute approximately 10-15% of all criminality, the same or slightly more than is found in other industrialized countries. Likewise, crimes against property contribute approximately the same proportion of total offenses as in other industrialized societies. The only distinguishing offense among American crime is the large proportion of criminality attributed to armed robbery. This anomalous situation may be explained by the greater materialism in the United States. The greater penchant for goods combined with the readiness to use violence to achieve one's goals may lead to the greater frequency of armed robbery in the United States.

The differences between the United States and the other developed countries are not of long standing. A survey of American crime patterns in this century suggests that American crime patterns have diverged from those of other industrialized countries in the last forty years. The United States has not always had higher rates of crime. Sixty years ago it was possible to walk the streets of New York and other major cities without the fear of crime. The crime picture in the United States changed dramatically after World War II.

1 The Development of Social Factors Influencing American Crime

National crime statistics are not available for the entire United States prior to 1933 (Graham 1969). But more limited data is available from different cities and very good descriptive data is available concerning the American crime picture (Ferdinand 1967; Lane 1969; Monkkonen). Together these data present a very consistent picture of American crime. They suggest that American crime at this time was not an international anomaly. As in Europe, crime patterns rose at the onset of industrialization. A growing proportion of all crimes were property offenses and violent crimes were receding in importance. Prior to World War I this data suggests that the United States had neither dramatically higher crime rates nor different patterns of crime commission. The United States had not escaped the societal dislocations that had accompanied industrialization but the problem in the United States was not as severe as in England.

During the 1930's, the period of the great depression, American crime patterns remained similar to those in other industrialized countries. This was a period of generally low crime rates compared to that of the previous century. The figures were not consistent, certain categories of crime rose while others declined. The same phenomenon was observed elsewhere in the industrialized world (Gurr 1977). Yet at this time, violent crime in the United States appeared to assume a larger share of total crime commission than in many other industrialized societies (Henry/Short 1954). In the 1930s, 45% of the United States population still resided in rural areas (U.S. Department of Commerce 1975, p. 11) where violent crime rates are usually higher. In urban areas, violent offenses assumed 9 to 10 percent of all crime commission (U.S. Department of Justice 1936, pp. 134-135).

A dramatic differentiation in American crime patterns occurred after the War. Therefore, it is necessary to look to some of the social dynamics of American society in the past forty years. There are several principal areas in which American society has changed in this period. They are: post-war urbanization and population mobility, class structure of the urban population, American participation in wars, greater female involvement in the labor force, the growth of an endemic drug problem and the growth of a welfare system.

Although World War II was not fought on the mainland of the United States, American involvement in the war sparked many domestic changes which had a direct impact on crime rates. Increased urbanization by rural whites and blacks changed the character of American cities. Beginning in 1940, there was a mass exodus of rural blacks to the industrial north, a figure calculated at 160,000 annually between 1940 and 1950 and at 100,000 annually through the mid 1960s (Report of the National Advisory Commission 1968, p. 240). This mass migration had a significant impact on daily life. Earlier than in many other industrialized societies, large numbers of individuals moved to the suburbs, depriving cities of their economic base. Urban decay and urban renewal crippled city life. Cities were thus filled with a large minority population. Poor training and a decline in jobs left many black youths unemployed. Some individuals unaccustomed to urban life and feeling frustrated by the lack of opportunities turned to crime commission (Murray 1984, p. 113).

American cities were not alone in undergoing massive change in the post-war period. Numerous immigrants arrived in cities in Europe, Canada and Australia. But while poor American blacks who had recently arrived in the cities were left without jobs, immigrants to the United States as well as their counterparts in other industrialized countries often found work or started their own businesses. While many were not immediately financially successful, it is believed that their immigrant status deterred their criminality. Yet many European cities are experiencing rapidly growing crime rates as the children of these immigrants are beginning to commit crimes in significant numbers. In the United States, however, it is the inner city blacks cut out of the labor force who are now committing street crime disproportionately, while the offspring of immigrants are not contributing as significantly to the crime phenomena.

Compounding the dislocations of the rural to urban migration was American involvement in the Vietnam War and the accompanying social strife. The Vietnam War followed in close sequence American involvement in Korea. Research suggests that homicide rates increase when a country is involved in war. This might explain the higher level of violence in the United States (Archer/Gartner 1978, p. 226). Throughout the 1960s there was considerable social protest in the industrialized nations. But the social protest in the United States was aggravated by the mass opposition to the Vietnam War. This exacerbated the level of social conflict as the middle class population protested American involvement. Yet it was the lower class, particularly black youths, who went and fought in the war.

An important dynamic in American family life was the entrance of large numbers of women into the labor force. This has occurred in other industrialized countries as well but in the United States there were more mothers of younger children who entered the labor force than in many other societies. Many of these children, particularly in less affluent areas, are left unsupervised. With little supervision of school attendance or after school behavior, many juveniles have become part of an urban street culture that has seen crime as a normal element of its way of life.

American family life is also unstable for other reasons. The United

States has had a uniquely high divorce rate during the last two decades (United Nations 1983, pp. 517-519). Furthermore, many children have been raised in single family homes as the existing welfare system provides payments more easily to mothers without fathers. This system means that many women raise children on their own. Some social critics suggest that the welfare system has provided a social network that has discouraged social mobility in the population (Murray 1984, p. 113).

Yet there has been a growth of a significant underclass in the United States that is outside the reach of the authorities. The schools, social institutions and the intervention of the justice system have failed to make a dent in the deterrence of crime among this population group. Exacerbating this problem is the increased drug consumption in the urban ghetto areas. This is both a manifestation of the declining social control within the community as well as a factor that is further contributing to urban decay and urban violence. The most visible symbol of this is the nation's capital, Washington, D.C., which at present has a homicide rate of over 60 per 100, 000 – a level that surpasses many of the developing countries in the world. The United States is a developed country that has urban areas with crime and demographic indicators (such as infant mortality) similar to those observed in developing countries.

The post-War affluence affected both the haves and have nots in society. It created a society with unprecedented material goods and a striving to obtain these items as a symbol of success. The post-War baby boom brought millions of young individuals into the most crime prone age group. For the poor, it led to a rise in street crime whereas for the affluent it has led to the growth of securities fraud and other "get rich" schemes. All of these conditions, as well as many others, help explain the rapid growth of crime in the United States since the 1950s.

2 The Dynamics of Crime

At present crime rates in the United States, after taking the lead in the industrialized nations, appear to have leveled off. Yet crime rates continue to grow in much of Western Europe. The explanation for this situation may be that the United States experienced first many of the conditions which have led to exacerbating crime problems in Western Europe – the settlement of many rural individuals from different cultures in major cities, societal affluence and a loosening of social controls in a more impersonal society.

Two sources of crime data, the Uniform Crime Report (UCR) and the

National Crime Survey (NCS), provide insight into the dynamics of American criminality. They are in many respects consistent but do provide a different picture of the overall level of criminality and trends in crime rates in the last fifteen years.

Certain important differences exist between the NCS and UCR data. NCS measures crime reported to the police as well as that not reported while the UCR represents only data that is reported. The NCS ist based on a survey of thousands of citizens queried across the United States, concerning their victimization. The UCR counts all crimes while the NCS counts crimes only against those over 12 and those offenses committed against individuals. The NCS counts multiple crimes committed simultaneously as separate offenses. Homicides must naturally be excluded from the NCS data set based on victim reports (Territo et al. 1989, pp.70-71). Observing crime rates in the United States in the post-War period reveals that crime rates for the seven offenses included in the Uniform Crime Report changed dramatically (see tables 1-4). Crime rates for homicide, assault, rape, robbery, burglary and larceny grew consistently and significantly in these decades. Especially dramatic growth was observed after the tumultuous 1960s. The NCS data, initially collected only in 1973, reveals a very high level of total crime that has fluctuated only by plus or minus ten percent in the intervening decades (see table 5).

Significant increases in criminality were already observed in the late 1950s. According to data, the reported number of offenses for 1960, was 20 percent above that of the average for the previous three years. Furthermore, the rate in 1960 was up a full 14 percent over the previous year. The greatest rate of increase was noted in the property offenses of robbery, burglary and larceny over $50 (see table 1).

In 1960, there was a total crime index of 1869.7 offenses per 100,000. By 1973, that figure had increased to 4,116.4 or a growth of 120 percent. In actual numbers there was a growth in the number of offenses from 3,352,800 in 1960 to 8,638,400 offenses in 1973 or an increase of 157 percent. Examining the figures in more detail, it is apparent that from 1961 on, crime rates rose approximately 7 to 8 percent a year. The most significant rise was noted in the years 1966-70 when social turmoil in the United States was at its greatest. In that short period of time the crime index went up 50%. But as the level of social tension diminished, the crime rate did not decline. Rather the rate of growth merely slowed.

Between 1960 and 1973 certain offenses had growth rates that exceeded the general growth rate and certain crimes grew more slowly. Homicide grew much less rapidly than the general crime index. Significant numbers were being killed at a rate that far exceeded that of other industrialized countries. But the growth in this category was much less than in the area of property crime. The other major violent offense was aggravated assault which exceeded the general growth rate per 100,000 by 16%. Reported rape also grew at a significantly higher rate but this might be an artifact of the women's movement which was instrumental in this period in setting up many treatment centers for rape victims and encouraging the reporting of assaults. The greatest growth occurred in robberies which tripled in number and doubled in frequency on a per capita basis.

Examining American crime data in the first half of the 1970s permits us to make some international comparisons. In the United States in 1970 the rate per 100,000 for index offenses was 3,949 whereas in 1975 it was 5282, a growth of approximately 33% in this five year period. The United Nations collected international crime data in this period for both developed and developing countries. It found, on average, that crime grew worldwide at a rate of 15% during this time period. In the developing countries the crime rate increased 2.5% annually while in the developed countries it increased by 1 percent (Report of the Secretary General 1977). The rate of increase in the United States during this time period was thus double that in the rest of the developed world and even exceeded that in the developing world.

The phenomenal growth in crime was, fortunately, not sustained. If crime had continued to grow at this rate throughout the 1970s, there would have been approximately 8000 crimes per 100,000 recorded in 1980. But in 1980, the figure was less than two-thirds of that. The crime total index was 5,900 per 100,000 in 1980, a figure approximately 50% above what it was in the previous decade (see tables 2 and 3). The NCS data in 1980 reveal a slight rate of decrease over the beginning of the decade. (see table 4) Examining the dynamics of the individual crimes for this period reveals very different patterns than in the previous decade. The greatest increase in the UCR data was noticed in the crime of rape but this could be explained by increasing female readiness to report this offense. Homicide grew at a much lower rate than other offenses and the rate of increase for robbery slowed, increasing by less than a third in that decade. The most notable increase was in aggravated assault and in the most common crime of larceny-theft. In contrast, the NCS data revealed a constancy in the rates of commission for the violent offenses (see table 6).

The most recent crime figures of 1986 show an annual rate of 5,479.9 per 100,000 or a figure approximately ten percent below the rate at the beginning of the decade. If one, however, compares the present day figure with that of a decade ago one finds that, according to the UCR, the rate has increased 7.9% from 1977. In contrast, the NCS data indicate that during this period there was even a decline in total criminality (see tables 4 and 5).

Several notable features are observable. Property crime has increased more gradually than the general rate of criminality. Whereas the rate of violent crime has increased as a share of total crime commission according to both the UCR and NCS data. According to the UCR data, in the decade between 1977 and 1986 the number of violent crimes increased by 44.5%. Calculated on a per capita basis the increase was 29.7%. The rate of growth for violent crimes far exceeded that for any other category of criminality. Property crimes increased moderately with the largest increase noted in the category of the violent property offense, robbery. Following such a significant increase, violent crimes against the person slightly exceed their ten percent contribution of the previous decade. According the NCS data, their contribution is over 16%. This difference may be explained by the fact that individuals are more likely to report property crimes for insurance reasons but may decline to report violent offenses that are often perpetrated by known individuals.

The high proportion of violence in total crime commission makes American crime anomalous in the developed world as violent crime rates generally decline with development (Shelley 1981). This occurred initially in the United States, but this trend has not been sustained. Rather a noticeable increase has occurred very recently according to the UCR. Furthermore, the NCS shows no decline in the number of reported violent offenses. Examining the location and the perpetrators of these violent offenses provides some possible explanation for this situation. Violent crime is increasing within the inner cities that house the poor and uneducated who have been left behind in the increasingly high technology society. The American underclass in many ways resembles the poor population of a developing country that does not find a place for itself in society and resides in neighborhoods with high levels of violence. The major difference is that in certain developing countries this underclass might comprise as much as 50% of the population whereas in the United States it is no more than ten to twenty percent.

The Uniform Crime Report is based on national figures and does not reflect some of the important changes in the dynamics of crime in the recent period within individual cities. The influence of the drug epidemic is most noticeable in the cities of New York, Washington and other major urban centers. In many poor urban neighborhoods, crack, a cocaine derivative, is the predominant drug and by its nature makes the user more prone to violence than do other drugs. It can be anticipated that until there is a change in patterns of drug usage, violent crime will continue to rise in the United States as a proportion of total criminality.

The UCR and NCS, national statistical sources, collect data on the major violent and property offenses. They do not provide data on new and emerging areas of criminality such as computer crime, securities frauds and racketeering. There is no data provided on the extent of criminality perpetrated by members of organized crime. Although rough estimates can be made as to the existence of this crime, much of it falls into the area of undisclosed criminality. With the growth of drug usage in the United States, much of it controlled by traditional and new forms of organized crime, it is clear that this criminal activity is an important component of the country's large shadow economy.

Despite the absence of major data on these types of offenders and offenses, there has been an increased willingness to treat as offenders not just those known as "street criminals" but also the higher status offender who is engaged in stock market manipulation, fraud and violation of worker safety laws. Part of this can be explained by a changing perception of crime that has made the society and the justice system sensitive to the fact that the criminal is not only the individual who mugs you on the street or enters your house but also the person who violates the ethical standards and the laws governing public office or regulating the security markets.

The recent prosecutions that have been mounted against some of the major Wall Street financiers are indicative that the government is no longer focusing exclusively on the crimes of the indigents. The decision to prosecute one of the major American financiers, Michael Milliken, under the RICO statutes (used against members of organized crime) indicates that crime is no longer only equated with a tangible victim. American society is no longer focusing exclusively on the crimes that do harm to a specific individual, but is broadening its enforcement net to include crimes that do harm to numerous, less tangible victims.

Evaluation of the extent to which American crime has moved away from the personal to the impersonal victim is hard to calculate. Both the UCR and victimization surveys, the prime methods of crime data collection, are still geared to gathering information on the losses and suffering of the individual rather than the corporation. Although the NCS provides data on burglary and robberies in the commercial sector, these data are generally of smaller business. The victimization of the department store, insurance company or the investment house is not discernable from the existing crime data. No national picture exists but each business must anticipate the loss that it will suffer as a result of employee and customer theft or cheating. Certain rough guidelines exist within each industry but these figures yield only rough estimates of losses. Some suggest that the cost of this criminality exceeds that lost to street crime.

The victimization of large corporations does not generally figure in the crime data, but neither do the crimes committed by the large corporations. Only estimates exist as to the cost or frequency of price fixing, stock manipulation, exceeding pollution standards or illegally shipping technology to countries that can not legally acquire these products. Discussion of such crimes is confined primarily to newspaper accounts of individual cases rather than a survey of the extent of such practices.

A very clear example of this is the recent case of the Exxon oil tanker's pollution of the highly delicate Alaska environment. The captain of the tanker is now being prosecuted. The discussion has focused not only on the specifics of this case but also on the issue of corporate accountability. Stockholders have questioned the company's action and it has raised awareness of the responsibility of the large corporations to the community.

The United States in the post-War period has been demoralized by the growth of crime. It has had some profound influences on the society, changing individuals' outlooks, the way they raise their children and their perception of their neighbors. The security of American life that was reflected in the literature of the United States in the first part of this century is no as longer representative of the culture. A certain openness has been lost as individuals feel that they cannot trust their neighbors.

In many industrialized countries, the growth of crime in the post-War period has shaped the way individuals live. This change has been particularly pronounced in European cities in the last decade. But the precipitous rise in crime rates early in the post-War period, made Americans shift their lifestyles several decades earlier. Crime rates in American rural areas, although significantly below those of major cities, are high compared to those of western European countries. Consequently, Americans in all areas are careful leaving their homes at night and many restrict the freedom of their children to play and move outside the home.

In surveys of their daily patterns of behavior, Americans discuss the way that they respond to crime and how it affects their lives (U.S. Department of Justice 1978). Politicians, aware of the importance of crime to the citizenry, have made it a major topic on the national political agenda. Various presidents have declared a war on crime. While in office, former President Reagan appointed a drug czar to coordinate American efforts to combat drug abuse and trafficking.

In summary, the preceding discussion of American crime indicates that it is distinctive in four respects. First, crime is much more frequent in the United States. The chances of being a victim of a violent or property offenses are several times as great in the United States as elsewhere in the developed world. The magnitude of crime severely detracts from the quality of life of Americans, particularly those residing in urban areas.

Second, American crime up until the most recent decade has been growing at a faster rate than in other industrialized nations. The growth rate of American crime up until the mid-1970s was not only higher than that observed in other industrialized nations but was greater than that recorded in the developing countries. The precipitous growth of American crime preceded that of the other industrialized nations. With each post-war year up until a decade ago, the gap between American crime

Table 1: Crime Index from 1957-60

Crime index classification	Estimated number of offenses 1957-59 average	1960	Change 1960 Over 3-year average Number	%	Over 1959 Number	%
Total	1,547,590	1,861,300	+313,710	+20	+230,870	+14
Murder	8,290	9,140	+850	+10	+560	+6
Forcible rape	14,240	15,560	+1,320	+9	+400	+3
Robbery	72,540	88,970	+16,430	+23	+13,770	+18
Aggravated assault	116,020	130,230	+14,210	+12	+6,640	+5
Burglary	663,500	821,100	+157,600	+24	+122,800	+18
Larceny $50 and over	388,800	474,900	+86,100	+22	+59,100	+14
Auto theft	284,200	321,400	+37,200	+13	+27,600	+9

Crime index Classification	Crimes per 100,000 inhabitants Rate 1960	1960 percent chance Over 1959	Over 5-year average
Total	1,037.9	+13	+24
Murder	5.1	+6	+6
Forcible rape	8.7	+2	+10
Robbery	49.6	+17	+24
Aggravated assault	72.6	+4	+11
Burglary	457.9	+17	+29
Larceny $50 and over	264.8	+13	+27
Auto theft	179.2	+8	+16

Source: FBI, Uniform Crime Reports for the United States, Washington,D.C.: U.S. Department of Justice, 1961, p. 2.

rates for conventional offenses and those of the other developed nations broadened.

Third, robbery rates are significantly higher in the United States than in other industrialized nations.

Fourth, the United States simultaneously shares the crime patterns of both developing and developed countries. Major American cities share the crime characteristics of many third world cities while the national data share the attributes of developed nations.

Table 2: Index of Crime, United States, 1960-73

Year	Total Crime Index	Violent crime[a]	Property crime[a]	Murder and nonnegligent manslaughter	Forcible rape
1960	3,352,800	286,220	3,066,600	9,050	17,050
1961	3,455,500	287,120	3,168,400	8,680	17,080
1962	3,717,400	299,150	3,418,200	8,480	17,410
1963	4,071,200	314,490	3,756,700	8,580	17,510
1964	4,522,300	361,350	4,161,000	9,300	21,250
1965	4,695,500	384,340	4,311,200	9,900	23,230
1966	5,175,200	426,830	4,748,300	10,970	25,620
1967	5,849,200	496,150	5,353,000	12,160	27,410
1968	6,658,900	590,640	6,068,200	13,720	31,410
1969	7,343,300	657,050	6,686,200	14,670	36,880
1970	8,024,100	733,530	7,290,500	15,860	37,690
1971	8,509,800	810,680	7,699,100	17,670	41,940
1972	8,173,400	828,820	7,344,600	18,550	46,480
1973	8,638,400	869,470	7,768,900	19,510	51,000
Percent change[b] 1960-1973	+157.6	+203.8	+153.3	+115.6	+199.2

3 The Response to Crime

In the post World War II period, several notable trends can be observed in the treatment of street crime. First, an activist Supreme Court has pushed through greater rights for the defendant during the investigatory and prosecution stages of a case. Second, the number and qualifications of law enforcement personnel have increased. Third, there has been a marked increase in the number of incarcerated individuals. In many areas, the growth in prison populations and law enforcement personnel has exceeded the growth in crime. Fourth, on the federal level, there has been an increasingly punitive sentencing policy implemented that has been followed by some of the states.

The response to economic offenses and political corruption has not been so consistent. In several states, there have been activist attorney generals who have made these crimes their priority. There has been no concerted attack waged against these offenses on the federal level. But this may change with the new head of the U.S. Justice Department who seeks to shift the enforcement effort away from street crime to the more sophisticated corruption crimes. With a prosecution background in this

Table 2 (Continued): Index of Crime, United States, 1960-73

Year	Robbery	Aggra-vated assault	Burglary	Larceny-theft	Auto theft
1960	107,410	152,720	903,400	1,836,800	326,400
1961	106,240	155,130	940,400	1,893,800	334,200
1962	110,410	162,850	984,800	2,068,700	364,800
1963	116,000	172,400	1,076,000	2,274,800	406,000
1964	129,860	200,940	1,201,600	2,489,300	470,200
1965	138,130	213,090	1,270,200	2,546,900	494,100
1966	157,350	232,890	1,396,500	2,793,700	558,100
1967	202,100	254,490	1,616,500	3,080,500	656,100
1968	261,780	283,720	1,841,100	3,447,800	779,300
1969	297,650	307,850	1,962,900	3,849,700	873,600
1970	348,460	331,480	2,183,800	4,183,500	923,200
1971	386,150	364,920	2,376,300	4,379,900	942,900
1972	374,790	389,000	2,352,800	4,109,600	882,200
1973	382,680	416,270	2,540,900	4,304,400	923,600
Percent change[b] 1060-1973	+256.3	+172,6	+181.3	+134.3	+183.0

area, there may be a different policy response to crime at the national level (Wines 1989, p. 23).

A most significant change occurred in the development of defendant's rights following the appointment of Earl Warren as Chief Justice of the United States Supreme Court. Many landmark decisions were issued which gave the offender great rights in relationship to the law enforcement apparatus and in judicial proceedings.

Since the Miranda decision (1966) was issued by the Supreme Court over two decades ago, defendants have been guaranteed the right to counsel from the moment of arrest. It holds that the "privilege against self-incrimination is fully applicable during a period of custodial interrogation" (Israel/LaFave 1975, p. 213). Subsequent decisions expanded the right to counsel. The police complain that the Miranda decision as well as other protections that limit searches hamper their operations. But there is no concrete evidence that restrictions on the rights of law enforcement personnel have increased the numbers of offenders on the streets, thereby contributing to the rise in crime.

The defendant is now assured access to counsel in the courtroom. Following the Gideon decision in 1963, indigent defendants are to be provided lawyers to assist them in trials. Initially interpreted as assuring

Table 2 (continued): Index of Crime, United States, 1960-73 / Rates per 100,000 inhabitants

Year	Total Crime Index	Violent crime[a]	Property crime[a]	Murder and nonnegligent manslaughter	Forcible rape
1960	1,869.7	159.6	1,710.1	5.0	9.5
1961	1,888.8	156.9	1,731.8	4.7	9.3
1962	2,000.5	161.0	1,839.5	4.6	9.4
1963	2,159 4	166.8	1,992.6	4.5	9.3
1964	2,363.6	188.9	2,174.7	4.9	11.1
1965	2,422.6	198.3	2,224.3	5.1	12.0
1966	2,646.0	218.2	2,427,7	5.6	13.1
1967	2,956.2	218.2	2,427.7	5.6	13.9
1968	3,331.8	295.5	3,036.2	6.9	15.7
1969	3,636.7	325.4	3,311.3	7.3	18.3
1970	3,949.2	361.0	3,588.1	7.8	18.6
1971	4,125.8	393.0	3,732.8	8.6	20.3
1972	3,925.2	398.0	3,527.1	8.9	22.3
1973	4,116.4	414.3	3,702.1	9.3	24.3
Percent change[b] 1960-1973	+120.2	+159.6	+116.5	+86.0	+155.8

counsel only in the more serious felony cases, it later was applied to misdemeanor offenses (those carrying less than one year's incarceration) as well.

At the same time that the criminal has been granted greater rights, the state and federal governments have increased the numbers and sophistication of law enforcement personnel. The state and federal government have responded to the rising crime rate by increasing the number of justice personnel on state and federal payrolls (U.S. Department of Justice 1987, p. 6). For a decade starting in the late 1960s, hundreds of millions of dollars were spent by the Law Enforcement Assistance Administration, a now defunct branch of the Department of Justice, to provide higher education to law enforcement and correctional personnel. The creation of this program was based on the philosophy that education would make the police more sensitive to the needs of the population and more aware of their legal obligations. As a result, the ranks of students in criminal justice programs swelled. Within a short period of time two to three percent of all undergraduate degrees in the United States in the late 1970s were offered in the criminal justice field. Although this assistance was curtailed, it left the country with a more highly educated police population that was at times more sensitive to the laws that they were to uphold.

Table 2 (continued): Index of Crime, United States, 1960-73 / Rates per 100,000 inhabitants

Year	Robbery	Aggra-vated assault	Burglary	Larceny-theft	Auto theft
1960	59.9	85.2	508.8	1,024.3	182,0
1961	58.1	84.8	514.0	1,035.2	182.7
1962	59.4	87.6	530.0	1,113.3	196,3
1963	61.5	91.4	570.7	1,206.6	215.3
1964	67.9	105.0	628.0	1,301.0	245.7
1965	71.3	109.9	655.4	1,314.0	254.9
1966	80.4	119.1	714.0	1,428.4	285.3
1967	80.4	119.1	714.0	1,428.4	331.6
1968	131.0	142.0	921.2	1,725.1	389.9
1969	147.4	152.5	972.1	1,906.5	432.7
1970	171.5	163.1	1,074.8	2,059.0	454.4
1971	187.2	176.9	1,152.1	2,123.5	457.2
1972	180.0	186.8	1,129.9	1,973.6	423.7
1973	182.4	198.4	1,210.8	2,051.2	440.1
Percent change[b] 1960-1973	+204.5	+132.9	+140.3	+100.3	+141.8

Source: FBI, Crime in the United States Uniform Crime Reports 1973, Washington, D.C.: U.S. Government Printing Office, 1974, p. 59

Notes:

(a) Violent crime is offences of murder, forcible rape, robbery and aggravated assault. Property crime is offences of burglary, larceny theft and auto-theft.

(b) Percent change and crime rates calculated prior to rounding number of offences. Revised estimates and rates based on changes in reporting practices.

The change in the governmental sector of policing was matched by a remarkable evolution in the non-governmental side. The tendency of individuals to victimize the impersonal corporations has led to an even more dramatic upsurge in the number of law enforcement personnel on corporation payrolls. Private security personnel retained by corporations and retail enterprises presently total 1.1 million and outnumber governmental law enforcement personnel (Marx 1987, p. 174). This growth is not confined to the United States as private security has also expanded significantly in Western Europe. In the United States, there has been a diminution in the distinction between private and public control as the two types of law enforcement often join efforts to combat criminality particularly in the economic arena, drug trafficking and the illegal export of technology (Marx, p. 172-193).

Table 3: Index of Crime, 1971-1980/Absolute Figures

Year	Total Crime Index	Violent crime	Property crime	Murder and non-negligent manslaughter	Forcible rape
1971	8,588,200	816,500	7,771,700	17.780	42,260
1972	8,248,800	834,900	7,413,900	18,670	46,850
1973	8,718,100	875,910	7,842,200	19,640	51,400
1974	10,253,400	974,720	9,278,700	20,710	55,400
1975	11,256,600	1,026,280	10,230,300	20,510	56,090
1976	11,304,800	986,580	10,318,200	18,780	56,730
1977	10,935,800	1,009,500	9,926.300	19,120	63,020
1978	11,141,300	1,061,830	10,079,500	19,560	67,130
1979	12,152,700	1,178,540	10,974,200	21,460	75,990
1980	13,295,400	1,308,900	11,986,500	23,040	82,090

Year	Robbery	Aggra-vated assault	Burglary	Larceny-theft theft	Motor vehicle
1971	387,700	368,700	2,399,300	4,424,200	948,200
1972	376,290	393,090	2,375.500	4,151,200	887,200
1973	384,220	420,650	2,565,500	4,347,900	928,800
1974	442,400	456,210	3,039,200	5,262,500	977,100
1975	464,970	484,710	3,252,100	5.977,700	1,000,500
1976	420,210	490,850	3,089,800	6,270,800	957,600
1977	404,850	522,510	3,052,200	5,905,700	968,400
1978	417,040	558,100	3,104,500	5,983,400	991,600
1979	466,880	614,210	3,299,500	6,577,500	1,097,200
1980	548,810	654,960	3,759,200	7,112,700	1,114,700

A major change has recently occurred on the federal level in the sentencing of offenders. Tremendous disparities in sentences among judges were observed. Federal Sentencing Guidelines were recently introduced to rectify this problem and were upheld by the Supreme Court. They provide that for a particular offense and for offenders with a particular criminal history, a very limited range of sentences can be imposed. Under these new guidelines, many white collar offenders will find themselves subject to prison terms rather than the probation they have traditionally enjoyed. This sharp deviation is not the only major change brought by their introduction; they also eliminate the possibility of parole for sentenced offenders. Many states are planning or are already following these federal guidelines. With harsher sentences and no chance of parole, it can be expected that federal prison populations will continue to rise.

Table 3: Index of Crime, 1971-1980 / Rates per 100,000 inhabitants[c]

Year	Total Crime Index[a]	Violent crime[b]	Property crime[b]	Murder and non-negligent manslaughter	Forcible rape
1971	4,164.7	396.0	3,768.8	8.6	20.5
1972	3,961.4	401.0	3,560.4	9.0	22.5
1973	4,154.4	417.4	3,737.0	9.4	24.5
1974	4,850.4	461.1	4,389.3	9.8	26.2
1975	5,281.7	481.5	4,800.2	9.6	26.3
1976	5,266.4	459.6	4,806.8	8.8	26.4
1977	5,055.1	466.6	4,588.4	8.8	29.1
1978	5,109.3	486.9	4,622.4	9.0	30.8
1979	5,521.5	535.5	4,986.0	9.7	34.5
1980	5,899.9	580.8	5,319.1	10.2	36.4

Table 3 (continued): Index of Crime, 1971-1980 / Rates per 100,000 inhabitants[c]

Year	Robbery	Aggravated assault	Burglary	Larceny-theft	Motor vehicle
1971	188.0	178.8	1,163.5	2,145.5	459.8
1972	180.7	188.8	1,140.8	1,993.6	426.1
1973	183.1	200.5	1,222.5	2,071.9	442.6
1974	209.3	215.8	1,437.7	2,489.5	462.2
1975	218.2	227.4	1.525.9	2,804.8	469.4
1976	195.8	228.7	1,439.4	2,921.3	446.1
1977	187.1	241.5	1,410.9	2,729.9	447.6
1978	191.3	255.9	1,423.7	2,743.9	454.7
1979	212.1	279.1	1,499.1	2,988.4	498.5
1980	243.5	290.6	1,668.2	3,156.3	494.6

Notes:
(a) Due to rounding, the offenses may not add to totals.
(b) Violent crimes are offenses of murder, forcible rape, robbery and aggravated assault. Property crimes are offenses of burglary, larceny-theft and motor vehicle theft. Data are not included for the property crime of arson.
(c) Crime rates calculated prior to rounding number of offenses.
Source: FBI, Crime in the United States Uniform Crime Reports 1980 Washington, D.C.: U.S. Government Printing Office, 1981, p.41

A marked expansion has already been noted in the number of individuals incarcerated in the United States in recent decades. Adding together those incarcerated on the federal, state and local levels, approximately 600,000 individuals are confined in the United States at any one time. The prison population has doubled in the 1980s and has tripled since the 1960s

Table 4: Index of Crime, United States, 1977-1986

Year	Total Crime Index[a]	Violent crime[b]	Property crime[b]	Murder and non-negligent manslaughter	Forcible rape
1977	10,984,500	1,029,580	9,955,000	19,120	63,500
1978	11,209,000	1.085.550	10,123,400	19,560	67,610
1979	12,249,500	1.208,030	11,041,500	21,460	76.390
1980	13,408,300	1,344.520	12,063,700	23,040	82,990
1981	13.423,800	1,361,820	12.061,900	22,520	82,500
1982	12,974.400	1.322,390	11.652,000	21,010	78,770
1983	12,108,600	1,258.090	10.850.500	19,310	78.920
1984	11.881.800	1,273,280	10,608,500	18,690	84,230
1985	12.430,400	1,327.770	11,102,600	18,980	87,670
1986	13,210,800	1,488.140	11,722.700	20,610	90,430

Year	Robbery	Aggra-vated assault	Burglary	Larceny-theft theft	Motor vehicle
1977	412,610	534,350	3,071,500	5,905,700	977,700
1978	426,930	571,460	3,128,300	5,591,000	1,004,100
1979	480,700	629,480	3,327,700	6,601,000	1,112.800
1980	565.840	672,650	3,795,200	7,136.900	1,131,700
1981	592,910	663,900	3,779,700	7,194,400	1,087.800
1982	553,130	669,480	3,447,100	7,142,500	1.062,400
1983	506,570	653,290	3,129.900	6,712,800	1,007,900
1984	485,010	685,350	2,984.400	6,591.900	1,032,200
1985	497,870	723,250	3,073,300	6,926,400	1,102,900
1986	542,780	834,320	3,211,400	7,257,200	1,224,100

(Skolnick 1989, p. A17), whereas there has been minimal growth in the total population. The United States presently has one of the highest rates of incarceration in the industrialized world (Lauen 1988, p. 4).

The increase in incarceration has coincided with the stabilization of crime rates. One might ascribe the positive trend to this increased use of incarceration. But much of the growth in incarceration rates can be ascribed to the increased tendency to imprison drug offenders, many of whom could be better served by placement in treatment programs. Examining the geography of incarceration in the United States reveals great variations; the highest rates of incarceration are not in those states with the highest crime rates but often in those with the highest rates of unemployment. These data suggest that the policy of locking up more offenders does not necessarily produce a positive impact on crime rates.

Table 4 (continued): Index of Crime, United States, 1977-1986 / Rate per 100,000 inhabitants[c]

Year	Total Crime Index[a]	Violent crime[b]	Property crime[b]	Murder and non-negligent manslaughter	Forcible rape
1977	5.077.6	475.9	4,601.7	8.8	29.4
1978	5.140.3	497.8	4,642.5	9.0	31.0
1979	5,565.5	548.9	5.016.6	9.7	34.7
1980	5.950.0	596.6	5,353.3	10.2	36.8
1981	5.858.2	594.3	5,263.9	9.8	36.0
1982	5.603.6	571.1	5,032.5	9 1	34.0
1983	5.175.0	537.7	4,637.4	8.3	33.7
1984	5.031.3	539.2	4,492.1	7.9	35.7
1985	5.206.7	556.2	4,650.5	7.9	36.7
1986	5.479 9	617.3	4,862.6	8.6	37.5

Table 4 (continued): Index of Crime, United States, 1977-1986 / Rate per 100,000 inhabitants[c]

Year	Robbery	Aggra-vated assault	Burglary	Larceny-theft	Motor vehicle
1977	190.7	247.0	1,419.8	2,729.9	451 9
1978	195.6	262.1	1,434.6	2,747.4	460.5
1979	218.4	286.0	1,511.9	2,999.1	505.6
1980	251.1	298.5	1,684.1	3,167.0	502.2
1981	258.7	289.7	1,649.5	3,139.7	474.7
1982	238.9	289.2	1,488.8	3,084.8	458.8
1983	216.5	279.2	1.337.7	2,868.9	430.8
1984	205.4	290.2	1.263.7	2,791.3	437.1
1985	205.4	290.2	1.263.7	2,791.3	437.1
1986	225.1	346.1	1,344.6	3,010.3	507.8

Notes:
(a) Due to rounding, the offenses may not add to totals.
(b) Violent crimes are offenses of murder, forcible rape, robbery and aggravated assault. Property crimes are offenses of burglary, larceny-theft, and motor vehicle theft. Data are not included for the property crime of arson.
(c) Crime rates calculated prior to rounding number of offenses.

Source: FBI, Crime in the United States Uniform Crime Reports 1986 Washington, D.C.: U.S. Government Printing Office, 1987, p. 40

Table 5: From National Crime Survey Data Total Crime and Total Violent Crime 1973-1986

Year	Total Crime	Total Violent Crime
1973	37,007,800	5,493,600
1974	37,872,000	5,399,000
1975	38,685,000	5,448,000
1976	39,317,000	5,599,000
1977	40,315,000	5,902,000
1978	40,412,000	5,941,000
1979	41,249,000	6,159,000
1980	39,329,000	5,974,000
1981	41,454,000	6,582,000
1982	39,329,000	6,459,000
1983	37,001,200	5,903,440
1984	35,476,360	5,953,990
1985	34,863,960	5,822,650
1986	34,118,310	5,515,450

Table 6: Personal and Household Crimes: Victimization Rates, 1973-1986 per 100,000 Population

Year	Violent Crime	Rape	Robbery	Aggravated Assault
1973	3,400	[a]	700	1,000
1974	3,200	30	700	1,000
1975	3,200	30	600	900
1976	3,200	20	600	900
1977	3,300	30	600	1,000
1978	3,300	30	590	970
1979	3,400	40	630	990
1980	3,300	20	650	920
1981	3,500	30	740	960
1982	3,400	30	710	930
1983	3,100	30	[b] 370	800
1984	3,100	30	[b] 390	870
1985	3,000	40	[b] 340	830
1986	2,800	20	[b] 320	790

Notes:

a) Only given as "less than .5" per 1,000 population. Since an exact number was not given, it seemed artificial to transform it into a rate per 100,000.

b) From 1983 and on, robberies were broken down into attempted and completed.

Table 7: Personal Property and Household Crimes: Rates per 100,000 Population

Year	Total Property Crimes Theft	Burglary	Larceny	Motor Vehicle
1973	31,400	9,300	22,100	1,900
1974	32,960	9,260	23,700	1,870
1975	33,190	9,150	24,040	1,940
1976	32,560	8,890	23,670	1,650
1977	32,610	8,850	23,760	1,700
1978	32,020	8,600	23,420	1,750
1979	32,720	8,410	24,310	1,750
1980	31,020	8,420	22,600	1,670
1981	31,110	8,790	22,320	1,710
1982	29,080	8,720	20,360	1,620
1983	26,670	7,000	19,670	1,460
1984	25,050	6,410	18,640	1,520
1985	24,380	6,270	18,110	1,420
1986	23,750	6,150	17,600	1,500

Total Property Crimes includes total crimes of theft under personal sector category and total household sector crimes.

4 Discussion

Why are American crime rates so high? Why did they increase so rapidly in the post-War period despite intense legislative efforts to fight crime? Various explanations have long found favor in explaining the high rate of violent offenses. These include the endurance of a frontier mentality, the existence of a southern regional culture of violence, and the vestiges of a slave-holding society. These theories, however, attempt to explain only the distinctly high rates of crime against the person and provide no insight as to why there are also high rates of property crime. The materialism of the United States, the role of the mass media in promoting a consumer society and the emphasis on money as a sign of success are all theories used to explain the high rates of property offenses. Yet are there more general explanations that simultaneously explain the high rates of both property and violent crime?

Several possible explanations for America's high crime rate exist and most of these have been articulated. These are the areas where American life diverges most from that of other industrialized countries. They are: the early post-War urbanization and population migration from rural to urban areas, the class structure of the urban population, the drug problem, family structure, and social values.

Yet a significant change has occurred more recently with the national drug crisis. Apart from the establishment of a cabinet level position to fight the drug problem, significant resources have been allocated to fight this problem at home and abroad. The high rates of robbery in the United States may be explained by the large number of drug users as well as the availability of arms. The need of so many addicts to obtain large sums of money forces many individuals into criminal activity, a phenomenon less common in societies where drug addiction is treated as a medical problem and drugs have been decriminalized. Furthermore, the ready availability of firearms which are less controlled than in many other industrialized societies contributes to the very high level of violent crime.

These many factors have probably contributed to the high crime rates of the United States. But it is difficult to isolate the relative importance of these different influences without comparative analysis. Then it may be possible to understand more clearly the forces that affect the development of internationally recognized forms of crime and delinquency.

In the United States, as elsewhere in the industrialized world, there is a growing realization that crime does not consist entirely of the street crimes of the generally lower class offender. Rather crime is an increasingly international phenomena that touches the financial markets and manifests itself in the power games of the politicians. Although political corruption has always existed, it has been given unprecedented visibility by the current ethics investigation of the Speaker of the House of Representatives. The willingness to bring leading figures within public scrutiny may mark a change in the perception of crime.

Even though there are stirrings in a new direction, there is no indication of a major redirection of law enforcement efforts away from the prosecution of those who harm tangible individuals to those with impersonal victims. The prisons of the United States are swelling in size with members of the underclass. Until the United States turns the corner on its current drug problem, there is no reason to believe that American priorities in the criminal arena will change dramatically. Furthermore, there can be no expectation that crime rates, particularly for violent offenses, will remain at current levels.

References

Archer, Dane and Rosemary Gartner (1978) "Legal Homicide and its Consequences", in: Violence: Perspectives on Murder and Aggression, I.L.Kutash and L. B. Schlesinger eds., San Francisco: Jossey-Bass.

Ferdinand, Theodore (1967) "The Criminal Patterns of Boston Since 1849", in: American Journal of Sociology, vol. 73, pp. 84-99.

Gurr, T.R. (1977) "Contemporary Crime in Historical Perspective: A Comparative Study of London, Stockholm and Sydney", in: Annals of the American Academy of Political and Social Science, vol. 434, pp. 114-136.

Graham, Fred "A Contemporary History of American Crime" in: Violence in America, Hugh D. Graham and Ted R. Gurr eds., Washington, D.C.: U.S. Government Printing Office, pp. 371-385.

Henry Andrew F. and J. F. Short. Jr. (1954) Suicide and Homicide, New York: Free Press.

Israel Jerold H. and Wayne R. LaFave (1975) Criminal Procedure Constitution Limitations, St. Paul, Minn.: West Publishing Co.

Lane, Roger (1969) "Urbanization and Criminal Violence in the 19th Century: Massachusetts as a Test Case," in: Violence in America, Hugh D. Graham and Ted R. Gurr eds., Washington, D. C.: US Government Printing Office, pp. 359-370.

Lauen, Roger (1988) Community-Managed Corrections And Other Solutions to America's Prison Crisis, Laurel, Md.: American Correctional Association.

Marx, Gary T. (1987) "The Interweaving of Public and Private Police in Undercover Work", in: Private Policing, Clifford D. Shearing and Philip C. Stenning eds., Newbury Park: Sage.

Monkkonen, Eric H. The Dangerous Class: Crime and Poverty in Columbus, Ohio 1860- 1885. Cambridge, Mass.: Harvard University Press.

Murray, Charles (1984) Losing Ground: American Social Policy, 1950-1980 New York: Basic Books, p. 113.

Report of the National Advisory Commission on Civil Disorders (1968) New York: Bantam, p. 240.

Report of the Secretary General (1977) Crime Prevention and Control, September 22.

Shelley, Louise I. (1981) Crime and Modernization: The Impact of Industrialization and Urbanization on Crime, Carbondale, Ill.: Southern Illinois University Press.

Skolnick, Jerome H. (1989) "7 Crack Dilemmas in Search of An Answer", in: New York Times, May 22, p. A17.

Territo, Leonard, James Halsted and Max Bromley (1989) Crime and Justice in America St. Paul: West Publishing Co.

United Nations (1983) Demographic Yearbook, New York: United Nations.

U.S. Department of Commerce (1975) Historical Statistics of the United States Part I. Washington, D.C.: U.S. Government Printing Office.

U.S. Department of Justice (1936) Uniform Crime Reports 1934-1936, Washington, D.C.: U.S. Government Printing Office, pp. 134-135.

U.S. Department of Justice (1978) Myths and Realities About Crime Washington, D.C.: U.S. Government Printing Office.

U.S. Department of Justice (1987) Sourcebook of Criminal Justice Statistics, Washington, D.C.:U.S. Government Printing Office.

Wines, Michael "Shaking up Justice", in: New York Times Magazine, May 21, 1989.

Part II
Crime and Control in Developing Nations

Crime and Control in Venezuela

Christopher Birkbeck[1]

Simón Bolívar, the foremost hero of the struggle for Venezuelan independence, once said that "Venezuelans love their country, but do not love their laws" (Venezuela 1919, p. 34). One hundred and seventy years later, the continued popularity of Bolívar's critical posture (Carrera Damas 1973) reflects a deeply ingrained pessimism among Venezuelans concerning the prospects for achieving orderly social life. It is a pessimism founded on the belief that law is the principal instrument for regulating social relations but that Venezuelans, as the popular phrase goes, "make laws so as to break them." It is a pessimism that colors perceptions of crime and influences policies for crime control. But it is also a pessimism that may not be entirely justified.

This study is a description of crime and crime control in Venezuela, focusing mainly on the period since 1970.[2] First, I examine social perceptions of crime and compare them with what can be learned from official statistics and victim survey data. While crime rates are perceived to be inordinately high and still on the increase, the available, albeit limited, criminological data do not always support such perceptions. Second, I examine the consequences of these perceptions for policies of crime control. While there has been a gradual evolution towards professionalism among criminal justice personnel and rehabilitative programs for offenders, the periodic manifestation of public concern over crime leads to

---

1 Portions of this research were funded by the CDCHT – Universidad de Los Andes; and the Dirección de Prevención del Delito of the Venezuelan Ministry of Justice. I would like to thank Carmelo Boada for extensive and valuable assistance with data collection and analysis; Quin-Mar Manrique for additional work in compiling police statistics; Harvey Williams for information on drug use; and Luis Gerardo Gabaldón and Gary LaFree for their help in locating documents.

2 Venezuela is a nation of approximately 19 million people located on the northern coast of South America. It is bordered on the east by Guyana, the south by Brazil and the west by Colombia. Economic growth throughout this century has rested mainly on the exploitation of the country's prodigious oil reserves. Since 1958, there has heen democratic government. For further information on Venezuela, see Waddell (1990).

governmental responses that run counter to these trends. I conclude with some brief observations on the wider implications of the analysis.

1 The Crime Problem in Venezuela

As in other parts of the world, the definition of crime in Venezuela is complex because legal and social definitions of deviant behavior do not coincide exactly. Following the Napoleonic tradition, criminal law in Venezuela is largely contained in a Código Penal (Code of Criminal Law) that classifies and lists crimes and the corresponding sanctions. The present Code was enacted in 1926 and draws heavily on the Codes of 1873 and 1897, which in turn were strongly influenced by the Spanish Code of 1870 and the Italian Code of 1889 (see, for example, Clagett 1947). Despite pressures for a new Code that would take account of the vast social and economic changes in the country since 1926 and address new forms of crime, the governmental response has been to enact complementary criminal legislation to deal with specific problems as they arise (Chiossone 1980). Recent notable examples are the Anti-Corruption Law of 1982 and the Drug law of 1984.[3]

While many legally defined crimes, such as murder, theft and robbery, are subject to widespread social disapproval (Gabaldón and García Sucre 1978), some, such as adultery and contraband, are not. Moreover, some activities not legally defined as crime are treated as if they were. Thus, the Vagrancy Law of 1939 effectively implies penal sanctions for people who have not committed a crime, in particular for the malandros (ruffians, hooligans) that cause problems in many low income barrios (neighborhoods) (Hernández 1977).

Social concern regarding crime in Venezuela varies over time in intensity and specific focus. An enduring preoccupation involves personal safety and the risk of predatory crime[4], but during the last decade the themes of corruption and drugs have also been prominent.

---

3 Criminal procedure is governed mainly by the Código de Enjuiciamiento Criminal, enacted in 1926. Complementary criminal legislation also includes specific norms regarding criminal procedure.

4 Glaser (1971, p. 4) defines predatory violations as acts in which "someone definitely and intentionally takes or damages the person or property of another."

1.1 Predatory Crime

Concern for personal safety and the perception of high rates of predatory crime are not new in Venezuela (Gómez Grillo 1982).[5] Opinión surveys consistently reveal that lack of safety figures prominently among the country's problems. Table 1 shows data from household surveys[6] conducted in Mérida (1981, 1983), a city of 275,000 located in the Venezuelan Andes, and Caracas (1983), the capital, with an estimated population of 3.4 million (OCEI 1987). Respondents were asked to name the three most serious problems they felt citizens were facing. Despite differences in questionnaire design, lack of personal safety was among the three problems most frequently mentioned in all surveys and was considerably more important than other issues such as health, transport or education. The same surveys also revealed substantial fear of predatory crime. When asked how safe they felt on the streets at night, on a scale of 1 (very safe) to 4 (very unsafe) Mérida respondents averaged 3.2 in 1981 and 3.1 in 1983; Caracas respondents averaged 3.5 (1983).[7]

The perception of high crime rates is also evident in many statements made by politicians, journalists and even academics. For example, in 1974 the President convened a meeting of Governors to discuss crime control, at which he spoke of the "moving" and "dramatic" "avalanche of crimes" (MRI 1974, p. 378). The same metaphor -"an avalanche of crimes"- was used by a sociologist in 1980 (Alvarez Bernee 1980, p. 5); and in his first message to Congress in 1985, President Lusinchi stated that "In recent years there has been an explosion of crime" (Lusinchi 1985, p. XLVII). Elsewhere, I have examined in more detail the perceptions of crime as evidenced in Venezuelan newspapers and found similar characteristics (Birkbeck 1981a).

In addition, crime rates are not only perceived as high, but also to be increasing. Thus, 73% of respondents in the Mérida opinion surveys and 79% of respondents in the Caracas survey felt that crime had increased in their city over the previous two years.

Finally, collective perceptions are marked by short periods during which predatory crime is seen to have reached crisis levels. Their appearance is

---

5 "The streets of Caracas are completely unsafe at night, because of the large number of assaults and knifings." This was the observation made in 1802 by the famous French traveler Francois Depons (Gómez Grillo 1982, p. 22).

6 Where no documentary reference is given for survey results, the data come from the author's own files.

7 According to these data, Venezuelan respondents appear more fearful of predatory crime than respondents in many U.S. cities (see Skogan and Maxfield 1981, pp. 47-58).

Table 1: WHAT DO YOU THINK ARE THE THREE MOST SERIOUS PROBLEMS THAT CITIZENS FACE TODAY?

	Mérida 1981		Mérida 1983		Caracas 1983	
	N[a]	%	N	%	N	%
Unemployment	–[b]	–	479	20.9	832	23.2
Cost of Living	811	26.3	449	19.6	795	22.1
Housing	653	21.2	151	6.6	359	10.0
Public Health	161	5.2	140	6.1	111	3.1
Transport	314	10.2	21	0.9	34	0.9
Education	140	4.5	191	8.3	204	5.7
Crime/Safety	588	19.1	420	18.3	867	24.2
Corruption	–	–	181	7.9	247	6.9
Other	414	13.4	256	11.1	133	3.7
Total	3081	100.0	2288	100.0	3582	100.0

Notes:
(a) N = number of times mentioned.
(b) – = not measured.

normally linked to serious crimes committed against members of the upper class. For example, in February 1981 a prominent member of the armed forces, General Fernández Escobar, was killed in the course of an armed robbery at his home. As a result, the armed forces, businessmen and other members of the upper class made public demands on the government to strengthen policies for crime control. One of the arguments used was that crime was out of hand, a theme taken up by the newspapers and reflected in increased attention to crimes of violence over the next few weeks. A similar but lesser crisis occurred in February 1982 following the murder of the wife of ex-President Caldera's physician (Birkbeck 1982).[8]

How do these perceptions compare with available evidence on predatory crime rates? Such data derive from police statistics and victim surveys, and each source has its own strengths and weaknesses.

The best series of police statistics is that compiled by the Judicial Police (PTJ) and published annually since 1969 (Ministerio de Justicia, 1971-). This gives information on crimes reported to the Judicial Police (PTJ), which, under the Code of Criminal Procedure, is the principal agency encharged with receiving such reports. However, estimates from victim

8 Available evidence suggests that the Venezuelan press pays much greater attention to serious victimizations of the wealthy than to comparable victimizations of other groups. A study of kidnappings during the 1970's revealed significantly greater press coverage if the victim belonged to a wealthy family (Vera 1985).

surveys in Caracas and Mérida indicate that between 20 and 30% of reports made by victims are directed to police forces other than the PTJ. These are the uniformed police in each State, the political police (DISIP) and the National Guard. Thus, the PTJ statistics probably underestimate the number of crimes reported to the police.

A second problem is, of course, that not all crimes are reported. Victim survey data for Caracas and Mérida show that the proportion of thefts, robberies and assaults reported to the police varies from 17 to 28%, depending upon crime type, city and survey date (Birkbeck 198lb; Ministerio de Justicia n.d.; 1986; Gabaldón, Birkbeck and Bettiol 1990). This is lower than reporting rates for similar kinds of crime in the United States and other industrialized countries (Birkbeck, Gabaldón and LaFree 1990).

It is clear, therefore, that PTJ statistics substantially underestimate the real crime rate. However, if the proportion of crimes reported to the police has not varied greatly over time, these statistics may be indicative of trends in crime rates. Research in industrialized nations shows that the characteristics of the crime incident, particularly seriousness, are a far stronger determinant of reporting than other variables, such as the victim's attitude towards the police (Skogan 1984; Gottfredson and Gottfredson 1988). This suggests that the proportion of reported crime may be relatively stable, at least for more serious crimes. A preliminary analysis of data from an attitudinal study of reporting in the city of Mérida finds similar results (Gabaldón, Birkbeck and LaFree 1990). Thus, although caution should be exercized, police statistics may be an acceptable indicator of trends in more serious crime.

The second type of data for studying predatory crime in Venezuela is provided by victim surveys. At least nine surveys have been carried out during the last decade, two at the national level in 1981 (Venezuela, OCEI 1983) and 1987[9], one in the Guayana region (CVG 1983), five in the city of Mérida in the years 1981, 1983, 1985, 1986 and 1987 (Birkbeck 1981b; Ministerio de Justicia n.d.; 1986; Gabaldón, Birkbeck and Bettiol 1990), one in the city of Caracas in 1983 (Ministerio de Justicia n.d.) and one in the city of Maracaibo in 1987 (LaFree and Birkbeck 1991). Considerable variations in objectives, sampling frame, questionnaire design and quality control make it difficult to use these surveys for examining geographic or temporal variations in crime rates. However, they allow an assessment of the extent of unreported crime and provide important information on the characteristics of both victims and crime incidents, at least for thefts, robberies and assaults.

---

9 The results of the second national victim survey conducted by the OCEI in 1987 are still unavailable.

Table 2 shows aggregate crime rates for Venezuela between 1962 and 1987 and specific crime rates for 1970-1987, based on crimes reported to the PTJ. Assuming that these figures reflect real crime rates, it is clear that the latter rose substantially during the period under study. In 1962, the rate for all crimes was 474/100,000, but by 1987 it had increased to 1,111. Superimposed on this general trend are three periods in which crime rates temporarily declined: 1962-65, 1974-78 and 1980-84. Property crimes represented 51.8% of all crimes known to the police in 1971, but had increased to 66% in 1987. By contrast the proportion of violent crimes remained almost constant: 24.8% in 1970 and 26.1% in 1987.[10] Thus, the overall crime rate has increasingly become a reflection of the property crime rate, as figure 1 shows. In particular, an examination of the homicide rate in table 2 shows a divergent pattern, with a sustained increase during the 1970's and a general decline during the 1980's.

As we have seen, Venezuelan victim surveys reveal that a substantial amount of crime is not reported to the police. Hence real crime rates are appreciably higher than those calculated from police statistics. For example, PTJ figures for Caracas show crime rates of 1,151 for theft and 652 for robbery during 1983, but the victim survey carried out in Caracas during the last quarter of 1983 indicates a rate of 3,356 for theft and 8,593 for robbery.[11] Since direct comparison of victim survey results and police statistics is extremely difficult, these findings should be treated as indicative, rather than definitive.

We saw above that Venezuelans perceive predatory crime rates to be both inordinately high and on the increase. Analysis of the available data suggests that this perception is in some respects concordant with the evidence on crime rates, but in other respects markedly divergent. Venezuelans are correct in asserting that crime rates are on the increase, for such has been the general tendency over the last 25 years. Nevertheless, it is not clear that such increases warrant the metaphor of an "avalanche" of crimes. Moreover, Venezuelans have not distinguished between the marked rise in property crime and the slower increases in violent crime, for the latter undoubtedly represent the more serious threat to personal safety.

---

10 Property crimes include burglary, larceny, personal larceny with contact, personal larceny without contact, vehicle theft, extortion, cattle rustling, and kidnapping. Violent crimes include homicide, assault, rape and robbery.

11 The large number of robberies reported in the Caracas victim survey may in part reflect problems in survey design. While the Código Penal distinguishes between robbery (hurto) and robbery (robo), the average citizen refers to both crimes as robo. Unless interviewers are carefully trained and monitored they are likely to register many thefts as robberies.

Table 2: Crime Rates (/100,000 Inhabitants), Venezuela, 1962-87

Year	All	Property	Violent	Homicide	Corruption	Drugs
1962	474	–[a]	–	–	–	–
1963	414	–	–	–	–	–
1964	347	–	–	–	–	–
1965	335	–	–	–	–	–
1966	366	–	–	–	–	–
1967	472	–	–	–	–	–
1968	495	–	–	–	–	–
1969	547	–	–	–	–	–
1970	575	–	–	–	–	–
1971	600	311	149	6.2	–	–
1972	709	374	177	6.0	–	15.0
1973	768	438	250	7.5	–	–
1974	864	463	236	7.1	–	19.3
1975	862	470	283	7.4	–	20.1
1976	817	466	251	8.3	2.5	15.8
1977	743	413	238	8.8	2.4	16.6
1978	684	381	215	9.6	1.8	17.2
1979	744	417	238	10.7	2.9	23.0
1980	855	460	297	12.5	2.6	26.9
1981	797	420	280	11.0	1.8	27.7
1982	819	425	303	10.9	1.4	27.4
1983	874	437	349	12.5	1.3	26.6
1984	837	440	308	9.9	1.3	30.9
1985	921	525	304	9.7	1.5	35.6
1986	988	607	291	8.4	2.1	34.4
1987	1111	734	290	8.1	2.1	31.1

Source: Ministerio de Justicia (1980; 1988)
Notes:
(a) – = data unavailable

Given that police statistics are rarely used in public discussions of crime, it is not surprising that perceptions diverge from the available evidence. For example, although crime rates fell between 1975 and 1978, when the President addressed Congress in 1977 he spoke of the "dramatic situation" with regard to crime and the "extreme anxiety" that Venezuelans felt (Pérez 1977, p. XLI); and in early 1979 he told Congress that crime had reached "alarming levels" (Pérez, 1979, p. XCVIII). Similarly, in his 1978 report to Congress, the Minister of Justice spoke of the need to find solutions to the "grave and complex problems (...) relating to the increase in crime" (Ministerio de Justicia 1979). These statements are clearly contradicted by crime rates as reflected in police statistics.

Figure 1:
Crime Reported in Venezuela 1962 – 1987
Rates per 100,000 Inhabitants

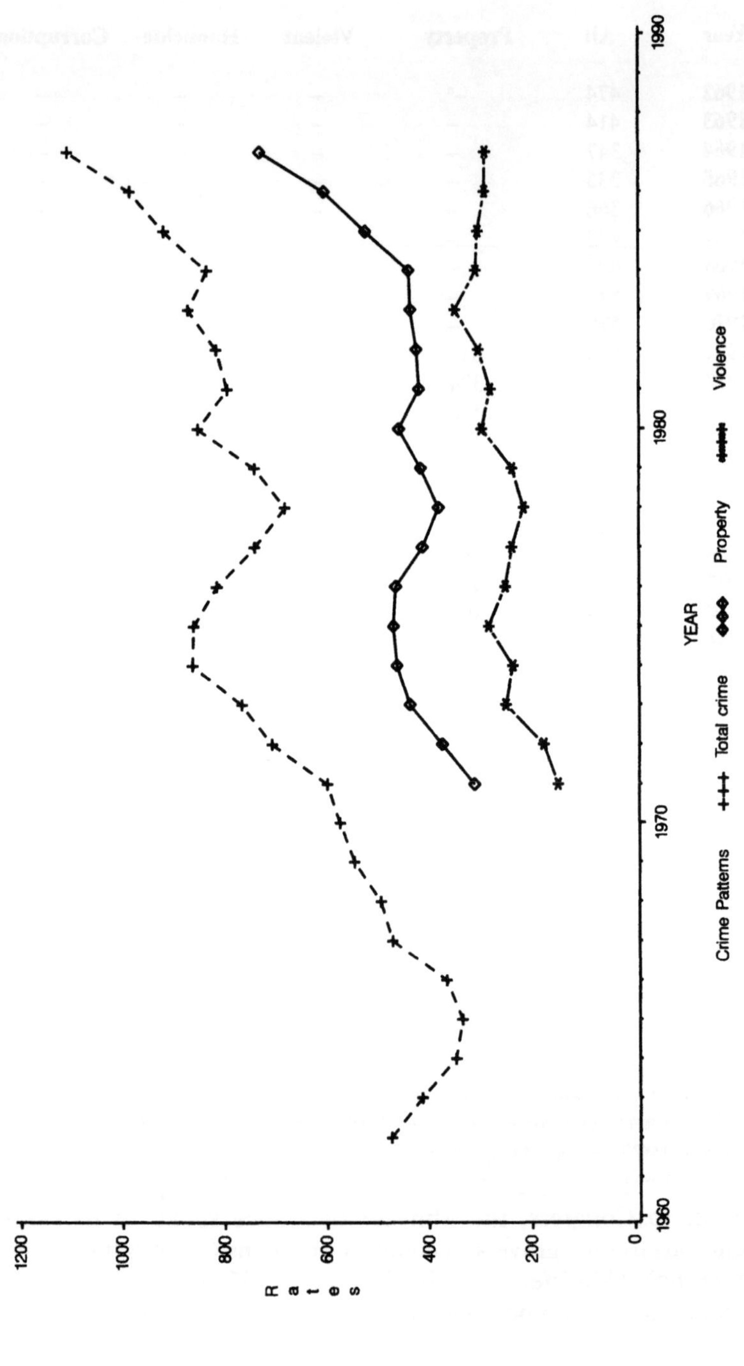

Table 3: Victimization Rates (/100,000)[a] for theft, robbery and assault, Venezuela and the United States

	Mérida 1981	Mérida 1983	U.S.[b] 1983	Caracas 1983	U.S.[c] 1983
Theft[d]	3870	2887	18,541	3356	23,623
Robbery[e]	796	1004	839	8593	2,196
Assault	-[f]	41	2,602	299	3,509

Notes:
(a) Rates for Venezuela are calculated for population 10 years of age or older. Rates for the U.S. are calculated for population 12 years of age or older.
(b) Refers to areas within Standard Metropolitan Statistical Areas but outside of core cities. Calculated from the U.S. National Crime Survey, 1983 (U.S., Bureau of Justice Statistics 1984).
(c) Refers to core cities within Standard Metropolitan Statistical Areas. Calculated from the U.S. National Crime Survey, 1983 (U.S., Bureau of Justice Statistics 1984).
(d) Includes personal larceny without contact, larceny, burglary and vehicle theft.
(e) Includes robbery and personal larceny with contact.
(f) Not measured in 1981.

While Venezuelans are not always correct in their perceptions of crime rates, the relatively low proportion of predatory crimes reported to the police might give weight to their feeling that real crime rates are inordinately high. Nevertheless, victimization rates may be no higher in Venezuela than they are in other countries. Although a systematic analysis of this question is currently impossible, table 3 shows a comparison of victimization rates for theft, robbery and assault in two Venezuelan cities and urban areas in the United States. This evidence indicates that victimization rates for theft and assault are substantially lower in Venezuela than in comparable urban areas in the United States. By contrast, the victimization rate for robbery is much higher, although perhaps not so high as the Caracas figures indicate.[12] Thus, Venezuelans may be justified in their alarm over predatory crime rates if the focus of their concern is robbery, but not if they are referring to other crimes.

1.2 Corruption

As with predatory crime, concern over corruption is not new in Venezuela (Rangel and Pulgar 1975; Malavé Mata 1987; Ochoa Benítez 1988). It

12 See note 10

becomes a particular focus of attention in the year following national elections, as the previous government's activities become a target for political attack (Malavé Mata 1987). Most observers see corruption as widespread, particularly since the inception of the democratic period in 1958, but the average citizen views it as less serious than do politicians and academics.

For example, in 1975 a prominent leftwing politician suggested that corruption was so generalized that "not only have people become hardened to it, they themselves are wondering how to get part of the booty" (Rangel and Pulgar 1975, p. 25). In 1982, a criminologist described a "chaotic panorama of institutional anarchy" that resulted from a "vortex of (illegal) enrichment" (Aniyar de Castro 1982, pp. 146-147). And in 1985 the President declared to Congress that "corruption, both public and private, is today one of the gravest potential threats to our democratic system and to our identity as a people" (Lusinchi 1985, p. XLVIII).

An opinion survey conducted in 1983 revealed that a high proportion of respondents felt there was a lot of corruption in politics (79.3%), that its current level was intolerable (77%) and that its prevalence threatened the stability of the democratic regime (79.7%). Moreover, compared to a survey in 1973, a much greater proportion of the 1983 respondents felt that many government officials were crooked (Baloyra 1986).

However, the average citizen seems to perceive corruption as less serious than other forms of crime. Thus, surveys have found that respondents judge personal victimization through predatory crime to be more serious than the social losses incurred through embezzlement and corruption (Gabaldón and García Sucre 1978; Gabaldón and Murúa 1981). Similarly, table 1 shows that respondents in Caracas and Mérida view corruption as far less of a problem than personal safety from predatory crime.

Empirical evaluation of the perception that corruption is widespread is difficult for a number of reasons. First, in Venezuela the term corruption is frequently used in a very broad and ill-defined sense. For example, a recent discussion of the problem (Ochoa Benítez 1988) includes failure to pay taxes, presidential pardons for prisoners, excessive and inefficient bureaucracy, and the establishment of a national salary scale for Universities. It is clear that, with such free-ranging definitions as these, corruption can be found practically anywhere. Second, measurement is difficult because, unlike most predatory crime, the victims of corruption are frequently unaware that they have been victimized. Thus it is most likely discovered through official checkups within public administration, or through accusations made by enemies of bureaucrats. Unlike predatory crime, neither police statistics nor victimization data are likely to be appropriate sources for measuring the extent of corruption and its trends over time.

Third, the existence of corruption is less easily determined than is the case for many predatory crimes. With the exception of some rape cases, both nonlegal and legal observers have little problem in recognizing predatory crimes when they occur. However, the identification of corruption is much more complex, in part because there may only be circumstancial evidence available (e.g., the government paid more than the market price on a given purchase, but there is no direct evidence of kickbacks to government officials), in part because it may not be clear whether the law has been broken.

Until adequate measures are developed, the extent of corruption and its trends over time in Venezuela will remain largely unknown. However, it is worth noting that the available evidence does not support the perception of high and increasing rates. As table 2 shows, not only is the rate of cases reported to the police extremely low when compared to predatory crime, but it is also relatively stable.[13] Hence, there may be less corruption than many Venezuelans claim.

1.3 Drug Trafficking and Drug Use

Whereas concerns over predatory crime and corruption are a relatively permanent feature in Venezuela, concern with drugs has been more sporadic. At the beginning of the 1970's, Congress devoted some attention to a perceived increase in marihuana and LSD consumption, but interest soon waned (Sánchez Peláez 1974; Morales Bello 1986). Drugs became prominent in 1984, when law enforcement agencies began to discover relatively large transhipments of cocaine. This sparked intense concern among politicians, businessmen, religious leaders and others over the rise in drug trafficking and its effects on crime, morals and politics (Aniyar de Castro 1985).

The prevalent conception of the problem was well summarized by opposition Deputy Alvarez Paz in the debate he initiated in Congress in

13 This is not to deny that corruption may cause substantial financial losses. For example, in 1983 two lawyers accused managers of the Andean Cement Company (CASA) of misusing funds originally assigned to CASA by the Venezuelan Corporation for Development. They claimed that the managers were using the funds to finance their own businesses (Malavé Mata 1987). If this accusation was correct, it involved a loss to the nation of approximately 250 million dollars. The total losses from poverty crimes reported to the police in 1983 were approximately 530 million dollars (Ministerio de Justicia 1988).

February 1984. Given the rise in drug production in other Andean countries, Venezuela's convenient geographic location and the country's worsening economic situation, there were many incentives for Venezuelans to engage in the international drug trade. One particular danger resulting from this, said Alvarez Paz, was that of political subversion. In relation to drug use, the fact that 64% of Venezuela's population was under 18 meant that there was a large market of potential consumers within the country. Alvarez Paz claimed that there were 500,000 drug users in the country and that 85% of crimes were linked to drug use. He concluded that drugs were "the most serious, profound and dramatic problem that Venezuelans have ever faced" (Alvarez Paz 1988).

Concern over drugs continued until 1988, when left-wing politician José Vicente Rangel accused the opposition candidate in the forthcoming presidential election of maintaining links with members of the international drug cartels. Since then, drugs have been relegated to a secondary position in discussions of the problems facing the nation.

As with corruption, measurement of the extent of drug trafficking in Venezuela is difficult, since the cases brought to light depend almost entirely on the diligence and organization of the country's police forces. Moreover, there is no mechanism for coordinating either the activities or the statistics of these forces. While the PTJ has the principal responsibility for preparing cases for court, interdiction is largely the work of the National Guard.

The only consistent data on trafficking are the number of cases known to the PTJ. Prior to 1975, no case of trafficking was recorded (Ministerio de Justicia 1980). In that year 44 cases were recorded and the figure grew to 1,741 in 1987, with a notable increase between 1983 (550 cases) and 1985 (1450 cases). However, the fact that a special Drug Law was enacted in July 1984 may well have stimulated police activity, such that these figures probably do not reflect real trends in drug trafficking. Figures on drug seizures by the National Guard during the 1980's (U.S. Department of State, Bureau of International Narcotics Matters 1984) are so inconsistent that they provide no reasonable estimates of trends in trafficking. Furthermore, they exclude drug seizures made by other police forces in Venezuela, and seizures of drugs from Venezuela made in other countries.

Data on domestic drug use are scarce but more reliable. In 1986 the Ministry of Justice conducted a national self-report survey among high school students which revealed that 1.5% of respondents had used marihuana at least once, and even lower percentages had used other drugs.[14] In 1988 the Ministry for Family Affairs undertook a similar survey which found that the proportion of high school students reporting use of

14 Harvey Williams, personal communication.

marihuana over the previous six months varied from 0.8% in the eastern region to a high of 2.3% in the central region (Ministerio de la Familia n.d.). These figures suggest that drug use among Venezuelan youth is much lower than many observers claim.[15]

Thus, while the general increase in drug production and shipment from Latin America to North America and Western Europe since the 1970's has undoubtedly affected Venezuela, it is not clear how much transhipment occurs within the country. While consumption may have increased, drug use appears to be relatively low. The claims by Deputy Alvarez Paz that there are 500,000 drug users in the country and that 85% of crimes are related to drugs cannot be substantiated (Aniyar de Castro 1985). Finally, table 2 includes a drug "crime rate" based on cases of possession or trafficking of drugs known to the PTJ. While the rate of drug related offences doubled between 1972 and 1987, much of this increase had already occurred by 1980, four years before Congress and the media began paying attention to the problem. Furthermore, although strict comparison is not possible, it is evident that predatory crimes are much more numerous than drug related offenses, making it harder to accept that the latter constitute "the most serious, profound and dramatic problem that Venezuelans have ever faced".[16]

We see therefore, that perceptions of predatory crime, corruption and drug offenses do not always coincide with the available evidence. Nevertheless, these perceptions have been influential in pressuring governments to act. In the following section, I describe changes in crime control in Venezuela over the last 60 years and then examine responses to the perceived problems of predatory crime, drugs and corruption.

---

15 There is some evidence that use of marihuana is lower among Venezuelan high school students than among comparable groups in other countries. Using a similar questionnaire, Williams found that 16.9% of students in Managua (Nicaragua) private schools in 1976 reported having ever used marihuana (Williams 1977) and that 40,1% of high school juniors in San Joaquin County (California) in 1989 reported having used marihuana during the previous six months (Williams 1990). However, differences in sample characteristics between Venezuela, Nicaragua and the United States mean that these comparisons should be treated as indicative rather than definitive.

16 Aniyar de Castro (1985) reaches a similar conclusion to mine.

2 Crime Control in Venezuela

2.1 A General Perspective

As in other countries, the marked economic, social and political changes that have occurred in Venezuela over the last 60 years have had a substantial impact on policies for crime control. In 1930, the only police forces were the State and Municipal uniformed police and the national political police. Training and professionalism were almost absent, and these forces were heavily controlled by those in power at national or local level (Agudo Freites 1973). Each State had its own judicial system, and judges were appointed by local politicians. In some States, judges had no legal training (Méndez 1952). The prison system was organized at two levels: a national system of penitentiaries under the control of the Ministry of Interior Relations, and locally run jails in the main cities of each State (Méndez 1952). All matters relating to crime and justice were under the supervision of the Minister of Interior Relations or the Governor of each State.

Changes began in 1937 when the National Guard was founded. In 1938, the government created the National Security Service, which integrated the activities of the National Guard and the forerunner of the judicial police. In 1950, The Ministry of Justice was created and this assumed control of the courts and prison system. In 1951, an inter-ministerial Commission for Crime Prevention was created, and in 1970 its activities were assigned to a new Devision within the Ministry of Justice. With the initiation of the democratic period in 1958, the Government set up a specialized judicial police (PTJ) under the Ministry of Justice and reorganized the political police (later to become the DISIP). The Courts were given administrative autonomy in 1970 and an independent and professional judiciary was guaranteed by new legislation in 1984. There are plans to bring the uniformed police into a national administrative structure, but these have not yet materialized.[17]

Institutional changes has therefore involved centralization, the separation of judicial and political powers and increased professionalization. In contrast to these relatively rapid changes, crime control policies have been more static. Despite new legislation, many traditional practices have proved remarkably resistant. For example, although there have been attempts to integrate police and community in crime control (e.g., Cordiplán 1976), these have generally been shortlived and have produced

17 For the more detailed description of changes in the criminal justice system since 1935 see Birkbeck (1982).

ambiguous results (Gabaldón 1986-1987). Policing is still based more on the hunt for offenders than the prevention of crime.

Although the judiciary are now an independent and professional body, the failure to modernize Court procedures results in long delays and low conviction rates. Thus, Garrido (1980) found that during 1979 the Courts only completed 30% of cases admitted for investigation; García Iturbe (1968) found that between 1959 and 1964, the average time from arrest to sentencing doubled to 18 months (more than twice that prescribed by the law on criminal procedure); and Gabaldón (1987) estimates that in 1979 45% of court cases ended without a sentence (in part because prescribed time limits had been exceded).

Finally, the Penitentiary Law of 1961 was designed to replace the punitive and frequently inhuman prison regime of pre-democratic times with individualized treatment for the offender. However, adequate classification of prisoners, work and educational opportunities, and medical and psychological attention are still lacking in many prisoners (Linares 1977).

A particular problem arises from the practice, common in many Latin American countries (Carranza et al. 1983), of the preventive detention of the accused. Thus, in 1987 67% of all prisoners were awaiting trial (Ministerio de Justicia 1988), and although there is a broad institutional segregation according to legal status, most observers agree that prisoners awaiting trial are treated as if they were convicted offenders.

Concern over the state of the nation's prisons led to the introduction of probation in 1980, as an attempt to reduce the amount of preventive detention and increase community based treatment for some convicted offenders (Bravo Dávila 1983; Jiménez 1988). This program, which is probably the most radical innovation in criminal justice in this century, has grown rapidly from 1,361 probationers in 1980 to 14,979 in 1987 (Ministerio de Justicia 1988). However, it has not slowed the growth in prison population, which increased only 7.8% during the 1970's but 130% between 1980 and 1987.

2.2 Responding to Crises

The history of crime control in Twentieth Century Venezuela is thus one of progressive and uneven change towards a more professional and humanitarian model. These advances have generally gone unnoticed by Venezuelan criminologists, who have taken a cross-sectional perspective and, consequently, found much to criticize (e.g., García Iturbe 1968; Gabaldón 1979; Bravo Dávila 1981; Gabaldón 1987). Part of that criticism concerns the response to perceptions of crime such as those described above, for these responses are overwhelmingly regressive.

For example, the typical response to concern over predatory crime has involved the deployment of police in massive search and arrest operations in low income neighborhoods (Hernández 1984; 1989) and use of the Vagrancy Law to deal with "dangerous" individuals. For example, following the murder of General Fernández Escobar in 1981, the Minister of Interior Relations met with the chiefs of the PTJ, DISIP, National Guard and uniformed police and agreed to implement a special operation named the "Plan Unión." According to Gabaldón (1987, p. 185), during the next seven months in Caracas, more than 150,000 people were searched or checked by the police, nearly 8,000 were arrested, and 251 were processed under the Vagrancy Law.

Policies such as these have drawn criticism. The Vagrancy Law gives the police wide discretion in the definition (and detention) of "dangerous" individuals. It involves an administrative procedure overseen by Prefects and Governors rather than a legal procedure handled by the courts and the judiciary. And the most frequent measure is to imprison the individual for anything from a few months to five years. In short, the Vagrancy Law is used as a rapid and highly repressive instrument for punishing selected lower class males (Hernández 1977). Finally, it is not clear that special operations are an efficient method of locating offenders or preventing crime. Despite these criticisms, government and police officials universally claim that such operations are effective in reducing crime rates.[18]

Similarly, the response to concern over drugs can hardly be called progressive. Following the discussions of the early 1970's, in 1975 the Supreme Court decided that possession of even small quantities of drugs was a crime and thus changed the status of drug users from that of clinically ill to that of criminal offenders (Martínez Rincones 1984-1985). The intense debate initiated in 1984 led to the enactment, in the same year, of a new drug law which substantially increased the severity of sanctions (Venezuela 1984). This law widened the definition of illegal drugs (e.g., to include barbiturates), and increased the number of activities defined as crimes (e.g., by including those who finance illegal drug production). Prison sentences were increased from a previous maximum of 11 years (for supplying drugs to juveniles) to the current maximum of 30 years (for those who cultivate or traffick in drugs for subversive purposes). Finally, drug offenders are denied the benefits of probation or parole. The net result has been to channel more individuals through the overburdened judicial system and into a prison system that is widely acknowledged to be defective.

Finally, in response to concern over corruption, the government intro-

18 See, for example El Nacional (Caracas) 12/22/81, p. D-11, "El Plan Unión logró controlar el auge del hampa y el terrorismo."

duced a new anti-corruption law in 1982 (Venezuela 1982). Like the drug law, this increased the number of activities defined as crimes (for example, to include cases where public administrators make unauthorized use of funds even in the public interest). Sanctions were also increased, generally through the simultaneous application of both fines and imprisonment, rather than extending prison sentences.

3 Conclusion

The implications of the preceding analysis should now be apparent. Perceptions of crime in Venezuela convey an image of crises. Crime rates are not only unacceptably high, but they are on the increase. When these concerns are articulated in public debate, they trigger governmental responses that variously emphasize increased policing of citizens, fewer legal guarantees, and more punitive sanctions. Such responses move counter to a general trend, observable over the last sixty years, towards the development of a more professional and humane system of criminal justice. In that sense, they are both regressive and repressive.

What is striking is that the public discussion of crime problems rarely acknowledges the issue of measurement. Thus, perceptions of crime are weakly anchored in available evidence and in some cases contradicted by such evidence. Furthermore, the efficacy of repressive responses can frequently be questioned. As a result, we observe a process in which the public, the media and the politicians construct a problem which does not necessarily exist, while the government responds with measures which would not necessarily resolve the problem. A clue to the reasons for this apparently illogical process may well lie in the "success" the government claims for itself in effectively responding to a serious social problem. The negative image of crime and the responses by government to perceived crises in crime control may be manifestations of doubts concerning the ability of the Venezuelan political system to live up to democratic ideals, and the attempt by those in power to reinforce support for that system (Hernández 1989). But this is a theme that leads far beyond the confines of the present paper.

References

Agudo Freites, Esteban (1973) "Notas sobre la Guardia Nacional.", in: Revista de la Escuela Superior de las Fuerzas Armadas de Cooperación (Caracas) 1, pp. 263-294.

Alvarez Bernee, Sandra (1980) "Lineamiento sobre el auge delictivo.", in: Boletín de la Academia de Ciencias Políticas y Sociales (Caracas), Nos. 58-59.

Alvarez Paz, Oswaldo (1988) El Círculo Vicioso de la Droga, Caracas: Ateneo de Caracas.

Aniyar de Castro, Lola (1982) La Realidad Contra los Mitos: Reflexiones Críticas en Criminología, Maracaibo: Universidad del Zulia.

Aniyar de Castro, Lola (1985) "Legitimación interna y estrategias de dominación en la campaña contra las drogas de 1984 en Venezuela", in: Capítulo Criminológico (Maracaibo) vol. 13, pp. 1-28.

Baloyra, Enrique A. (1986) "Public opinion and support for the regime: 1973-83", in: Venezuela: The Democratic Experience, John D.Martz and David J. Myers eds., New York: Preager, Revised edition, pp. 54-71.

Birkbeck, Christopher (1981a) "Apuntes para una investigación sobre la inseguridad en Venezuela", in: Revista Cenipec (Mérida), 6, pp. 9-40.

Birkbeck, Christopher (1981b) "Informe metodológico sobre la encuesta de víctimas: Mérida, octubre de 1981", in: Revista Cenipec (Mérida), 6, pp. 205-213.

Birkbeck, Christopher (1982) "La planificación de la política antidelictiva en Venezuela: balance y perspectivas", in: Revista Cenipec (Mérida), 7, pp. 67-123.

Birkbeck, Christopher, Luis Gerardo Gabaldón and Gary LaFree (1990) "Reporting crime to the police in the United States and Venezuela: an attitudinal study", Paper presented at the the 12th World Congress of the International Sociology Association, Madrid, Spain.

Bravo Dávila, Luis (1981) Bases para el Desarrollo de un Sistema de Probación en Venezuela, Caracas: Ministerio de Justicia, Dirección de Prisiones/Universidad Central de Venezuela, Facultad de Ciencias Jurídicas y Políticas, Instituto de Ciencias Penales y Criminológicas.

Bravo Dávila, Luis (1983) La Ley de Sometimiento a Juicio y Suspensión Condicional de la Pena: Fundamentos y Aplicación del Tratamiento en Libertad, Caracas: Universidad Central de Venezuela.

CVG (Corporación Venezolana de Guayana) (1983) Encuesta sobre Hechos Delictivos para la Región Guayana – Area Urbana 1980, Puerto Ordaz: CVG.

Carranza, Elías, et al. (1983) El Preso sin Condena en América Latina.

San José, Costa Rica: Instituto Lationamericano de Naciones Unidas para la Prevención del Delito y el Tratamiento del Delincuente.

Carrera Damas, Germán (1973) El Culto a Bolívar: Esbozo para un Estudio de la Historia de las Ideas en Venezuela. Caracas: Universidad Central de Venezuela.

Chiossone, Tulio (1980) Formación Jurídica de Venezuela en la Colonia y la República. Caracas: Universidad Central de Venezuela, Facultad de Ciencias Jurídicas y Políticas, Instituto de Ciencias Penales y Criminológicas.

Clagett, Helen L. (1947) A Guide to the Law and Legal Literature of Venezuela, Washington, D.C.: The Library of Congress.

Cordiplán (Oficina Central de Coordinación y Planificación) (1976) V Plan de la Nación, 1976-80, Caracas: Cordiplán.

Gómez Grillo, Elio (1982) La Historia Fea de Caracas y Otras Historias Criminológicas, Caracas: Academia Nacional de la Historia, Colección El Libro Menor, No. 22.

Gabaldón, Luis Gerardo (1979) "Criminología académica y praxis criminológica en Venezuela", in: Revista Cenipec (Mérida), 4, pp. 9-32.

Gabaldón, Luis Gerardo (1986-1987) "Presencia policial en zonas residenciales urbanas: hacia la evaluación de la interacción estable entre la policía y el público", in: Revista Cenipec (Mérida), 10, pp. 39-63.

Gabaldón, Luis Gerardo (1987) Control Social y Criminología, Caracas: Editorial Jurídica Venezolana.

Gabaldón, Luis Gerardo, Christopher Birkbeck and Daniela Bettiol (1990) La Policía en el Vecindario, Mérida: Gobernación del Estado Mérida/Universidad de Los Andes.

Gabaldón, Luis Gerardo, Christopher Birkbeck and Gary LaFree (1990) "La decisión de denunciar a la policía: un estudio actitudinal en Venezuela y los Estados Unidos." Paper presented at the 7th Annual Research Seminar, Centro de Investigaciones Penales y Criminológicas, Mérida.

Gabaldón, Luis Gerardo and Víctor García Sucre (1978) La Percepción Social de la Ley Penal: Una Primera Aproximación, Mérida: Universidad de Los Andes, Centro de Investigaciones Penales y Criminológicas.

Gabaldón, Luis Gerardo and Mario Murúa (1981) Gravedad Social del Delito e Imágenes del Delincuente en la Población Venezolana. Mérida: Universidad de Los Andes, Centro de Investigaciones Penales y Criminológicas.

García Iturbe, Arnoldo (1968) "La administración de justicia penal como causa de delincuencia", Ministerio Público (Caracas), 6-8, pp. 13-35.

Garrido, Pilar (1980) "Estadísticas judiciales", Paper presented to the Fourth National Criminology Meeting, Mérida.

Glaser, Daniel (1971) Social Deviance. Chicago: Markham.

Gottfredson, Michael R. and Don M. Gottfredson (1988) Decision Making in Criminal Justice: Toward the Rational Exercise of Discretion, New York: Plenum Press.

Hernández, Tosca (1977) La Ideologización del Delito y de la Pena, Caracas: Universidad Central de Venezuela.

Hernández, Tosca (1984) "Los operativos policiales extraordinarios en Venezuela." Paper presented to the Seventh Eastern Seminar on Criminal Justice, Puerto Lacruz (Venezuela).

Hernández, Tosca (1989) "Los problemas de la legitimación: le legitimación de los problemas sociales", in: Legitimidad y Sociedad, Luis Gerardo Gabaldón ed., Caracas: Alfadil/Trópicos, pp. 114-168.

Jiménez, María Angélica (1988) La Probación: Una Medida Eficaz de Prevención Social. Maracaibo: Universidad del Zulia, Instituto de Criminología. Serie Investigadores.

LaFree, Gary and Christopher Birkbeck (1991) "The neglected situation: a cross-national study of the situational characteristics of crime", in: Criminology (forthcoming, February issue).

Linares, Myrla (1977) El Sistema Penitenciario Venezolano. Caracas: Universidad Central de Venezuela, Facultad de Ciencias Jurídicas y Políticas, Instituto de Ciencias Penales y Criminológicas.

Lusinchi, Jaime (1985) I Mensaje al Congreso de la República. Dr. Jaime Lusinchi, Presidente de Venezuela. Caracas: Ministerio de Información y Turismo.

Malavé Mata, Héctor (1987) Los Extravíos del Poder. Caracas: Universidad Central de Venezuela, Ediciones de la Biblioteca.

Martínez Rincones, José Francisco (1984-1985) "Retroactividad e irretroactividad en materia penal, un caso referido al artículo 367 del Código Penal venezolano y la Ley Orgánica sobre Sustancias Estupefacientes y Psicotrópicas", in: Revista Cenipec (Mérida), 9, pp. 121-138.

Méndez, José Agustín (1952) "Política penal y penitenciaria", in: Revista del Ministerio de Justicia (Caracas), Año 1, No. 1, pp. 19-35.

Ministerio de Justicia (1971-) Estadística Delictiva. Caracas: Ministerio de Justicia.

Ministerio de Justicia (1979) Memoria y Cuenta, Caracas: Ministerio de Justicia.

Ministerio de Justicia (1980) Estadística Delictiva 1979, Caracas: Ministerio de Justicia.

Ministerio de Justicia (1986) Estadística Policial Referida a la Ciudad de Mérida y al Estado Mérida, 1985, Mérida: Ministerio de Justicia, Dirección de Prevención del Delito del Estado Mérida.

Ministerio de Justicia (1988) Resumen de Ia Estadística Delictiva 1980-1987, Caracas: Ministerio de Justicia.

Ministerio de Justicia (n.d.) Informe sobre Encuesta de Victimización. Caracas/Mérida, 1983. Caracas: Ministerio de Justicia, Dirección de Prevención del Delito.
Ministerio de la Familia (n.d.) Encuesta Nacional sobre Consumo de Drogas Lícitas e Ilícitas en Estudiantes de Educación Media. 1987-1988, Caracas: Ministerio de la Familia/Fundación José Félix Rivas.
Morales Bello, David (1986) El Delito de Droga y la Ley Anti-Droga en Venezuela, Caracas: Ediciones Aculpueblo.
MRI (Ministerio de Relaciones Anteriores) (1974) Política Antidelictiva. Política Presupuestaria. XVII Convención Nacional de Gobernadores. Caracas: MRI.
OCEI (Oficina Central de Estadística e Informática) (1983) "Población víctima de delitos, 1981", Caracas: OCEI, Unpublished document.
OCEI (Oficina Central de Estadística e Informática) (1987) Proyecciones de Población 1980-2000, Caracas: OCEI.
Ochoa Benítez, Arturo E. (1988) El Comportamiento Folklórico del Venezolano y de las Instituciones Públicas, Caracas: Editorial Panapo.
Pérez, Carlos Andrés (1977) III Mensaje al Congreso de la República. Carlos Andrés Pérez, Caracas: Ministerio de Información y Turismo.
Pérez, Carlos Andrés (1979) V Mensaje al Congreso de la República. Carlos Andrés Pérez, Caracas: Ministerio de Información y Turismo.
Rangel, José Vicente and Juvencio Pulgar (1975) ¿Quién Encubre a los Culpables? Caracas: Colección Parlamento y Socialismo.
Sánchez Peláez, Abel (1974) Drogas. Cultura Comercial y Alienación, Caracas: Universidad Central de Venezuela.
Skogan, Wesley G. (1984) "Reporting crimes to the police: the status of world research." Journal of Research in Crime and Delinquency 21(2): 113-137.
Skogan, Wesley G. and M.G. Maxfield (1981) Coping with Crime, Beverly Hills: Sage.
U.S. Bureau of Justice Statistics (1984) Sourcebook of Criminal Justice Statistics – 1983. Washington: U.S. Bureau of Justice Statistics.
U.S. Department of State, Bureau of International Narcotics Matters (1984-) International Narcotics Control Strategy Report, Washington: Department of State.
Venezuela (1919) An Address of Bolívar at the Congress of Angostura (February 15, 1819), Washington, D.C.: Byron S. Adams Press.
Venezuela (1982) Ley Orgánica de Salvaguarda del Patrimonio Público, Caracas: Gaceta Oficial No. 3.077, extraordinaria del 23/12/82.
Venezuela (1984) Ley Orgánica Sobre Sustancias Estupefacientes y Psicotrópicas, Caracas: Gaceta Oficial No. 3.411, extraordinaria del 17/07/84.

Vera Rivas, María Maidola (1985) "El secuestro en Venezuela." Unpublished thesis, Universidad de Los Andes, Facultad de Ciencias Jurídicas y Políticas, Escuela de Derecho.
Waddell, D.A.G. (1990) Venezuela, Oxford: Clio Press. World Bibliography Series, vol. 110.
Williams, Harvey (1977) Progressive Drug Involvement: Marihuana Use Careers among Nicaraguan Private Secondary School Students. Ph.D. Thesis, Vanderbilt University.
Williams, Harvey (1990) A Report of Drug Use Patterns among High School Juniors in San Joaquin County, Mimeo.

Crime and Control in the English-Speaking Caribbean: A Comparative Study of Jamaica, Trinidad[1], Tobago and Barbados 1960-1980

Hyacinthe Ellis

Jamaica, Trinidad and Barbados are the three largest of the English-speaking Caribbean territories. They are also the most highly industrialized to date with Jamaica concentrating on the production of Bauxite-Alumina, Trinidad, and now Barbados on the production of oil and natural gas. As a consequence, perhaps, they are more advanced economically and politically than the other territories. Jamaica and Trinidad achieved political independence from Britain within months of each other during 1961-1962. Barbados became independent in 1966.

Jamaica, Trinidad, Barbados are among Third World societies that have been subjected to the experiences of slavery and colonial exploitation. Economic dependence and foreign domination continue despite the achievement of political independence. Relative poverty and deprivation, overpopulation and underemployment are common to all three.

Writers and analysts claim that over time, these experiences result in the emergence of negative structural and psycho-social features which affect the vitality of these societies. The main problems pin-pointed identified are: economic, social and psychological dependency; conflicting loyalties and value systems; instability in political and/or economic relationships; political patronage or clientism. Each of these, in one respect or another, is the basis for the development and maintenance of negative patterns of behaviour that sometimes qualify or define a society.

Third World societies, including the Caribbean are marked by a high level of criminality. Explanations attempted by Third World scholars point to the emergence of distinctive forms of crime and justice, that are a consequence of historical processes that promote and maintain the underdevelopment of these societies (Pryce 1976; Mahabir 1980; Sumner 1982). Other explanations cite such factors as theris to modernize (Clinard & Abbott 1978; de Albuquerque 1984) and the indigenous system of socio-political/economic organization (Stone 1983). Relatively few studies

---

1 Trinidad and Tobago will be referred to as Trinidad

consider the problem of crime in relation to the functioning of the criminal justice system.

It has been contended that crime levels and the growth of crime in developed societies are related to internal systems that reduce the risk of crime detection and weaken sanctions against criminals (Haferkamp 1985). Perhaps this is also true of developing societies. This article questions the evidence of such relationships in the Caribbean, with particular regard to the differences in crime levels among the societies under discussion. Internal systems examined in relation to the levels and growth of crime in the three Caribbean societies are described by the concepts of Decriminalization, Desinstitutionalization and Mitigation of Sanctions.

Decriminalization refers to a tendency to trivialize criminal behaviour by removing the stigma from certain offences. It also refers to a reluctance on the part of law enforcement officers to apprehended certain offenders and a low level of vigilance that allows criminal activities to escape detection. These features are categorised as Police Activity, and operationalized, here, as the proportion of crimes apprehended, prosecuted and cleared up.

Desinstitutionalization and Mitigation of Sanctions describe the tendency to reduce or abandon strong punitive measures against criminal offenders. Such may be inferred from changes in sentencing practices over time.

Desinstitutionalization is here indicated by declining conviction and imprisonment rates. Mitigation of sanctions is indicated by a reduction in the number of death sentences imposed.

Trends from 1960 to 1980 in the growth of crime, police activity, and sentencing practices are examined comparatively and in relation to each other. To this end, rates of reported crimes (total, personal, property) are shown alongside rates of crimes apprehended, prosecuted and cleared up; rates of imprisonment and conviction; and changes in the number of death sentences imposed. Rates of crimes apprehended, prosecuted and cleared-up are calculated as percentages of crimes reported. Rates of conviction and imprisonment are calculated as percentages of cases apprehended, prosecuted and cleared up.

1 Development in Criminality over Two Decades 1960-1980

1.1 Total Crimes Reported

Comparing data for Jamaica, Trinidad and Barbados, we find that the level and growth of total crimes, do not vary among these societies as widely as may be expected among these countries, given the level of anxiety about the problem of crime in Jamaica. In some years (1963, 1965, 1966, 1968, 1974) Trinidad recorded higher total crime rates than Jamaica. In 1973 and 1979, Barbados recorded higher crime rates than Trinidad. While Jamaica's crime levels were distinctly higher than the other societies from the mid - 1970's to the end of the decade (fig. 1). The actual increase in crime rates in Jamaica over the period (1960-1980) fell below that of Barbados. It is noted, too, that in Barbados the trend in crime increase continued into the 1980's with rates outstripping those of Trinidad and even Jamaica, in 1984. (see table 1)

Generally the rates of total crimes reported to the police in Jamaica, Trinidad and Barbados are relatively low in comparison to those of advanced societies. For example, the mean rates for crimes recorded by the police in England and Wales during the decades of the 1960's and the 1970's were 2443 and 4080 per 100,000 of population respectively (Council of Europe 1985, p.89), while the combined mean rates for two Caribbean territories - Barbados and Trinidad - over the same periods were 2479 and 3108 per 100,000 of population, respectively. The mean rates for Jamaica were 1576 and 1974 per 100,000 of population respectively. Total crime rates recorded by England and Wales are reported to be lower than those recorded by France, West Germany and of course, the United States of America.

Of greater concern than reported aggregate rates however, is the recorded crime increase in all three territories. In this context, Barbados with a net increase of 108% from 1960-1980 appears to have experienced greater problems than Jamaica or Trinidad whose rates of increase were 12% and 35%, respectively.

Research that considers overall crime trends only, yields results which obscure important details about specific crime patterns. This is clearly undesirable in comparative studies since their objective is not simply observation and comparison of overall trends but also, more importantly,

Figure 1:
Trends in Rates of Total Crimes Reported 1960 – 1984
Rates per 100,000 of the Population

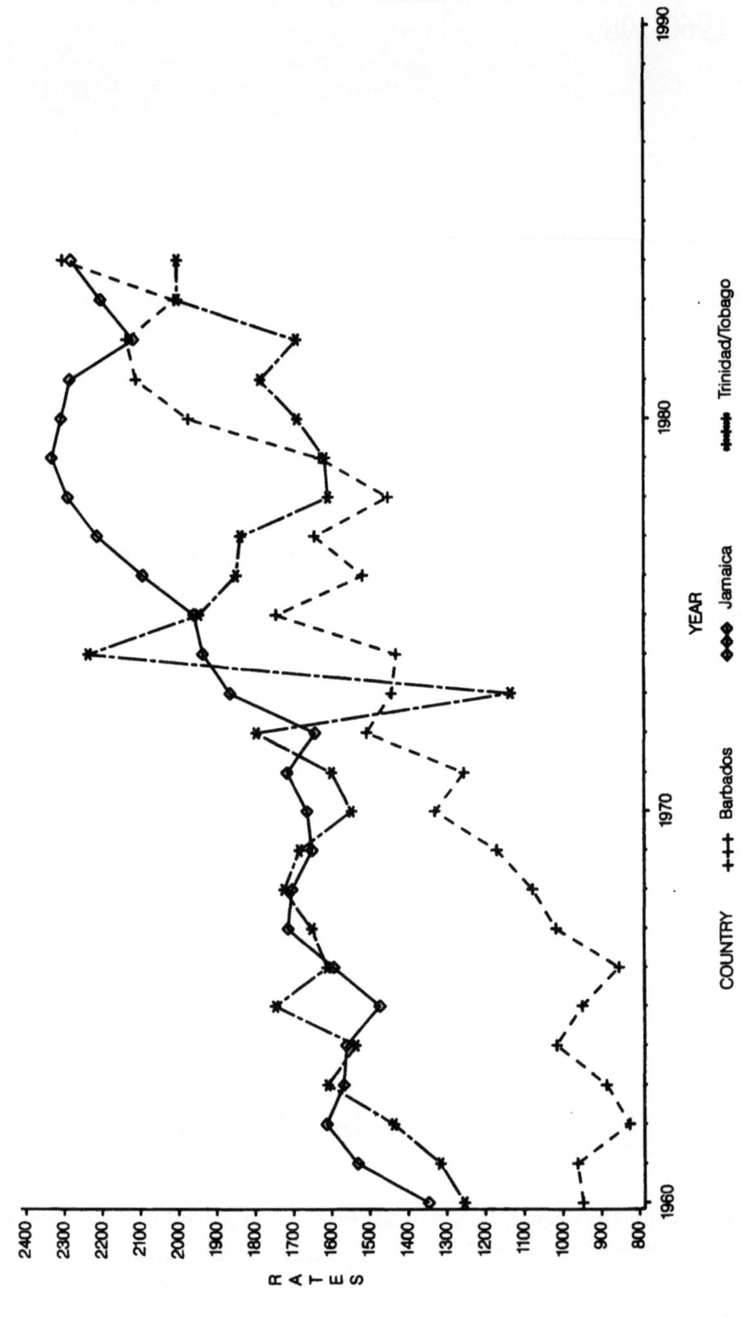

the examination of the dynamics of specific types of crimes over time. These more focused analyses help define the criminality of the societies compared. It is, therefore, appropriate to extend the analyses of crime trends in the English-speaking Caribbean to incorporate two sub-categories: Crimes against property and crimes against the person.

1.2 Crimes against Property[2]

The crimes considered in this category are burglary, breaking and entering, robbery, fraud, embezzlement and arson.

The data indicate that both Barbados and Trinidad report higher rates of crimes against property than Jamaica, and that Barbados took the lead in this category three times during the period 1977-1980. Barbados also shows a much steeper net growth in property crime rates over the period from 1960-1980 than either Trinidad or Jamaica. The net growth rates based on figures in table 2 are 104%, 35% and 3%, respectively. Table 2 also shows that Jamaica's relatively low property crime rates are fairly constant except for a possible decline during the late 1960's and early 1970's.

1.3 Crimes against the Person

Jamaica's reputation as a highly criminogenic society rests on its reported propensity for violence against the person. Over the period from 1960-1980, Jamaica's mean rate for total crimes against the person was approximately three times that for Trinidad and six times that for Barbados (see rates given in table 3). In the twenty-five years since 1960, Jamaica recorded, on average, more than twice the crime rate for murder/manslaughter than Trinidad or Barbados and in fact, more than the combined rates for these territories. The annual rates for the latter seem relatively stable, whereas Jamaica's rates have tripled. For example, in 1960 the murder/manslaughter rates per 100,000 of population were 4.7, 8.1, 7.3, for Barbados, Trinidad and Jamaica, respectively. In 1984, the corresponding rates were 5.9, 7.1 and 22.8. The difference among these territories is also similar in respect of rape. Jamaica for this category of crime between 1960-1980 recorded more than twice the mean rates for

2 Crimes against Property include: Burglary, Breaking and Entering, Larceny, Robbery, Fraud, Arson and Embezzlement. Crimes against the Person include: Murder/Manslaughter, Shooting with Intent, Rape/Carnal Abuse, Felonious Wounding, Infanticide, Suicide.

Figure 2:
Trends in Total Crimes Against Property 1960 – 1980
Rates per 100,000 of the Population

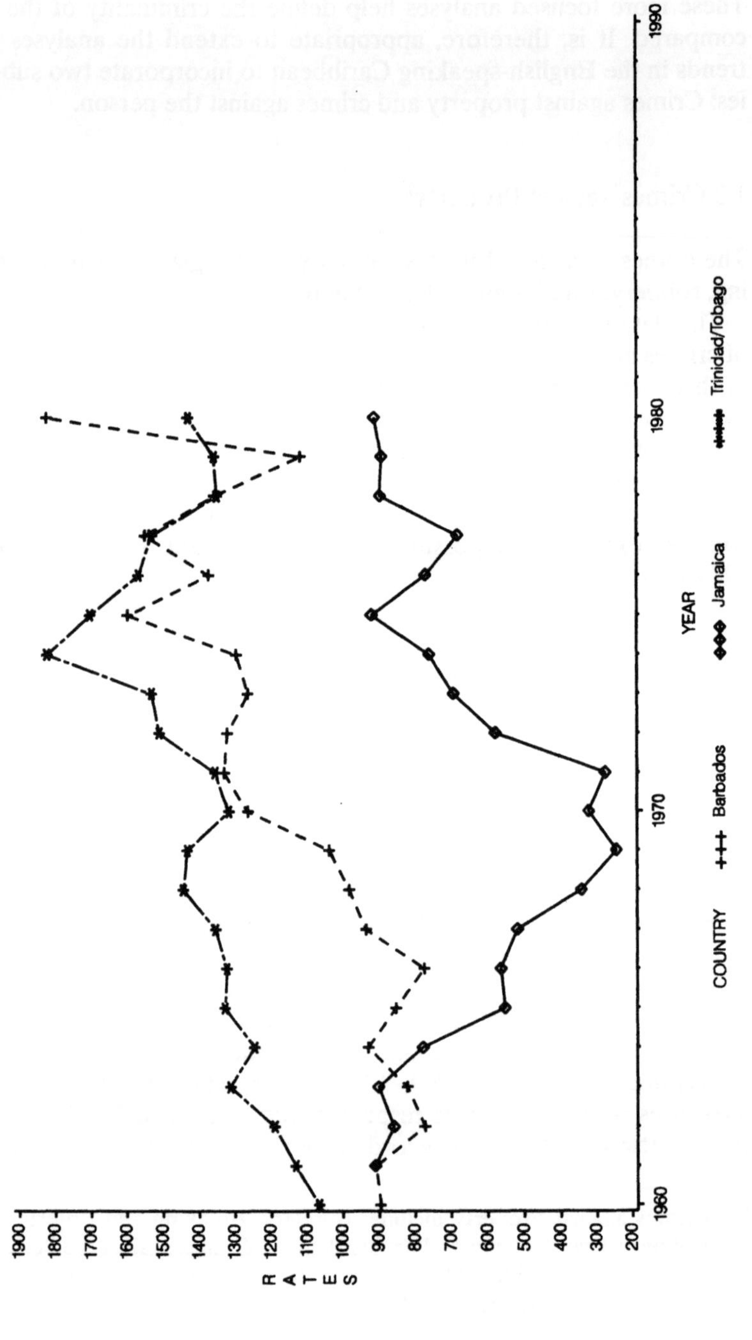

either Barbados or Trinidad. Over the ten year period from 1971-1980, crimes against the person as a proportion of all major and minor crimes recorded, averaged approximately 35%, 12% and 8% for Jamaica, Trinidad and Barbados, respectively.

Summing these statistical observations, it emerges that the major territories of the English-speaking Caribbean do not differ very greatly in respect to the rate of total crimes reported over the period from 1960 to 1980. They have, however, developed very different styles of criminal behaviour. While Barbados and Trinidad are likely to be concerned about relatively high and increasing levels of property crimes, Jamaica holds a reputation for dangerousness, compounded by the frequent use of the guns since the mid-1960's. In 1980, guns were used in over 70% of homicide cases and shooting with intent was recorded as 105 per 100,000 of population. The latter category of crime does not appear in the records of Trinidad and Barbados.

These differences will now be examined against the background of institutional practices that are common to the territories. In particular, trends in law enforcement and sentencing practices will be examined.

2 Trends in Law Enforcement and Crime

Total Crimes: Similarities as well as differences observed in this area of investigation could have important implications for the crime trends discussed earlier. Each of the three societies experienced not only a substantial growth in total crime rates over the period from 1960-1980, but also a corresponding reduction in the rate of police activity as a proportion of total crimes reported. Barbados, with the highest growth rate, also recorded the highest rate of decline in police activity as represented by the percentage of cases apprehended, prosecuted and cleared-up. The rates of decline were 43%, 39% and 28% for Barbados, Trinidad and Jamaica, respectively. Comparative trends in police activity are shown in fig. 6. Placing the trend in police activity alongside the growth of crime, one might hypothesize that crime levels in Barbados and Jamaica are positively related to offender detection thresholds which allow more or less freedom of criminal action. Figs. 7, 8 and 9 show the directions of crime trends and police activity between 1960 and 1980, for each territory. The relationship is less clear in Trinidad.

Property Crimes: Comparing police activity regarding crimes against property we observe (fig. 5) that Jamaica's clear-up rates are consistently higher than comparable rates for Barbados and Trinidad. Barbados

Figure 3:
Trends in Total Crimes Against the Person 1960 – 1980
Rates per 100,000 of the Population

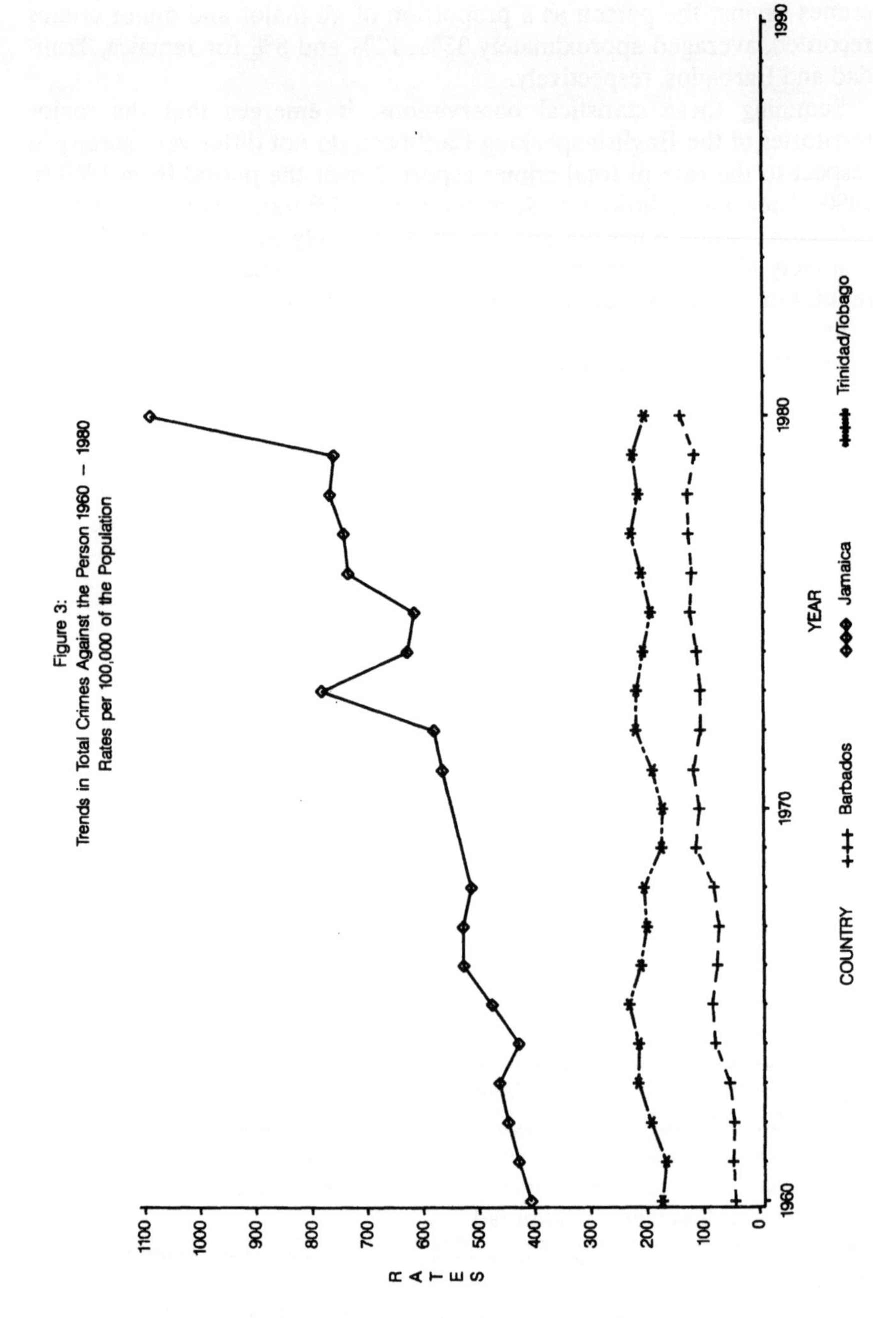

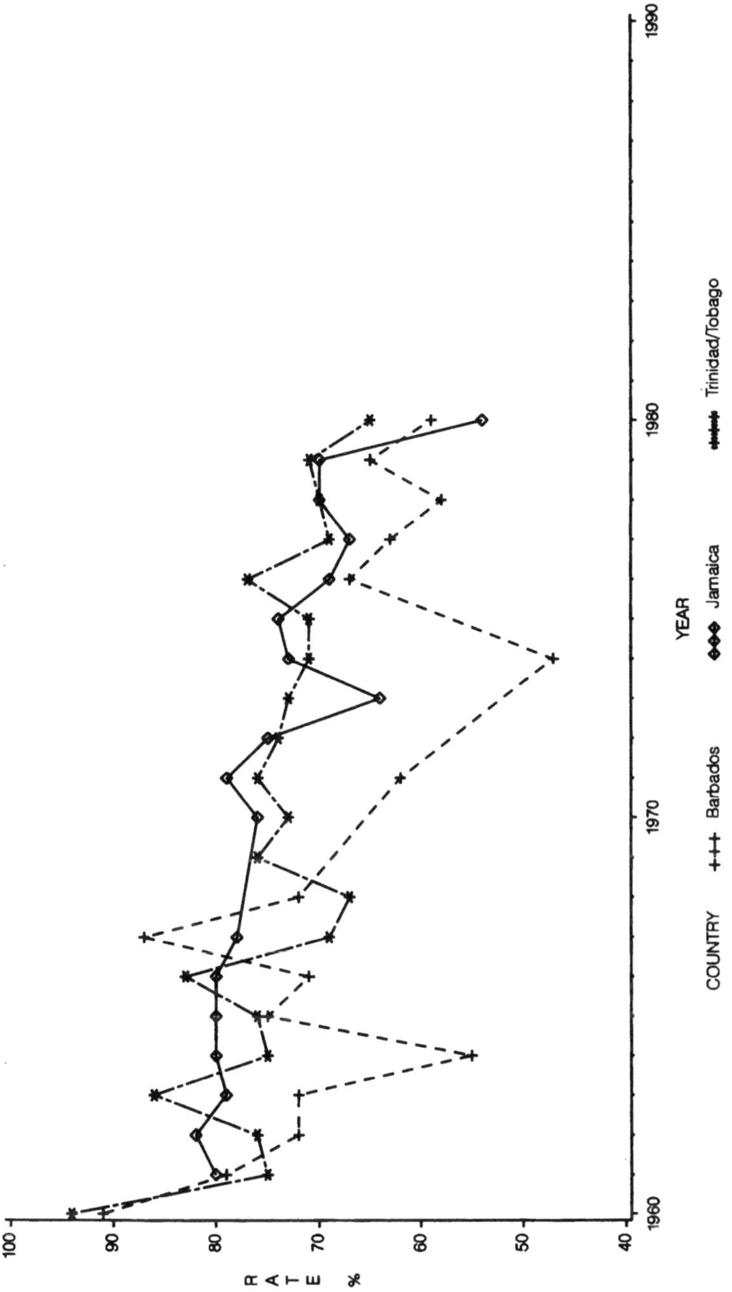

Figure 4:
Comparative Trends in Police Activity and Crime: 1960 – 1980
Crimes Against the Person

Figure 5:
Comparative Trends in Police Activity and Crime: 1960 – 1980
Crimes Against Property

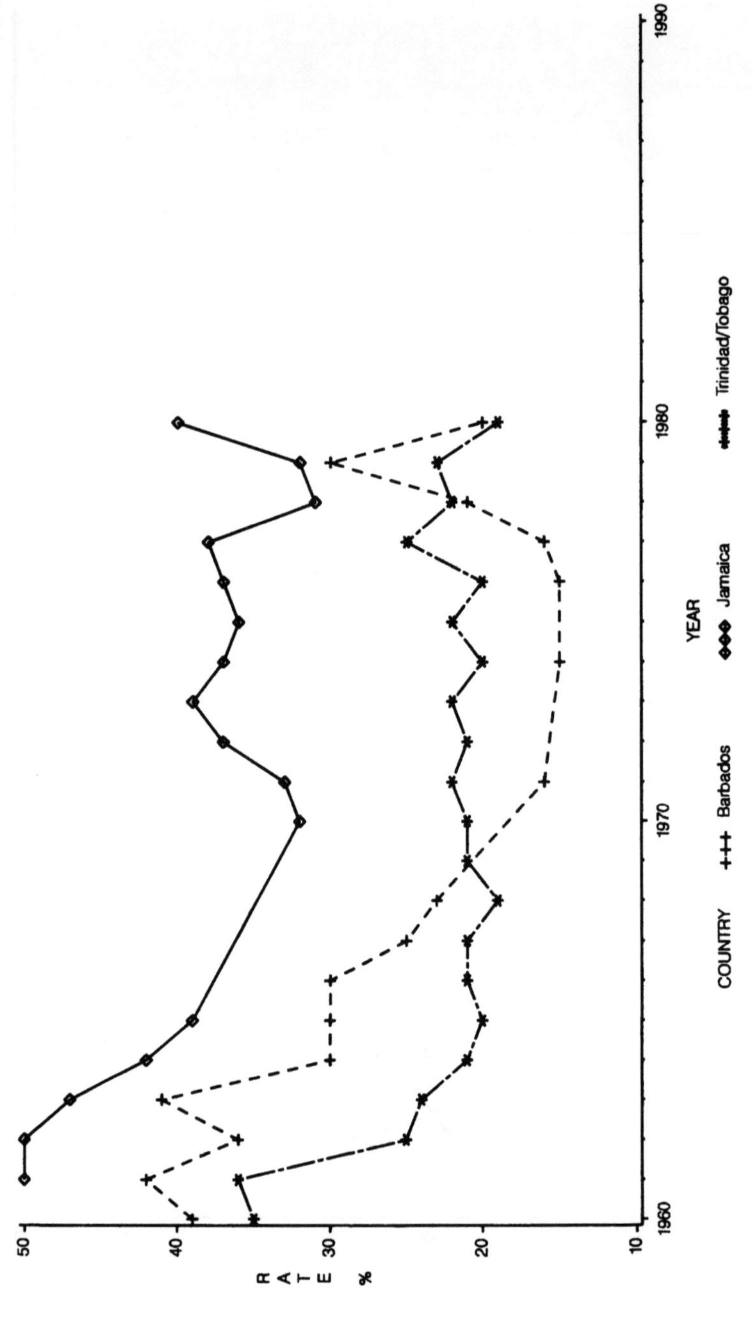

recorded the steepest decline in police activity during the decade of the 1960's but showed some improvement in the 1970's. Whereas Trinidad continued the downward trend with only a slight increase during the decade of the 1970's. It might be contended that Jamaica's superior police activity with respect to property crimes over the 1960-1980 period might have accounted for the low property crime rates in that territory relative to those of Barbados and Trinidad. The above hypothesis appears to be strengthened by the data.

Personal Crimes: The relationship between police activity and crime seems less valid with respect to crimes against the person. Fig. 4 shows that during the decade of the 1960's Jamaica's clear-up rate was more stable than the rates of corresponding activities for Trinidad and Barbados. Yet Jamaica's personal crime rates were considerably higher than those of the other two countries. On the other hand, Jamaica's critical period for crimes against the person (1972-1980) was also associated with critical decline in law enforcement activities. Jamaica's clear up rates declined by 18% between 1970 and 1980, while corresponding reductions for Barbados and Trinidad during the 1972-1980 period were recorded as only 3% and 11%, respectively.

The fact is, however, that even during the 1960's when police activity in Jamaica in the area of crimes against person was high – perhaps on average, higher than in Trinidad or Barbados – Jamaica's mean personal crime rate was approximately seven times that of Barbados and twice that of Trinidad. Despite the pattern of decade from 1970 to 1980 , it is obvious that a decline in police activity is not the important variable accounting for Jamaica's consistently high level of crimes against the person. It is conceivable that police activity may have an impact on the growth of some crimes. Alternatively, police activity may be associated with certain crimes through exogenous factors that determine trends in both phenomena. This is presumably the case with respect to crimes against the person.

Let us now look at the growth in crime against trends in sentencing.

3 Sentencing Practices and Crime

Conviction[3]: Examination of conviction rates provide some interesting insights. Barbados and Trinidad recorded roughly similar conviction rates for property crimes (an average of 50%; 53% respectively), with a slight

3 Represented as a percentages of crimes apprehended, cleared up, prosecuted each year.

Figure 6:
Comparative Trends in Police Activity and Crime: 1960 – 1980
Total Crimes

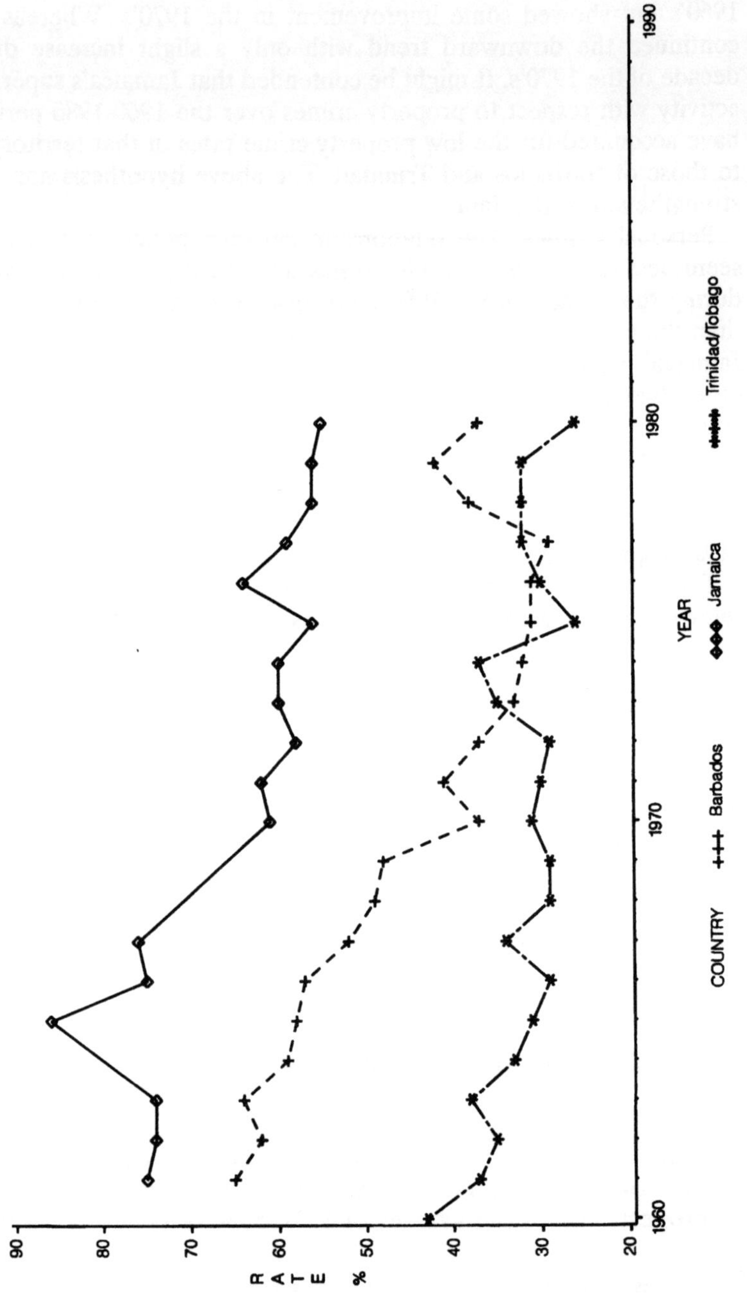

Figure 7:
Growth in Crime and Police Activity 1960 - 1984
Barbados, Total Crime Growth Rate and Apprehension Rate

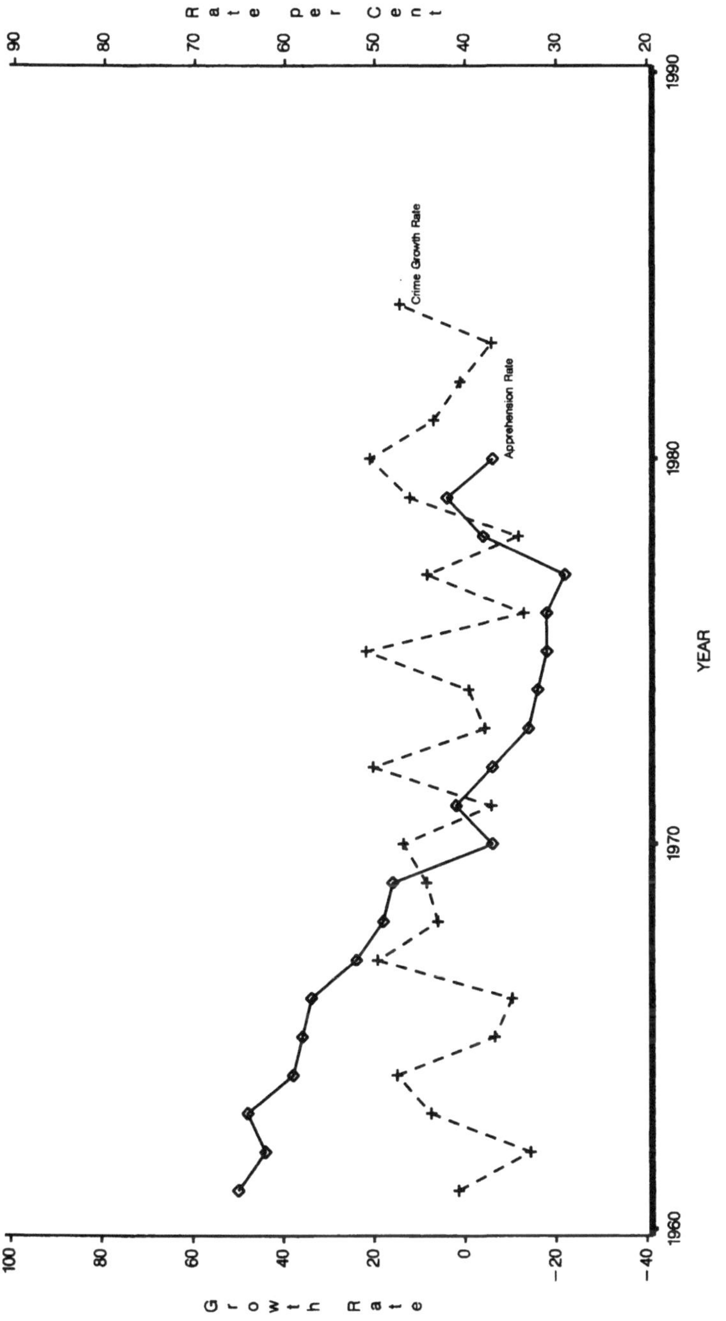

Figure 8:
Growth in Crime and Police Activity 1960 – 1984
Trinidad, Total Crime Growth Rate and Prosecution Rate

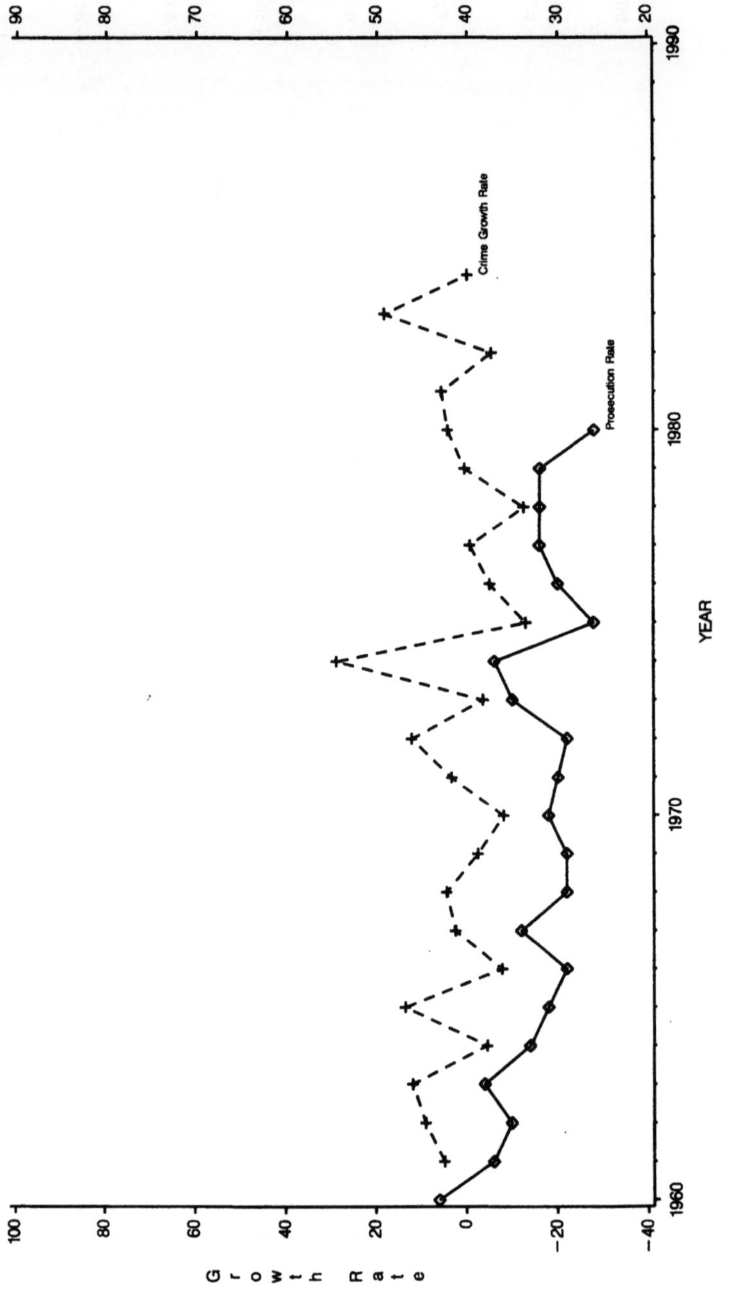

Figure 9:
Growth in Crime and Police Activity 1960 – 1984
Jamaica, Total Crime Growth Rate and Clear Up Rate

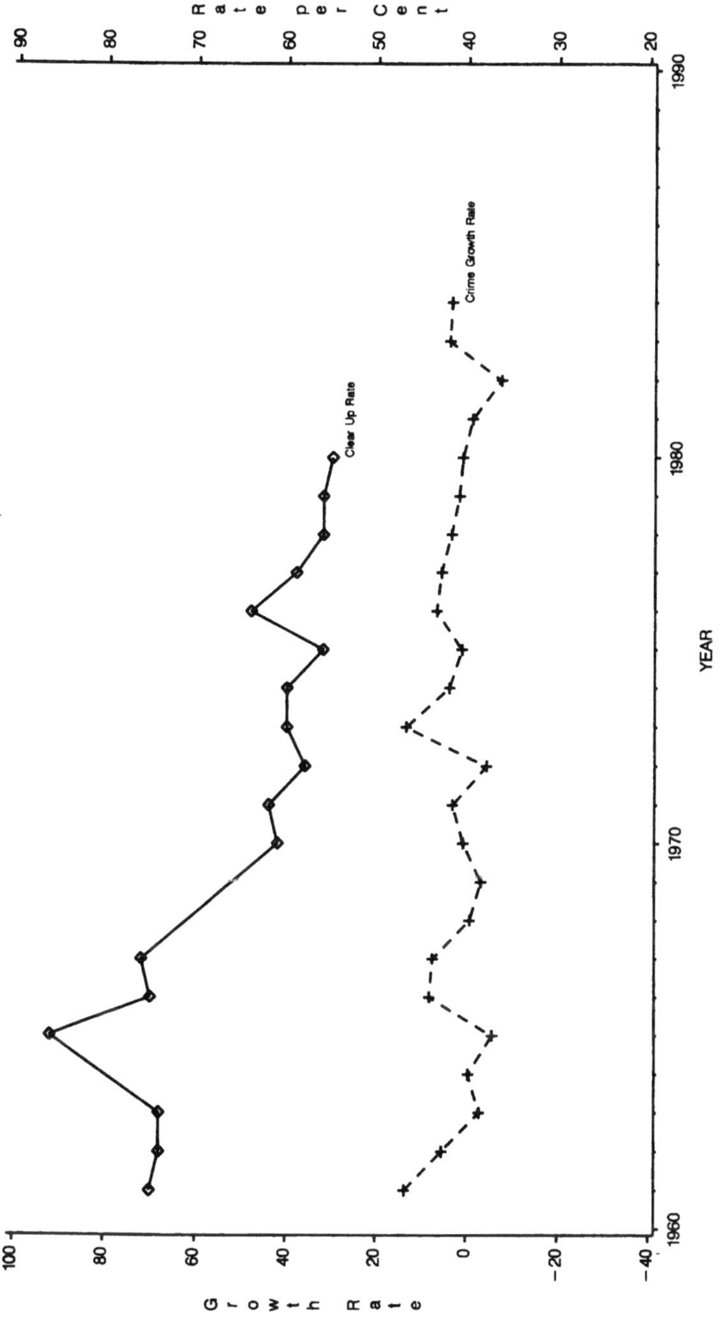

measured decrease over the period. Jamaica recorded high conviction rates during the early 1960's (82%) but these declined sharply by 1972. Thereafter, the increase was gradual. Despite an overall decline, Jamaica still showed in 1980, a substantially higher conviction rate than either Barbados or Trinidad. The rates recorded were 71%, 49% and 46% for Jamaica, Barbados, Trinidad, respectively.

The trends in conviction for crimes against the person describe a different situation. Jamaica maintained higher rates than Trinidad and Barbados up to 1979 but – recorded only 3% in 1980. Rates for Barbados and Trinidad were 18% and 34%, respectively. We note that superior conviction rates did not place Jamaica in a more favourable position regarding crimes against the person, than Trinidad or Barbados. With the lowest conviction rates, Barbados also recorded lowest rates of crimes against the person throughout the period (table 3).

Imprisonment[4]: Both Jamaica and Trinidad recorded substantial decreases in imprisonment rates over the period. Jamaica's highest rate which was recorded in 1970, declined by 70%. Trinidad's downward trend which commenced in 1967 was more gradual, showing a 50% decline by 1980. Barbados, somewhat surprisingly, recorded slight but relatively consistent rate increases in two waves (1969 – 1968: 1970 – 1980).

The contradiction suggested by the direction of Barbados' imprisonment rates diminishes the idea of a link between deinstitutionalization and crime. On the other hand, imprisonment rates were low in all three territories. Jamaica's rates peaked at just over 25%, Trinidad's at 19% and Barbado's fluctuated between 5% and 7%.

Death Sentence: The fact that all three territories have retained the death penalty permits further comparison of penal practices with respect to crimes against the person. From the data it appears that Barbados and Trinidad are more prone to deliver harsh punitive sentences than Jamaica. Barbados with less than 4% of the total number of murders recorded in Jamaica (1960-1984) issued the death sentence with greater frequency (14% and 12% of murders recorded, respectively). Trinidad, recording 25% of the number of murders occurring in Jamaica, issued the death sentence in 16% of murders recorded.

These trends indicate that there is in Jamaica, less severity of punishment for the most serious crime against the person than there is in Barbados or Trinidad. In the two and a half decades since 1960, there were a total of 5,850 murders. Over 5000 of these cases escaped the most severe penalty. It, therefore, follows that few offenders and potential offenders are likely to be anxious concerning the imposition of the ultimate

4 Represented as a percentages of crimes apprehended, cleared up, prosecuted each year.

Figure 10:
Comparative Trends in Penal Practices: 1960 – 1980
Imprisonment as Percentage of Crimes: Total Crimes

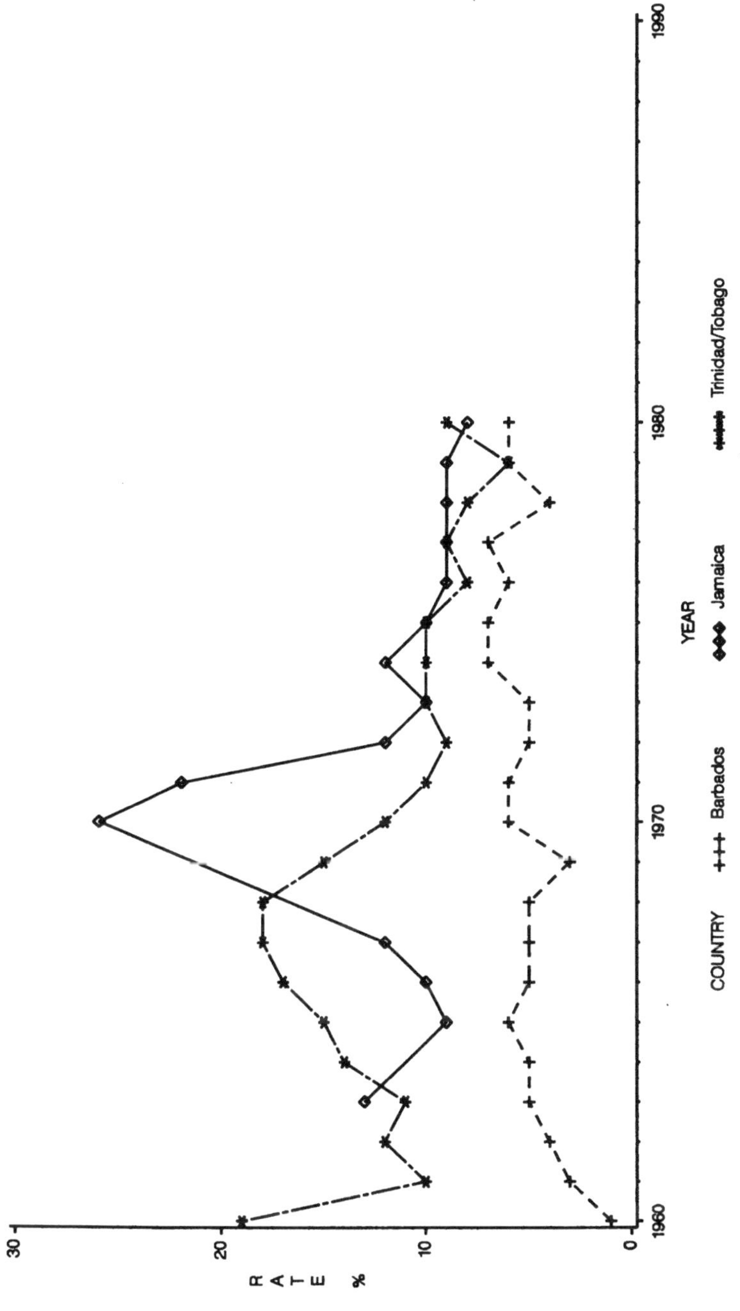

Figure 11:
Comparative Trends in Penal Practices: 1960 – 1980
Convictions as Percentage of Crimes: Crimes Against Property

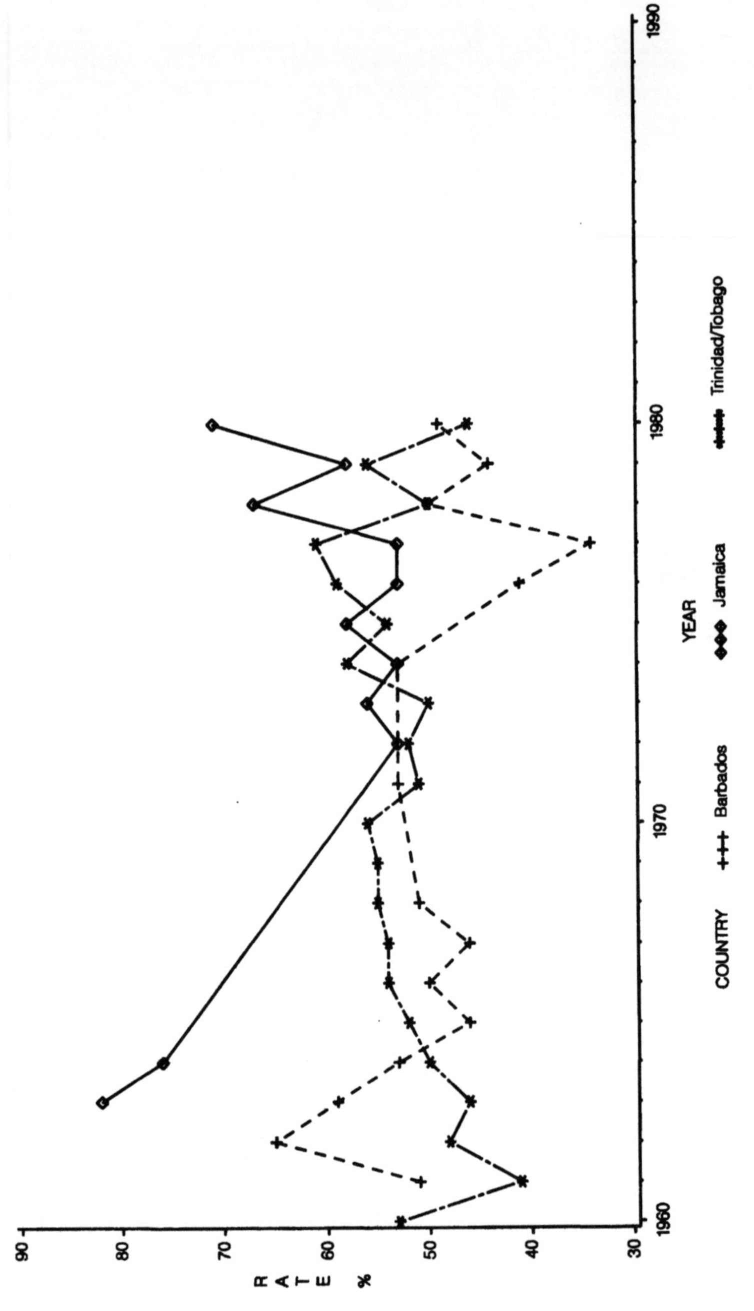

Figure 12:
Comparative Trends in Penal Practices: 1960 – 1980
Convictions as Percentage of Crimes: Crimes Against the Person

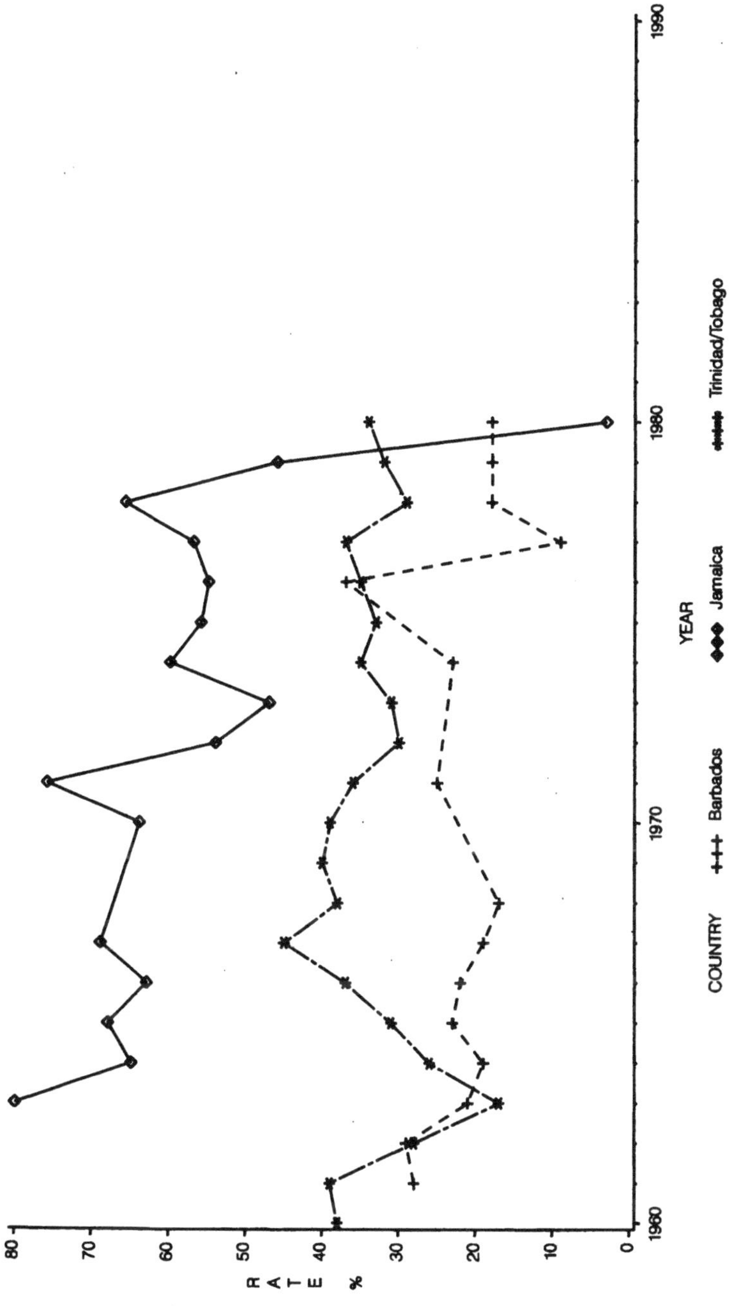

punishment for the crime of murder in Jamaica. It might be worth mentioning, too, that increasingly high rates of murder were recorded in Jamaica during the decade of the 1970's when the use of the death penalty was virtually abandoned. In 1980, the murder rate peaked at 42 per 100,000 of population. Accompanying the reactivation of the death penalty, there was a noticeable decline in the murder rate. The possibility of a link between mitigation of sanctions and crime – particularly crimes against the person – cannot be dismissed out of hand.

In comparing crime patterns in the English-speaking Caribbean territories one is not only able to point out differences and similarities but also to make certain general statements in relation to the decriminalization/deinstitutionalization hypotheses. This hypothesis suggests that increasing crime is the result of a low risk of arrest, a low risk of punishment and the mitigation of the severity of punishment. We find that trends in specific crime categories are associated with specific practices. It is not possible to make definitive statements about the relationship between decriminalization/deinstitutionalization and crime in general. A summary of findings from the analyses emphasizes the following points:

- Jamaica, Trinidad, Barbados all show a trend towards increasing crime, with Barbados outstripping Jamaica and Trinidad in rates of growth.
- Of the three territories, Jamaica has recorded the lowest rate of crimes against property. But its high rate of crimes against the person is hardly comparable with the other territories which still show relatively modest to low rates.
- Rates of growth in property crimes appear to be related to decriminalization represented by police activity in the area of apprehension, crimes cleared up, or prosecutions instituted.
- Rates of growth in crimes against the person appear to be more related to the mitigation or weakening of sanctions and the waiving of penalties. This observation, however, is based on trends in murder only.
- Increases in sanctions represented by increased institutionalization appear not to result in a decline in the growth of crime. Deinstitutionalization represented by declining imprisonment rates is found to be associated with increasing crime in Jamaica and Trinidad.

The comparative analysis of crime in the English-speaking Caribbean shows that decriminalization and deinstitutionalization offer better explanations of crimes within societies than between societies. This is observed particularly in the area of crimes against the person where Jamaica consistently recorded approximately twice the rate for Barbados and Trinidad, together, regardless of level or movements in the application of sanctions. Within the societies, however, increased criminal activities appear to be associated with a decline in the certainly and severity of punishment. This is consistent with findings in the criminological literature. But we must also be aware of the probability that crime and sanctions against crime have simultaneous effects. High crime rates may either be a response to or a cause of reduced effectiveness of the criminal justice system.

The comparison of Jamaica, Trinidad and Barbados crime raises question concerning the differential opportunities for crime commission. Are crimes against property more easily accommodated in Barbados and Trinidad than in Jamaica? Is murder or the use of the gun and other violent activities more venial in Jamaica than in Barbados and Trinidad? Our observations seem to affirm these observations.

More fundamental, however, are questions about those internal systems which promote the emergence of particular forms of crime and criminal justice. Looking more closely at Jamaica as a point of reference, we identify endemic characteristics that account for changes in both crime levels and institutional practices.

4 The Jamaican Problem

Throughout the Caribbean, Jamaica has gained notoriety as a high crime society. This reputation is not just a feature of the 1970's when fear of violence was rampant; it developed over time. In 1958, the rate of murder/manslaughter was 4 per 100,000; in 1968, it was 6 per 100,000; in 1978, it was 16 per 100,000; in 1980, it was 43 per 100,000. The fact that during this critical year (1980) the lowest apprehension and conviction rates were secured (54% and 3% respectively) calls attention to the relationship between crime and punishment – in particular, the increase in violent crimes and the mitigation of sanctions and waiving of punishments.

A proposition advanced by Haferkamp (1985) maintains that mitigation of sanctions and waiving of punishments occur where the political authority is losing or has lost power. It is also the result of the influence of modernity and social change. This reference is of course, to advanced societies such as West Germany, England and Wales, France and the United States of America. In Jamaica, we observe a loss of authority that is more associated with the continued dependency of an independent nation, than with modernity.

Independence in Jamaica, like elsewhere in emergent societies, was a landmark in the long struggle for the full rights of citizenship, for social

Table 1: Total Crimes per 100,000 of Population 1960 - 1984

Year	Barbados	Trinidad and Tobago	Jamaica
1960	949	1254	1347
1961	963	1316	1531
1962	824	1437	1613
1963	886	1610	1568
1964	1017	1537	1562
1965	951	1748	1474
1966	853	1612	1595
1967	1018	1152	1715
1968	1079	1726	1705
1969	1171	1685	1652
1970	1332	1549	1665
1971	1255	1601	1718
1972	1510	1799	1645
1973	1445	1136	1867
1974	1433	2239	1939
1975	1747	1949	1962
1976	1520	1852	2096
1977	1647	1841	2216
1978	1454	1611	2293
1979	1633	1620	2335
1980	1978	1692	2311
1981	2115	1790	2289
1982	2139	1695	2122
1983	2015	2008	2207
1984	2308	2008	2285

Sources:Barbados: Annual Review of Statistics, Annual Report of the Commission of Police, Barbados, Barbados Government Printing office.
Trinidad & Tobago: Annual Statistical Digest; Republic of Trinidad and Tobago, Central Statistical office, Trinidad
Jamaica: Annual Abstracts of Statistics, Department of Statistics, Jamaica.
Also: Demographic Year Book, United Nations.

justice, for a redistribution or sharing of political and economic power, for the questioning of norms and ideals, and for the restructing of values. But the promise was greater than the achievement -at least for certain sectors of the society. Since 1962, successive locally elected governments have tried, with very limited success to address the needs of the poorer sector of the society. In the face of persistent poverty and social backwardness, individuals as well as groups have chosen illegitimate routes to fulfillment.

Table 2: Total Crimes Against Property per 100,000 of Population 1960-1980

Year	Barbados	Trinidad and Tobago	Jamaica [a]
1960	896	1067	–
1961	908	1132	911
1962	773	1191	859
1963	823	1314	902
1964	930	1247	779
1965	853	1329	553
1966	775	1324	564 [b]
1967	936	1356	519 [b]
1968	983	1446	343 [b]
1969	1039	1435	244 [b]
1970	1265	1319	322
1971	1332	1358	276
1972	1324	1513	579
1973	1266	1534	694
1974	1299	1825	762
1975	1601	1706	921
1976	1376	1571	772
1977	1553	1535	683
1978	1361	1354	898
1979	1121	1363	894
1980	1828	1435	914

Sources: See notes, Table 1
(a) Property Crimes include Breaking and Entering, Robbery, Fraud, Embezzlement Arson, in accordance with the classification in Barbados, Trinidad & Tobago.
(b) Data suspect: error detected in records. Rates calculated from alternate source - Economic and Social Survey, Jamaica.

Governments have tried through strategies dictated by differing ideological positions to respond to different demands from different sectors of the population. Their failure to satisfy is due to dependence on advanced countries not only for material resources in the form of raw materials but also for aid for physical development that is predicated on foreign approval of their national development strategy. An example of the latter is seen in the circumstances surrounding the fall of the 1970s regime which flaunted a socialist rhetoric to justify social reforms.

A low level of economic power, declining economic power or even a loss of economic power is usually associated with declining political power. The socio-political scene in Independent Jamaica, over the 1960-1980 period, reflected a decline of political authority which was

Table 3: Total Crimes Against the Person per 100,000 of Population 1960-1980

Year	Barbados	Trinidad and Tobago	Jamaica[a]
1960	43	174	407
1961	47	167	429
1962	45	193	448
1963	53	216	464
1964	79	215	429
1965	84	232	477
1966	75	211	528
1967	72	200	529
1968	81	205	514
1969	113	174	–
1970	107	172	–
1971	117	190	566
1972	105	219	581
1973	105	218	783
1974	111	206	629
1975	122	192	616
1976	119	204	735
1977	125	227	743
1978	126	214	768
1979	114	224	761
1980	139	203	1091

Sources: See Note Table 1
(a) Not including Robbery, see Note 1, Table 2

particularly marked during the 1972-80 period. At this time, greatly reduced economic resources and activity rendered the government incapable of meeting the rising expectations of the masses. The outcome was a system of patronage which featured the trading of socio-economic benefits for party political support, victimization for non-support, discontent, jealousy and resultant hostility.

The effects of this were seen in high and constantly increasing levels of violent crimes as members of the most oppressed sector vied with each other for political attention and limited "hand-outs". This occurred particularly during pre-election and election years. The circulation of hand guns also employed the weapons for private vendettas and material gain. Experiencing or anticipating political intervention and reprisals from criminals, the police (informally) complained that their "hands were tied" with respect to bringing known criminals to justice. Feelings of powerless-

Table 4: Murder/Manslaughter per 100,000 of Population 1960-1980

Year	Barbados	Trinidad and Tobago	Jamaica
1960	4.7	8.1	7.3
1961	4.3	8.2	6.4
1962	4.7	7.6	6.1
1963	4.6	10.1	6.8
1964	2.9	8.6	6.5
1965	6.1	8.6	6.6
1966	4.0	8.0	9.4
1967	7.2	8.8	8.6
1968	4.3	7.1	9.9
1969	–	8.2	11.2
1970	–	7.5	11.2
1971	12.3	7.1	11.2
1972	–	8.0	14.2
1973	–	8.7	18.6
1974	6.8	7.6	13.6
1975	–	7.7	16.9
1976	10.1	8.0	20.3
1977	5.2	7.9	21.7
1978	5.2	7.1	18.8
1979	6.4	7.8	17.9
1980	6.4	5.8	45.3
1981	–	7.8	24.4
1982	7.6	8.1	20.0
1983	5.6	7.8	20.8
1984	5.9	7.1	22.8

ness were apparently reflected in the declining clear-up rates, and possibly in the conviction rates which were reduced to 3% of apprehension ("clear-up") rates in 1980, the year of highest reported murder/manslaughter rates, to date.

Accompanying steep increases in crime were sporadic attempts at control through stepped-up crime-fighting resources and more severe penalties. This situation which Haferkamp (1985) found in Federal Republic of Germany in the 1970's was regarded by the author as paradoxical. He later dismissed these as a brief diversion in the trend towards the mitigation and abandonment of sanctions. Haferkamp argued that at best, stronger penalties were merely half-hearted attempts to regain power which "cannot be sustained permanently" in the presence of

Table 5: Police Activity[a] 1960 - 1980

Year	Total Crimes Barbados	Total Crimes Trinidad	Total Crimes Jamaica	Crimes Against Property Barbados	Crimes Against Property Trinidad	Crimes Against Property Jamaica	Crimes Against Person Barbados	Crimes Against Person Trinidad	Crimes Against Person Jamaica
	%	%	%	%	%	%	%	%	%
1960	–	43	–	39	35	–	91	94	–
1961	65	37	75	42	36	50	79	75	80
1962	62	35	74	36	25	50	72	76	82
1963	64	38	74	41	24	47	72	86	79
1964	59	33	–	30	21	42	55	75	80
1965	58	31	86	30	20	39	75	76	80
1966	57	29	75	30	21	–	71	83	80
1967	52	34	76	25	21	–	87	69	78
1968	49	29	–	23	19	–	72	67	–
1969	48	29	–	–	21	–	–	76	–
1970	37	31	61	–	21	32	–	73	76
1971	41	30	62	16	22	33	62	76	79
1972	37	29	58	–	21	37	–	74	75
1973	33	35	60	–	22	39	–	73	64
1974	32	37	60	15	20	37	47	71	73
1975	31	26	56	–	22	36	–	71	74
1976	31	30	64	15	20	37	67	77	69
1977	29	32	59	16	25	38	63	69	67
1978	38	32	56	21	22	31	58	70	70
1979	42	32	56	30	23	32	65	71	70
1980	37	26	55	20	19	40	59	65	54

(a) Police Activity is calculated as a percentage of Apprehended, Prosecuted and Cleared-up cases in each of the categories.

Table 6: Imprisonment[a] as percentage of Cases Apprehended, Prosecutions Instituted or Cases Cleared up 1960 - 1980

Year	Barbados	Trinidad and Tobago	Jamaica
1960	–	19	–
1961	3	10	–
1962	4	12	–
1963	5	11	13
1964	5	14	–
1965	6	15	9
1966	5	17	10
1967	5	18	12
1968	5	18	–
1969	3	15	–
1970	6	12	26
1971	6	10	22
1972	5	9	12
1973	5	10	10
1974	7	10	12
1975	7	10	10
1976	6	8	9
1977	7	9	9
1978	4	8	9
1979	6	6	9
1980	6	9	8

(a) Refers to persons committed to penal imprisonment by all courts; does not include those awaiting trial in safe custody or awaiting deportation.

changing social norms values and expectations (Haferkamp 1985). This illuminates the Jamaican problem.

Between 1962 and 1980, many new crime fighting measures were introduced to tighten control and reduce criminal violence. These included: increases in the strength of the police force (number recruited); the introduction of harsh sanctions for gun-related crimes or association with gun offenders; the institution of the Suppression of Crime (Special Provisions) Act 1974 which allowed the police extended powers of arrest and intimidation in specially designated "criminal" areas; and the invocation of State of Emergency powers. But these measures were met with such criticisms as subversion of the court's jurisdiction, infringement of the rights of the individual, and breach of the Constitution. These were followed by reforms (in the case of the Gun Court Legislation and

Table 7: Convictions as percentage of Police Activity : 1960 - 1980

	Crimes Against Property			Crimes Against Person		
Year	**Barbados %**	**Trinidad %**	**Jamaica %**	**Barbados %**	**Trinidad %**	**Jamaica %**
1960	–	53	–	–	38	–
1961	51	41	–	28	39	–
1962	65	48	–	29	28	–
1963	59	46	82	21	17	80
1964	53	50	76	19	26	65
1965	46	52	–	23	31	68
1966	50	54	–	22	37	63
1967	46	54	–	19	45	69
1968	51	55	–	17	38	–
1969	–	55	–	–	40	–
1970	–	56	–	–	39	64
1971	53	51	–	25	36	76
1972	–	52	53	–	30	54
1973	–	50	56	–	31	47
1974	53	58	53	23	35	60
1975	–	54	58	–	33	56
1976	41	59	53	37	35	55
1977	34	61	53	9	37	57
1978	50	50	67	18	29	66
1979	44	56	58	18	32	46
1980	49	46	71	18	34	3

Sources: See notes, Table 1

Sentencing Practices) that favoured young offenders as well as limited or withdrew specially conferred crime-fighting powers that had been conferred on law enforcement officers before the middle of the 1980's. The trend towards mitigation continued. Evidence of this is the recognition of probation and parole, pre-release and diversionary sentences – institutional practices considered progressive by the Developed Western World.

An analyst may contend that in Jamaica, mitigation of sanctions is more apparent than real. The adoption of seemingly progressive, deinstitutionalization measures such as probation, parole, and community corrections including community service orders can be no more than a symbolic gesture in a society that favours strong coercive sanctions. The promulgation of Acts supporting 'progressive' mitigated sanctions in the absence of

Table 8: Death Sentence Imposed 1960-1984

Year	Barbados	Trinidad and Tobago	Jamaica
1960	–[a]	11	–
1961	3	6	–
1962	–	9	–
1963	–	16	18
1964	–	8	14
1965	3	11	13
1966	1	8	19
1967	3	24	11
1968	1	18	–
1969	1	16	–
1970	–	8	58
1971	2	6	32
1972	–	7	49
1973	5	10	28
1974	4	8	20
1975	–	14	11
1976	2	7	25
1977	1	5	–
1978	–	8	93
1979	4	4	52
1980	1	11	40
1981	-	7	31
1982	3	3	35
1983	-	1	51
1984	3	3	22

Notes:
(a) – No Data Available
Figures above represent number of persons receiving death sentences over the period.

physical and financial resources to ensure their efficacy is suggestive of "symbolic manipulation". According to Stone (1981), Jamaican politicians employ various symbolic representations as strategy to divert attention from failing or failed economic management and attendant loss of political power.

These observations may prove to be correct, however we cannot discount the intentions nor the unintended consequences of more liberal legislation. A tendency towards deinstitutionalization and mitigation of sanctions – however symbolic – has powerful psychological effects on both offender and law enforcer. They may elicit negative attitudes to law enforcement both among the police who are likely to relax efforts at surveillance and among the offenders who may grow bold. This boldness might easily translate into a contempt for perceived institutional weakness – resulting in more crime.

A juxtaposition of strong coercive measures and the weak application of crime control sanctions is not necessarily paradoxical. The former describes a societal reaction to crime whereas the latter, a societal action regarding crime. Both coercive political measures and weakening institutional practices contribute to crime levels in a society. They must be seen as independent variables operating independently to effect increases in crime. Strong coercive measures ensuing from a loss or weakening of political authority have the latent effect of creating crimes, especially crimes of violence. This occurs when those at risk respond in what they believe to be appropriate way of expression, defying authority. Thus we see, for example, an increase in violence against the police and private citizens regarded as potential "informers". Weakening institutional practices including the mitigation of sanctions have the immediate effect of condoning crimes through the creation of high thresholds for criminal activity. Each variable enhances the other in the production of increasing crime rates.

References

Clinard, M.B. and Abbott, D.J. (1983) Crime in Developing Countries: A Comparative Perspective, New York:Wiley.

Council of Europe (1985) Economic crisis and crime, T. Godefroy, H. Haferkamp, H.-G. Heiland, R. Hauge and C.G. Lewis eds., Strasbourg.

de Albuquerque, Klaus (1984) "A Comparative Analysis of Violent Crime in the Caribbean", In: Social and Economic Studies, vol. 33.

Haferkamp, Hans (1985) "Welfare State, Crime and Control", Unpublished paper, University of Bremen.

Mahabir, Cynthia (1980) "Crime and Nation-Building: The Emergency Powers Acts, 1970 Trinidad and Tobago", in: International Journal of the Sociology of Laws, vol. 8, pp. 129-148.

Pryce, Carl (1976) "Towards a Caribbean Criminology", in: Caribbean Issues, A Journal of Caribbean Affairs. Special Issue on Crime, vol. 2, pp. 3-19.

Stone, Carl and Brown Aggrey (eds.) (1981) Perspectives on Jamaica in the Seventies, Kingston, Jamaica.

Stone, Carl (1983) Democracy and Clientism in Jamaica, Institute of Social and Economic Research, University of the West Indies, Jamaica.

Stone, Carl (1986) Class, State and Democracy in Jamaica, Preger.

Sumner, Colin (1982) Crime, Justice and Underdevelopment, London: Heinemann

Crime and Control in Nigeria

Olufunmilayo Oloruntimehin

1 Introduction

Nigeria represents the largest single political entity in the West African Coast with 890,000 square kilometers of territory. Nigeria derived its name from the Niger River. It shares borders with the Republic of Benin, the Cameroon and Niger. Nigeria is the most populous state in Africa with about 113 million inhabitants.[1]

Nigeria has three major ethnic groups, Hausa-Fulani, Ibo and Yoruba and about two hundred other linguistic groups. Military conquests and cultural assimilations have contributed to the fusion of many groups into three large, culturally homogeneous groups and a few prominent 'minority' ones.

Nigeria, as a territorial entity, emerged in 1914 with the amalgamation of the then colony of Lagos and the Protectorate of Southern and Northern Nigeria. From then until 1960, Nigeria went through various stages of colonial rule when the British government granted the country its political independence. In 1963, Nigeria became a Republic within the Commonwealth. This experience was soon followed by a series of political crises which resulted in the loss of control by the existing civilian government and led in January 16, 1966 to a military take over. This was followed by a period of political confusion which culminated in a civil war which lasted until 1970. Since then the country has experienced a series of coup d'etats and attempted military insurrections sandwitched between periods of civilian rule. The present military government came into being in August, 1985 and the machinery has been set in motion for a possible transfer of power to a civilian government in 1992.

Nigeria has been divided into states at various stages – first into twelve states, then nineteen states and finally into twenty one states.[2] There was also the establishment of the federal capital city, Abuja. The creation of the various states was accompanied by rapid changes in the physical and

---

1 World Demografic Estimates and Projektions, 1990

2 Lagos, Bendel, Anambra, Imo, Benue, Bauchi, Plateau, Borno, Sokoto, Rivers, Kaduna, Kanọ, Kwara, Niger, Ogun, Ondo, Oyo, Gongola, Katsina, Cross River and Akwa Ibom

socio-economic spheres, especially in the capitals of these states. Of all the states Lagos state and, particularly its capital, Lagos has witnessed the most phenomenal of these changes. It continues to be the nerve centre of most of the political, as well as socio-economic activities of the country. This is due to the existence in metropolitan Lagos of the country's major airport and seaport, industries, multi-national corporations, foreign embassies, educational and cultural institutions and much of the Federal government including most of its ministries.

This situation has resulted in the Lagos city's disproportionate share of the country's output, income and employment. For example, metropolitan Lagos with less than 0.2 percent of the country's land area contributed 1,327.0 million naira or 20.4 percent out of the estimated total value for the country in 1975. Lagos city also employs 40 percent of Nigeria's skilled manpower while its ports handle 80 percent of the nation's total imports (Adeyemi et al. 1989).

The economy has undergone very serious changes in recent years. The changes were due to the huge debt burden created by mismanagement which has adversely affected the national economic order. This condition has led to drastic currency devaluation, decline in foreign reserves, increase in external debts, escalation of inflation and unemployment rates, reduction in Gross Domestic Product, massive rural to urban migration, significant dependency problems and growth in domestic poverty. According to the Nigerian National Paper (1990) presented at the "Eighth United Nations Congress on the prevention of crime and the treatment of offenders" the GDP/capita for the ten year period 1979-1988 was as follows: 1979: N 503.40($806.85); 1980: N 545.47($847.77); 1981: N 634.61($1,046.03); 1982: N 655.67($1,097.13); 1983: N 663.42($1,116.93); 1984: N 709.70($542.71); 1985 N 773.63 ($723.19); 1986 N 758.11($542.40); 1987: N 985.45($245.46) and 1988: N 349.19($278.95). A steady decrease can be observed since 1984, except for 1985, which has been followed by drastic decrease in 1987 and 1988.

The inflation rate for the same period is as follows: 1979: 11.8; 1980: 9.9; 1981: 20.8; 1982: 6.4; 1983: 23.2; 1984: 40.0; 1985: 5.4; 1986: 5.5; 1987: 10.2 and 1988: 38.8. The fluctuations in the inflation rate between 5.4 and 40 percent reveal clearly the economic instability.

The unemployment rate for the same period was as follows: 1979: 4.42; 1980: 4.40; 1981: 4.57; 1982: 4.74; 1983: 4.90; 1984: 6.30; 1985: 6.93; 1986: 7.25; 1987: 7.85; 1988: 4.75. There was a steady increase in the unemployment rate from 1979 to 1983 except for 1980, and from 1984 there was a very significant increase until 1988 when there occurred a phenomenal decrease. The unemployment rate can also be said to reveal the degree of economic instability in the country. Because of the economic situation just described, it has become very difficult for the average citizen to achieve a tolerable quality of life. Under this condition some able bodied men and women have resorted to begging, while the temptation to engage in criminal activities exists for many in these harsh economic conditions.

2 Crime Trends in Nigeria

Official crime statistics are a popular method of measuring crime. It measures crime known to the police and differs from measures of arrests made, prosecutions and convictions. The numbers decline as one moves farther from the original crime. The social processing of crime thus reduces the amount of crime being assessed.

Crimes known to the police, reflect social processing, because the majority of crimes they handle are the result of reports made to them rather than the result of crimes they disclose. Complaints to the police are subject to errors resulting from mistakes and even lies. Efforts are made by the modern criminal justice system to establish the actual amount of crime after discounting mistakes, frivolous complaints and maliciously reported injuries. Discretion is, however, involved in the compilation of all crime statistics. The amount of crime known to the police varies significantly and the figure of latent criminality ("hidden delinquency" or the "dark figure of crime") (Hood and Sparks 1970) is unknown. The "dark figure of crime" varies from one society to the other depending on the level of reporting of criminal cases to the law enforcement agents, the efficiency of these agencies, and the facilities available for the performance of their role. It is known that the level of the "dark figure of crime" varies with the kind of crime. For example, for serious offences like murder, armed robbery, the proportion of unsolved crimes is much smaller than in case of property offences.

The official crime statistics in Nigeria suffer from the inadequacies of social processing of crime. Due to the low level of citizen cooperation with the police, members of the public are reluctant to report criminal offences (even when they are victims) to the police. Thus a considerable number of minor offences and some serious ones such as murder and manslaughter are settled between the offenders and the victims without the knowledge of the police. In such cases the offenders make necessary restitution and provide compensation to the victims. This is in conformity with the traditional process of dispute settlement whereby "blood money" is paid as compensation in murder cases to the relatives of the victim (Elias 1973).

In addition, a considerable number of people have a significant degree of aversion to the modern criminal justice system because of its adversarial nature, its time consuming processes and its lack of consideration for the victim who is not provided restitution (Oloruntimehin 1977; 1978). Against this background the official crime statistics in Nigeria, like in many other countries, should be examined with caution. Whenever generalisations are made from such statistics, individuals should be fully aware of their shortcomings. However, the official crime statistics still remain and will continue to be the major means of explaining crime in this society, particularly since alternatives such as the victim survey and self-report-method have not yet been seriously considered.

Table 1 shows a steady increase in the volume of crime from 1960 to 1966 except for 1964. The crime rate varied for this period although the variation cannot be regarded as very significant. Between 1967 and 1969 there was a drastic fall in the volume and rate of crime. This is to be expected since this period covered the most serious years of the 1966-1970 civil war in Nigeria. During this period the attention of all the citizens of this country was on the war. The war thus created a diversion from the possibilities of engaging in criminal behaviour. More important, many able bodied young men who would have been tempted to engage in criminal activities as a result of unemployment and the desire for adventure, were drafted into the army. During this period there was also a break in communication among parts of the country, particularly the Eastern part. The Nigeria Police Force were, therefore, unable to keep track of the criminal activities particularly in the Eastern part. Such criminal activities were, therefore, lost to the police crime records (which is a central record for all crimes committed in the country) during this particular period.

From 1970 to 1982, with the exception of 1979 and 1980, the volume of crime and the rate increased steadily. The lower volume and rate of crime for the period 1979 and 1980 can be attributed to the renewed popular confidence in the state which was a result of the return of civilian government after approximately thirteen years of military rule marked by a series of coup d'etats and attempted military insurrections. The relatively peaceful situation as well as the compassion and the interest in solving problems shown by the civilian government might have inhibited the criminal behaviour of a considerable number of people.

The general increase in the level of criminality, especially from 1970 to 1982, can be attributed to the rapid rate of economic development in the country precipitated by the oil boom that began around 1970. Oil became the main source of revenue and agriculture, once the major revenue source, was virtually abandoned. As a result of the boom the various governments of the country engaged in gigantic capital projects such as building of bridges, airports, roads, hospitals, and educational institutions. Under these conditions, a class of nouveau riche enriched themselves through a system of contract awards involving price padding and the

Table 1: Official Crime Statistics 1960 - 1988

Year	Figure (all offences against person and property and Miscellaneous offences)	Rate per 100,000 of the Population
1960	106,165	220.24
1961	110,019	217.85
1962	118,475	224.39
1963	128,981	233.64
1964	123,243	217.70
1965	130,000	223.92
1966	151,850	255.05
1967	55,957	91.65
1968	57,984	92.60
1969	70,249	109.40
1970	112,943	171.52
1971	139,526	206.62
1972	146,331	211.30
1973	156,696	220.64
1974	182,832	251.03
1975	193,633	259.83
1976	214,286	280.44
1977	219,112	280.70
1978	220,475	273.56
1979	203,733	244.82
1980	210,908	245.48
1981	253,952	286.25
1982	271,240	296.11
1983	311,961	329.84
1984	372,558	381.50
1985	352,268	338.02
1986	330,957	279.29
1987	279,050	250.45
1988	325,861	282.84

Source: Nigeria Police Force Headquarters, Lagos, 1990.

payment of 'kick-backs' to politicians and government officials. This period also marked the development of a taste for foreign goods and services by a considerable number of people. This led to the smuggling of goods and currencies which later had serious adverse effects on the nation's economy and contributed to the present economic predicament whereby the country is highly indebted to other countries.

During the period 1970-1982, the years of the economic boom, drug trafficking and certain property offences, such as embezzlement, fraud, armed robbery, burglary, theft and smuggling of goods and currencies, were particularly pronounced (Oloruntimehin 1985; 1989).

During these years armed robbery became very visible in Nigeria, a situation which might have arisen as a result of the economic boom that resulted in much competition to own land, cars, houses, luxery goods like television, radiogrammes, video sets, and expensive clothing. With the end of the civil war in 1970, many of the able bodied young men drafted into the army in 1967, were discharged without proper provisions for economic survival. Many of them had access to guns and ammunition; they employed them to make a living for themselves by robbing individuals and corporations through the use of fire-arms (Nkpa 1976 and Rotimi 1984). This period also marked the emergence of syndicates and underworld criminal groups in this country.

The period 1983-1988, with the exception of 1987, has shown a tremendous increase in the volume and rate of criminality. This period has been remarkable for the downward economic trend, indicated most clearly by the inflation and high unemployment rates. During this period the huge debt burden led to a great devaluation of the currency. Some manufacturing industries which depend on foreign raw materials collapsed, which in turn led to the collapse of a considerable number of medium and small scale industries which depended on these larger industries. The situation also contributed to a low level of allocation of financial resources to institutions such as universities, schools, hospitals and other government establishments, resulting in significant retrenchment. Just as in the boom period, property offences were most affected by the adverse economic conditions that resulted in increased unemployment and underemployment. This is reflected in table 2.

Property offences include the following: Theft and other stealing, robbery and extortion, burglary, house breaking, store breaking, false pretences and cheating, forgery, receiving stolen property and unlawful possession. Offences against person include the following: murder, manslaughter, attempted murder, suicide, grievous harm and wounding, assault, child stealing, slave dealing, rape and indecent assault and unnatural offences (e.g. homosexuality). Other offences cover the following: forgery of central Bank notes, coining offences, gambling, offences against public order, perjury, bribery and corruption, and escape and rescue. The rise in property offences is consistent with America and Britain (Clifford 1974; Clinard and Abbott 1978).

Urban areas more than semiurban or rural areas are highly populated contain most of the industries, and the largest proportion of the country's labour force. The opportunities for criminal involvement, particularly property offences, abound in urban areas. The table which follows reveals the distribution of property crimes in the states between 1976 and 1983.

Table 2: Official Crime Statistics Reflecting the Status of Property Offences 1975 - 1988

Year	Total No. of Offences Against Person	Total No. of Offences Against Property	Total No. of Other Offences	Total No. of all Offences
1975	49,188	99,181	45,264	193,633
1976	51,670	105,748	56,868	214,286
1977	63,864	93,996	61,252	219,112
1978	59,183	99,486	61,806	220,475
1979	56,493	93,346	53,894	203,733
1980	65,856	90,791	54,261	210,908
1981	75,586	91,533	83,833	253,952
1982	76,203	93,224	101,813	271,240
1983	65,458	98,178	148,325	311,961
1984	72,022	144,810	155,726	372,558
1985	67,090	141,668	144,189	352,957
1986	88,104	146,616	96,237	330,957
1987	57,719	158,709	62,622	279,050
1988	83,687	163,720	78,454	325,861

Source: Nigeria Police Force Headquarters, Lagos, 1990.

Table 3 reveals that between 1976 and 1983, the highest volume of property offences were recorded in the most populous state of Lagos. This is followed by the fairly urbanized states like Anambra, Bendel, Kaduna, Oyo, Cross River, Rivers and Imo. These states are followed by the urbanized ones like Kano, Plateau and Ogun and then by the less urbanized ones such as Kwara, Borno, Gongola, Sokoto, Benue, Ondo and Bauchi. For example, according to a United Nations Social Defence Research Institute Publication (1984) in 1976 only 21.8 percent of the population in Lagos were Lagos born. This means that almost 80 percent of the population migrated into the city. Also between 1960 and 1965, 64.7 percent of the migrants in Lagos were in the 10 to 19 age group. Major

Table 3: Comparative Table of Property Crimes of all the States from 1976 to 1983

State	1976	1977	1978	1979	1980	1981	1982	1983	Remarks
Anambra	8,906	8,568	9,378	7,687	6,539	7,226	8,502	8,333	Fairly Urbanised
Bauchi	1,715	1,375	1,240	1,657	1,871	2,285	2,270	2,542	Less Urbanised
Lagos	24,686	17,380	23,143	18,322	21,120	18,858	20,731	25,797	Highly Urbanised
Bendel	8,181	9,663	5,001	5,880	9,645	2,576	4,330	6,045	Fairly Urbanised
Kwara	3,615	2,462	2,412	2,204	2,613	2,080	2,800	2,986	Less Urbanised
Benue	2,574	4,110	4,561	3,785	4,811	3,522	4,762	5,608	Less Urbanised
Borno	3,581	3,919	2,715	2,767	-	-	2,529	3,000	Less Urbanised
Imo	6,467	6,278	7,914	6,637	6,654	7,076	6,655	8,724	Fairly Urbanised
Gongola	2,566	3,254	3,166	2,042	4,201	3,176	3,176	4,828	Less Urbanised
Kaduna	8,310	7,993	8,429	9,098	8,848	6,890	7,216	6,966	Fairly Urbanised
C/River	7,553	7,202	5,452	6,706	7,271	7,375	7,198	9,214	Fairly Urbanised
Kano	4,616	2,598	14,740	8,872	9,033	6,160	7,441	7,492	Urbanised
Niger	742	147	1,242	400	1,801	1,907	1,754	1,755	Less Urbanised

Table 3 (continued): Comparative Table of Property Crimes of all the States from 1976 to 1983

Ogun	2,959	2,925	3,072	3,114	2,913	3,912	4,087	4,628	Urbanised
Ondo	2,704	2,666	6,647	2,586	376	390	3,196	5,533	Less Urbanised
Oyo	7,950	8,626	7,535	8,844	8,125	8,001	9,761	11,291	Fairly Urbanised
State	1976	1977	1978	1979	1980	1981	1982	1983	Remarks
Plateau	3,772	4,758	6,647	4,343	5,007	459	4,840	6,204	Urbanised
Rivers	6,493	6,183	6,456	5,989	1,152	4,180	5,715	6,191	Fairly Urbanised
Sokoto	2,785	1,862	2,811	1,176	1,756	1,506	1,192	2,618	Less Urbanised
Abuja	-	-	-	-	119	193	-	-	-

Source: Nigeria Police Headquarters, Lagos. 1987

factors which motivate migration are the search for employment opportunities, educational facilities, possibilities of lucrative trade and the glamour of the big city. Furthermore, the poor living conditions in many parts of the rural areas where there is no electricity, pipe-borne water, medical and recreational facilities contribute to the exodus. The influx of strangers into urban areas provides a degree of anonymity which aids the perpetration of criminal activities to an extent which cannot be experienced in the rural areas where the population is more homogeneous, relatively small and closely knit. As a result of the rapid migration into the cities, it has been difficult for the authorities to undertake proper planning of the urban centres. Thus there is often a remarkable shortage of employment, medical-care, communication and recreational facilities. These conditions tend to have adverse effects on the population and thus encourage involvement in criminal behaviour while making prevention and control of crime relatively difficult.

3 Juvenile Delinquency and Some Specific Types of Criminality

3.1 Juvenile Delinquency

Oloruntimehin (1974) has analyzed the nature of juvenile delinquency statistics including the official processing of juvenile delinquents. In a 1973 study of juvenile delinquents in Lagos, she gave some indications of the relationship between family structure and the development of juvenile delinquency. The study showed that the typical delinquent child belonged to a broken home, a consequence of either divorce, desertion or death of one of the parents. He was deprived of material and emotional needs and his parents belonged to lower/working class. It was also found that about 60 percent of the delinquents did not commit any crime but were found to be either 'beyond parental control' or in 'need of care and protection'. Thus juvenile delinquency was not a serious problem.

Odekunle (1986) corroborated some of the above findings when he stated that the typical institutionalized delinquent is usually a male in the 12 to 15 age bracket, and engaged in primary education which is terminated by an arrest or an earlier inability of his parents to bear the cost of his schooling. He further stated that his father typically has no meaningful employment, limited education, belong to the farming/artisan or junior/intermediate public service occupations. In about 40% of the cases, there was job and material instability. He concluded that the volume and seriousness of delinquency was in no way alarming since it is not ganglike nor conspiratorial as in countries like the United States of America.

This study was based on juvenile delinquents kept in the Approved Schools required by the Children and Young Persons Act of 1958. It has now been found that contrary to the Law, a substantial number of juveniles are kept in the prisons. For example, according to Nigeria Prison Service Statistics for 1985, the following number of children under 16 years of age were admitted into Nigerian Prisons: 1972: 555, 1973: 572, 1974: 252, 1975: 704, 1976: 39, 1977: 372, 1978: 468, 1979: 379, 1980: 821, 1981: 1,102, 1982: 916, 1983: 215, and 1984: 3,000. The presence of these juveniles in the prison signified the fact that they had been involved in serious crimes such as manslaughter, rape, armed robbery, burglary, drug offences, contrary to the claims made by earlier studies. Thus it is now clear that since the beginning of the oil boom in the early 1970s and until the early 1980s when the economy started to show a downward trend, juveniles have engaged in serious crimes. It is also clear that with the economic depression more young persons have become involved in gang-like criminal activities such as armed robbery and burglary. A considerable number of cases of armed robbery and automobile theft, reported to the police in recent times, have been known to involve young persons of about 16 and 18 years of age.

This situation is to be expected since a substantial proportion of migrants into the cities such as Lagos, Kaduna, Enugu, Port-Harcourt are young persons in search of educational and employment opportunities which may be difficult to obtain either because of their large number, lack of relevant qualifications or lack of resources during the recent economic depression. These young people are the most vulnerable to inflationary and employment fluctuations (Kibuka 1979; Kayode 1983). Juvenile delinquency can, therefore, be said to constitute a problem at present. Parents, authorities of educational institutions and even the government now express deep concern about the problem. The mass media also regularly feature public opinion on this issue. It is now recognised that juvenile delinquency is also a problem among children of the middle and upper classes who commit theft and drug offences.

3.2 Female Criminality

Until the early 1980s, female criminality in Nigeria was neither considered an issue of public concern nor a problem worthy of academic interest. The first published work on the subject, Oloruntimehin (1982), was a preliminary analysis focusing on the nature of female criminality and the types of crimes committed by women such as prostitution (particularly soliciting) child stealing, smuggling of prohibited goods and currencies, and theft. It was emphasized that women were seldom involved in serious crimes like armed robbery. Ebbe (1985), using this study as a reference point, carried out an empirical study of prostitution based on the data obtained from a female prison in Lagos. The public perceived that female criminality was not serious and did not disturb the smooth-running of the society. It did not realized that, although the level of female criminality is very low compared to that of men, it has increased rather steadily since the beginning of the oil boom in the 1970s when women acquired greater opportunities for economic and social activities. During this period, women had the unusual opportunity to take up occupations in banks and other financial institutions, to get jobs as contractors, and to travel overseas regularly. As a result of such exposure, women got involved not only in smuggling prohibited goods and currencies but also in drug trafficking. They also featured in cases of fraud and embezzlement. Some were involved in aiding and abetting armed robbers.

Table 4 shows that for the period 1975-1984, only 4 percent of prison inmates were women. However, it can be seen that the number of women entering prison tend to be relatively stable and may not reflect their actual criminality. Because of the 'masked' nature of female criminality, many of their crimes are not reported to or discovered by the police and are therefore not prosecuted (Polak 1961). This includes such offences as abortion, infanticide and child abandonment. Because most victims of female offenders are close relatives or friends, it is often easier to settle these cases privately without involving law enforcement agencies. Observational research at some police stations in Ibadan 1970 and Ile-Ife 1981 revealed that in minor assaults committed by women, the police often gave the female offender a warning after she had provided the victim some money to buy medicine to treat his wound. Such cases were never prosecuted nor reflected in the police crime records. A considerable amount of criminal cases are not prosecuted because the police tended to pity the women or compare them to their mothers, sisters, wives or daughters.

Women, when prosecuted, often receive fines instead of imprisonment. Observations in courts in Ibadan 1970 and Ile-Ife 1981 have revealed that judges and magistrates tended to be lenient with female offenders. Some of the offenders had been given a fine in cases which would have earned a male offender at least a short term of imprisonment. The judicial officers usually showed mercy, especially in cases of women who pleaded responsibility for young children. It is known from mass media reports and general discussions with members of the public that women aid and abet criminals, especially armed robbers, by helping to dispose off stolen goods and

Table 4: Prison Population Statistics (1975-1984)

Year	Figures	Sexes				Prison Population % of General Population	% Male Inreases	% Female Increases	% Total MF Increases
		Male No:	Male %	Female No.	Female %				
1975	87,947	84,989	96.64	2,958	3.40	0.12	3.6	40.6	4.5
1976	108,733	103,197	96.75	3,536	3.30	0.14	23.8	19.5	23.6
1977	112,713	108,941	96.65	3,772	3.40	0.14	3.6	6.7	3.7
1978	150,364	145,522	96.78	4,842	3.20	0.19	38.0	28.4	33.4
1979	159,551	154,722	96.97	4,829	3.00	0.19	2.9	0.3	6.1
1980	165,506	160,377	96.90	5,129	3.10	0.20	3.7	6.2	3.7
1981	169,930	164,485	96.80	5,445	3.20	0.20	2.6	6.2	2.7
1982	175,376	169,102	96.42	6,274	3.60	0.20	2.8	15.2	3.2
1983	202,153	194,986	96,45	7,167	3.50	0.22	15.3	14.2	15.3
1984	243,293	233,980	96.17	9,313	3.80	0.26	19.2	29.9	20.4

Source: Crime Prevention for Freedom, Justice, Peace and Development in Nigeria: The Nigeria National Paper for the 7th United Congress on Crime Prevention and Treatment of Offenders Held at Milan, Italy, 28th August to 6th September, 1985, p. 17.

preventing arrest. Thus women instigate and manipulate men to commit crimes but are seldom arrested, prosecuted or jailed for such offences.

Since 1983 and the economic downturn, currency smuggling has become much less profitable. Some women have been enticed into engaging in drug trafficking which is very lucrative; women figure prominently in this business. Nigerian women have been arrested at National and International Airports with various quantities of cocaine hidden in virtually every part of their bodies. This has embarrassed ordinary Nigerians as well as government officials who travel overseas, because they have been subjected to humiliating treatment by customs officials at airports (Oloruntimehin 1990).

3.3 Drug Offences

In the 1960s, Indian hamp and marijuana were planted in Nigeria and distributed for sale locally and overseas. Between the end of the 1970s and early 1980s, trafficking in hard drugs began. By 1984, hard drugs particualarly cocaine became prominent. Nigeria became an important transit country in the triangular trade between the producers of hard drugs in Latin America and Asia, and the consumers in the United States of America. Although the law enforcement agents have tried to control the illicit business, they have only been able to arrest and prosecute the couriers. The barons are virtually out of their reach because they use their wealth or influence to secure protection from people in power.

According to the Nigerian National Paper presented at the Eighth United Nations Congress on the prevention of crime and the Treatment of Offenders (1990), the number of people arrested between 1979 and 1988 abroad for drug trafficking were as follows: 1979: 1,261, 1980: 1,261, 1981: 1,321, 1982: 1,190, 1983: 1,423, 1984: 1,370, 1985: 1,540, 1986: 1,795, 1987: 1,788 and 1988: 2,032. During the same period the number of those convicted were as follows: 1979: 282, 1980: 315, 1981: 250, 1982: 301, 1983: 311, 1984: 497, 1985: 536, 1986: 762, 1987: 760, and 1988: 620. Some drug traffickers, particularly the couriers, are also arrested and convicted in Nigeria for attempting to smuggle drugs to other countries. Inspite of the efforts of the law enforcement agents, Nigeria is fast becoming a drug consuming nation. A significant proportion of both male and female citizens of different occupational statuses in such cities as Lagos, Ibadan, Enugu, Kaduna are on drugs. Drug addiction tends to be more rampant among young people of the middle and upper class particularly those in institutions of higher education. These young people have become involved in criminal activity as a side-effect of drug abuse or as a means of sustaining their habits. The admission of such young persons into psychiatric hospitals has also increased in recent times. This has been a source of great concern to parents, the general public and the government. This has led to serious considerations of the ways and means to control drug offences.

3.4 Corporate Offences

Offences related to banks, insurance companies and similar organizations emerged with the rapid establishment of these business institutions during the oil boom years of the 1970s. Such offences have become more common in the 1980s due to the introduction of computers into their operations.

3.5 Offences Related to Insurance Companies

Several offences are committed in connection with insurance companies. These include those committed by intermediaries such as brokers and agents who back-date insurance policies to cover a loss or accident which incurred before the inception of the contract and the misappropriation of premiums remitted through them to insurance companies. These problems have seriously hindered the solvency of many insurance companies.

Fraud is another crime problem in the insurance field. For example, a false age can be entered for the insured. For example, a women who is fifty years of age can pay a lower premium if she is listed as thirty years of age. Non-existent persons can be insured, pay the premium for a few months and after presentation of a forged or fraudulent death certificate can be file a claim. Fraudulent life insurance cases often involve the collusion of insurance agents, medical officers, local government functionaries and the police. As far as motor insurance is concerned, non-existent motor vehicles are insured or one vehicle is insured in more than one insurance office. Insured vehicles which have become derelict and unroadworthy have been deliberately set on fire. Some medical officers exaggerate the extent of injuries of motor accident victims in order to enhance the amount of compensation obtainable from the insurers. The incidence of fraud in motor insurance has contributed to its non-profitability.

Much fraud and misrepresentation also exists in the area of fire insurance. When their business declined, some burned down their shops in order to obtain money. From 1979 to 1987, the gross amount paid for fire losses according to the Nigerian Insurance Year book (1989) is as follows: 1979: 10,103,651, 1980: 14,264,758, 1981: 13,612,468, 1982: 18,622,468, 1983:

37,364,042, 1984: 39,648,869, 1985: 45,787,473, 1986: 42,657,311 and 1987: 40,729,069. Maritime insurance fraud often involves transnational syndicates spread out over two or three continents. Ships are purposely sunk, destroyed or their cargoes sold in order to falsely obtain insurance money from the insurers (Adeyemi, 1990).

3.6 Frauds Connected With Banks

According to Adeniji (1990), banking frauds include falsification of documents to benefit from customers excess proceeds and to fraudulently withdraw money from their accounts. There are also cases of deliberate cash theft by bank officials, cash officers, cashiers and customers. Telex frauds are usually committed by electronically transferring funds overseas to fictitious accounts or to genuine accounts under a fictitious or false mandate. Proceeds of such false transactions are usually cashed in by the overseas collaborators of the fraudulent persons, thereby draining Nigeria of foreign reserves needed for the development of the national economy.

The computer is creating new forms of crime and criminals among such categories of workers as computer programmers, operators, tape librarians and electronic engineers. These crimes include: computer frauds; the destruction of computers, data/programmes in them or the supportive facilities and resources; falsely crediting entries into customers' accounts and then making subsequent withdrawals; tampering with input systems; using computers for financial embezzlement; stealing money, property or confidential information through the manipulation of the computer output process.

The police receive reports of at least three cases of bank fraud daily, particularly from the Central Bank of Nigeria. Those who defraud the banks, do so in collusion with bank officials. Bank officials have been known to engage in unauthorised, reckless or fraudulent lending of money without collateral. It has been reported that sums up to 5.3 million Nigerian Dollars have been granted as an overdraft to a customer and 12.5 million Nigerian Dollars were granted to four customers by bank managers without authorisation (African Guardian 1990). Such fraudulent actions by bank officials have led to the near liquidation of some banks such as the National Bank of Nigeria Limited. Okonkwo (1990) gave the following record of bank staff dismissals or retirements for fraudulent activities in 1989: 27 supervisors/managers, 15 officers/accountants and executive assistants, 99 clerks and cashiers, 8 typists, technicians and stenographers, 50 messengers, drivers, cleaners, stewards and security guards, 5 temporary staff, and 67 uncategorized staff. There is no doubt that in recent times corporate frauds have featured prominently in the crime profile of this country. It is believed that the damage done to certain individuals and particularly the national economy is much greater than that accounted for by conventional crimes such as theft and burglary.

Along with corporate offences, corruption involving highly placed members of the society who manipulate their privileged positions to defraud the nation is the greatest drain on the national economy (Oloruntimehin, 1989). This unprecedented drain on the country's foreign exchange reserves has led to a huge debt burden, the devaluation of the nation's currency, tremendous inflationary tendencies, unemployment and underemployment. All of these have serious consequences for the state of criminality.

4 Crime Prevention and Control

Crime Prevention has become more important as such criminal activities as armed robbery have become a menace not only in the urban areas but also in the semi-urban and even rural areas. In some semi-urban and rural areas traditional rulers, supported by local government authorities, imposed curfews forbidding movement between nine o'clock at night and five o'clock in the morning. Hunters with dane guns moved around the community during this period. Any one found moving about without a convincing reason was apprehended and given a serious beating. This is reminiscent of past forms of crime prevention. Although there are police posts and stations in these communities, people believe that the police have lost control and they choose to rely on traditional approaches which proved effective. This approach is modified and applied even in urban areas like Ibadan and Lagos.

Through the joint efforts of the residents, a gate is constructed at the entrance of a street and is locked around nine o'clock in the night and opened only at five o'clock in the morning. The residents form vigilante groups and move about every night to ensure that no strange person is moving around the street. This method of crime prevention has been given official recognition by the state government and the police, particularly in Ibadan. The police have been charged with the duty of monitoring the activities of the vigilante groups and also giving them relevant information about crime prevention.

In the big cities such as Lagos, Ibadan, Kaduna, Kano, Enugu and Benin, the majority of those who reside in low density residential areas hire day and night guards. Some install burglary alarms in their houses while others keep fierce-looking and terrifying dogs. Still others erect high walls around their houses. They have huge iron gates and surround the windows and doors with burglar proof bars. In fact, some houses, especially in Lagos, look like prisons. In these cities many individuals also spend substantial amounts of money to install various safety gadgets in their cars. Store owners, besides installing burglary alarms, also use very strong locks on the doors of the stores and hire night guards. The governments of the states also try to install street lights on the major streets of important towns, especially state capitals. Police highway patrol vehicles, through their patrols, try to prevent the activities of criminals who might wish to rob travellers. Police public relations offices make requests on the radio and television that members of the public should report any suspicious persons they notice in their areas of residence, to the police. Customs and Immigration officials patrol the borders. Some even patrol the sea in order to stop the illicit activities of smugglers and pirates.

5 Crime Control

The criminal law in Nigeria is comprised of the Criminal Code (operative in the Southern part), the Penal Code (operative in the Northern part) and the Criminal Procedure Act. The criminal law adequately provides for all categories of criminal behaviour ranging from failure to pay a debt and tax evasion, to murder, rape, theft, drug offences, robbery, corruption, and corporate offences. With the rapid increase in the volume of such crimes as armed robbery, drug and corporate offences and the increasing menace they constitute to the society, the Federal government had found it necessary to promulgate new laws (sometimes in panic) to control such crimes. For example, as a result of the high rate of armed robbery immediately after the civil war in 1970, the Firearms Decree of 1970 was promulgated by the Federal Military Government. The law stipulated death by firing squad for anybody found guilty of armed robbery. In 1984, as a result of the phenomenal increase in the rate of drug trafficking, and the discreditation of Nigeria's image overseas, the Federal military government promulgated the Miscellaneous Offences (Special Military Tribunals) Decree No. 20 of 1984 which stipulated the death penalty for drug trafficking. A 1986 amendment to the Decree removed the death penalty in response to public pressure. After 1986, when drug trafficking was no longer punishable by the death penalty, (according to the Nigerian National Paper for the Eight United Nations Congress on the Prevention of Crime and Treatment of Offenders, 1990), drug offences rose from 1,946 in 1986 to 2,396 in 1987.

In relation to this offence unlike in the case of armed robbery. Although some members of the public also criticised the capitalization of armed robbery and particularly the public execution of the offenders, a substantial proportion of the people maintained a neutral attitude towards this form of punishment.

Since that time there have been serious arguments about the use of the death penalty. Many expressed the idea that the imposition of death penalty was inappropriate even in the case of armed robbery. It was emphasized that the death penalty merely expressed the vengeance of the society against the offender (retribution) and was no longer in line with modern philosophy of penology. Furthermore, it was pointed out that this penalty deters the particular offender but does not deter others from committing murder and armed robbery (Adeyemi 1987; Adeyemi 1990; Okagbue 1990).

To combat the rapid increase in crimes in the insurance area the Insurance Companies Act of 1961 was enacted. This was repealed and replaced by the Insurance Act of 1976. To more effectively control the insurance business, the Insurance (Special Provision) Decree 1988 was promulgated. To combat bank frauds, the Banking Act was enacted in 1969. This was amended by Decree No. 45 of 1972 which made the law more effective in controlling the actions of bank officials in the granting of loans and credits. The Companies and Allied Matters Decree 1990 contained provisions aimed at checking bank frauds in different ways (Adeyemi, 1990, Adeniji, 1990, Okonkwo, 1990). To deal with drug offences, a National Drug Law Enforcement Agency was established in December, 1989. Between 1988 and 1990 a series of national conferences were organized by the Federal Ministry of Justice under the leadership of the Federal Attorney-General and Minister for Justice, Prince Bola Ajibola, to discuss such critical issues in the area of criminal law as the Unification of the criminal and penal codes, economic crimes, and remedies for victims of crime and drug offences. The deliberations of the conferences have led to the establishment of various committees to draft policies and legislations on these issues. The ultimate aim is to promulgate relevant decrees.

6 The Criminal Justice System

The police, the judiciary and the prison system work together to control crime. To achieve effective crime control, these different sectors of the justice system need to cooperate.

6.1 The Police

The Police bear much of the burden of enforcing legal policy and legislations because they are expected by law to execute the law even when it is obviously faulty. The police are to prevent crime by proper surveillance of the community and by arresting and prosecuting offenders. These law enforcement agents, however, lack the necessary facilities to perform effectively. First, the level of police man power is low compared to the population. At present there is approximately one officer for every 1,200 citizens which is far from the United Nations requirement of 1 to 400 (Coker 1990). The level of police education is also low compared with what exists in other organizations. This seems to be a legacy of the colonial heritage when men who had no formal education were recruited into the Police Force in order to apply force and impose law and order on the indigenous population. The ever more sophisticated criminality, however, demands educated and well-trained personnel. Many policemen have only a primary school education. The remuneration of the police is also inadequate and is not commensurate with their onerous duties. Moreover, it is lower than that which is paid to workers in similar sectors of the economy. This may contribute to police corruption. The poor police training and their corruption have had a negative effect on police-community relations and has inhibited public cooperation in the area of crime control (Nigerian Institute of Advanced Legal Studies 1990; Coker 1990).

In addition, the police also lacks facilities and equipment needed to perform effectively. The absence of vehicles, communication systems, accommodation, and stationery seriously affects the level of police performance. For example, according to the Nigerian Prison Service Statistics (1986), over 60 percent of prison inmates between 1973 and 1985 were those on remand and awaiting trial. There have been cases of suspects who have been kept in prison awaiting trial for periods varying from some months to 8 years (Civil Liberties Organization 1988). The delays resulted from problems connected with lack of facilities to carry out investigations as well as police inefficiency. This situation has also resulted in the dismissal of criminal cases for lack of evidence and improper prosecutions. This in turn has led to the discharge of 'obvious' culprits on technicalites and has resulted in a loss of confidence of the common man in the criminal justice system. Some members of the public have, therefore, taken the law into their own hands by lynching suspects accused of armed robbery, child stealing, or manslaughter.

6.2 The Judiciary

The courts are given the responsibility to interpret and administer the law. The courts rely on cases presented to them by the police, the office of Director of Public Prosecutions as well as that of the Attorney-General. The Attorney General, both at Federal and State levels, is empowered by the 1979 Constitution to discontinue criminal proceedings at any stage before the final judgement (Tamuno 1985). Judges and magistrates have also been found to lack crucial facilities needed for the effective performance of their duties. For example, a considerable number of them lack suitable accommodations or secretarial assistance (they take down notes in court by long hand and write down judgements in the same manner). Intermediate and junior staff are also in short supply. The courts also lack stationery and related materials. Courts, especially the magistrate courts, also have heavy case loads. Combined with lapses in police performance, the granting of series of adjournments at the pleadings of lawyers and the absence of vital witnesses (who often refuse to serve as prosecution witnesses on account of their aversion for the court) often lead to delays in justice.

The delays keep many people who are presumed innocent in terrible, overcrowded, unhygienic prisons where they are poorly nourished for lengthy periods. The law stipulates that the Chief Judge of the State should periodically visit the prisons within his jurisdiction to oversee the inmates' welfare. He is empowered to release certain categories of inmates who have spent time in prison equal to that which they might have served if sentenced. But some chief judges hardly comply with this legal demand.

A major problem of the judges and magistrates is their ability to exercise discretion. Many exercise this discretion without considering the situation of those sentenced. Much discrepancy exists in the sentencing practices of the courts. Thus sentences for similar offences tend to vary from one judge to the other depending on the status, appearance, conduct, sex of the offender and even the mood of the judge. For example, although the law makes provision for suspended sentences, binding over and probation, most judicial officials hardly use them. They prefer to sentence offenders to a short term of imprisonment to serve as a deterrent. People have been sentenced to short terms of imprisonment for such offences as failure to pay debts and affray (Nigerian Prison Service Statistics 1985). The same report also revealed that between 1980 and 1984 about 80 percent of those sentenced to jail were given short term sentences. The report also revealed that some juveniles under 16 years of age as well as those between 16 and 17 years were sentenced to jail contrary to the provisions of the Children and Young Persons Law of

1958. The Supreme Court has recognised the need for more formal and informal training of judges, particularly those with less than five years experience.

6.3 The Prison

The prison is the last stage in the criminal justice system. The prison removes the offender from society. For many police and judicial officials, the prison is merely a place custody and a place that conveys society's negative reaction to the offender. However, prison officials believe that the prison could be a place for reform of the offender and an environment which helps prepare him for his eventual reintegration into society. There is an ever present conflict between the philosophies and objectives of the prison officials and those of other actors in the criminal justice system. Only limited rehabilitation facilities are provided in certain prisons. These include training for such various skills as carpentry, tailoring, and furniture making. Prison inmates are not classified and first offenders mix with recidivists. In the process, the hardened criminals have a negative impact on the first offenders. According to recidivism statistics of the Nigerian Prison service, about 40 percent of prison inmates between 1980 and 1984 had between one and eleven convictions.

According to available reports, prison population has increased at least threefold within the last two decades. But there has been no addition to the prison facilities or their provison of food, medical care or occupational training. Prison overcrowding has aroused concern among prison officials, the government and various humanitarian organizations, particularly the Civil Liberties Organization. For example, the rate of prison congestion has increased rapidly from 29.4 percent in 1980 to 93.7 percent in 1988 (Obot 1990). Under such conditions the inmates have become the victims of such diseases as tuberculosis, gastroenteritis, rheumatic fever, typhoid fever, chest infections, and scabies. Female inmates have been admitted into these terrible prisons with their young children and some have even had their babies in prison. In 1985, 400 women were admitted into the prisons with their children while 49 births were recorded among female inmates (Obot, 1990). Lunatics are also committed annually to the prisons even though there are no special facilities. For example, 663 lunatics were sent to the prisons in 1988 (Obot 1990).

Prison officials are paid poorly, lack essential vehicles or proper training. Even in developed countries where better prison conditions exist, imprisonment has been recognized as a great hinderance to the reintegration of offenders into the society. This situation should be more pronounced in the developing countries with their serious socio-economic problems. This calls for some thought about alternatives to imprisonment. The concern shown by the Federal government through the Federal Attorney-General and Minister for Justice has led to the decriminalization of wandering which had contributed significantly to the growth in the short term confinements which have swelled the prison population. Thus the Minor Offences Decree, No. 29 of 1989 decriminalized the offence of wandering. The National Seminar on Prison Reform in June, 1990 focused on alternatives to imprisonment other than the establishment of prison farms. It suggested the greater use of fines as well as restitution and victim compensation, penalties consistent with the traditional system of justice. The needs of the prison officials were also considered as crucial.

The police, judicial and prison officials have played a significant role in crime control. The hinderances placed on their proper performance of their roles have serious consequences for the satus of crime and criminals in this society.

Concern for crime victims, particularly victims of armed robbery, has resulted in the formation of a National Committee on Remedies for Victims of Crime, whose deliberations are likely to lead to the promulgation of Decrees on this vital issue. The establishment of a system of remedies for the victims of crime would do much to alleviate the suffering of victims and to restore citizen confidence in the criminal justice system.

7 Conclusion

An attempt has been made to highlight the state of crime and control in Nigeria in the context of post-1960 political and socio-economic conditions. The negativ impact to the post-1966 political instability, the mismanagement of the revenues from the oil boom and the consequent inflation, unemployment and underemployment have all been examined. These conditions have worsened the living standard of the population, particularly rural to urban migrants. These trends have been correlated with the growth in crime in rural and urban areas. Specific types of crime generated or aggravated by particular political and socio-economic conditions were identified and discussed. Special attention was paid to juvenile delinquency, female criminality, drug and corporate offences and their particular features.

Crime prevention and control were analysed within the context of Nigeria's growing crime rate. This included the analysis of self-help groups in the 'fight' against crime (the vigilant groups), the hiring of night guards, the use of dogs and burglary alarm gadgets. The problems of criminal justice system personnel in controlling the rising crime were scrutinized.

A thorough revision of the entire criminal justice system is necessary to address to existing crime problem. They must be provided with sufficient resources to perform their jobs. Suitable and practicable alternatives to institutionalization should be introduced. Remedies for victims of crime should be put into operation. The reform must be combined with major changes in political and socio-economic conditions in society.

References

Adeyemi, A. A. (1987) "Death Penalty: Criminological Perspectives, The Nigerian Situation", in: Revue Internationale de Droit Penal, vol. 58, Nos. 3 and 4.

Adeyemi, A. A. (1990), "Death Penalty in Nigeria: Criminological Perspectives", in: Narcotics: Law and Policy in Nigeria, Awa U. Kalu and Yemi Osinbajo eds., Lagos: Federal Ministry of Justice.

Adeyemi, A.A. et al (1989) "Lagos", in: Urban Crime: Global Trends and Policies, Hernando Gomez Buendia ed., Tokyo: The United Nations University.

Adeyemi, M.O. (1990) "Insurance Fraud and Criminal Justice Administration in Nigeria", Paper presented at the National Seminar on Criminal Justice Administration in Nigeria, Department of Public Law, University of Lagos, Lagos.

Adeniji, O.A. (1990) "Banking Frauds and Criminal Justice Administration in Nigeria", Paper presented at the National Seminar on Criminal Justice Administration in Nigeria, Department of Public Law, University of Lagos, Lagos.

African Guardian, April 23, 1990.

Children and Young Persons Law (1958), Lagos: Government Printers.

Civil Liberties Organization (1988) Annual Report.

Clifford, W.(1974) An Introduction to African Criminology, Nairobi: Oxford University Press.

Clinard M.B. and Abbott, Daniel J. (1978) Crime in Developing Countries, New York: John Wiley and Sons.

Coker, J. (1990) "The Role, Functions and Problems of the Nigeria Police Force in Criminal Justice Administration", Paper presented at the National Seminar on Criminal Justice Administration in Nigeria, Department of Public Law, University of Lagos, Lagos.

Ebbe, N.I. Obi (1985) "The Correlates of Female Criminality in Nigeria", in: International Journal of Comparative and Applied Criminal Justice, vol. 9, No. 1.

Elias, T.O. (1973) Law in a Developing Society Benin City, Nigeria: Ethiope Publishing Corporation.

Hood, R. and Sparks, R. (1970) Key Issues in Criminology, London: World University Library.

Kayode, Oluyemi (1983) "Nigeria", in: International Handbook of Contemporary Developments in Criminology: Europe, Africa, Middle East and Asia, Elemer H. Johnson ed., Westport, Connecticut, London: Greenwood Press, pp. 473-493.

Kibuka, Paul Eric (1979) "Crime in African Countries", in: International Review of Criminal Policy (United Nations No. 35).

Nkpa, N.K.U. (1976) "Armed Robery in Post Civil War Nigeria: The Role of the Victim", in: Victimology: An International Journal, vol. 1, No. 1.

Nigerian Institute of Advanced Legal Studies (1990) Report on Human Rights and the Administration of Criminal Justice, Lagos.

Nigerian Insurance Year Book, 1989.

Nigerian Prison Service Statistics (1985 and 1986), Federal Office of Statistics ed., Lagos.

Obot, Isidore, S. (1990) "Morbidity and Mortality Among Inmates of Nigerian Prisons: Causes and Solutions", Paper presented at the National Seminar on Prisons Reforms in Nigeria, Ministry of Internal Affairs, Abuja.

Odekunle, F. (1986) "Patterns of Delinquency and Formalized Control Policy in Nigeria", in: Youth Crime Social Control and Prevention: Theoretical Perspectives and Policy Implications. Studies from Nine Different Countries, M. Brusten, J. Graham, N. Herriger and P. Malinowski eds., Pfaffenweiler: Centaurus-Verlagsgesellschaft.

Okagbue, Isabella (1990) "The Death Penalty As An Effective Deterrent To Drug Abuse and Drug Trafficking", Paper presented at the National Seminar on Drug Law Enforcement, Nigerian Law School, Lagos.

Okonkwo, C.O. (1990) "Corporate Frauds and Criminal Justice Administration", Paper presented at the National Seminar on Administration of Criminal Justice in Nigeria, Department of Public Law, University of Lagos, Lagos.

Oloruntimehin, O. (1973) "A Study of Juvenile Delinquency in a Nigerian City" in: British Journal of Criminology.

Oloruntimehin, O. (1974) "A Note on Juvenile Delinquency Statistics in a Nigerian City", Ghana Journal of Sociology, vol. 8, No. 1.

Oloruntimehin, O. (1977) "The Difference Between Real and Apparent criminality", in: Nigerian Criminal Process, A. A. Adeyemi ed., Lagos: University of Lagos Press.

Oloruntimehin, O. (1978) “Operational Problems of Modern Penal Justice in Nigeria”, in: Ghana Social Sciences Journal, vol. 5, No. 1.
Oloruntimehin, O. (1982) “A Preliminary Study of Female Criminality in Nigeria”, in: The Incidence of Female Criminality in the Contemporary world, Freda Adler ed., New York: University Press.
Oloruntimehin, O. (1985) “Crime and Development”, in: Social Science, Ouest Summer, vol. 1, No. 1.
Oloruntimehin, O. (1989) “Crime and the Abuse of Power: The Experience of a Developing Nation”, in: International Annals of Criminology, vol. 27, Nos. 1 and 2.
Oloruntimehin, O. (1990) “Social and Psychological Implications of Drug Trafficking”, in: Narcotics: Law and Policy in Nigeria, Awa U. Kalu and Osinbajo eds., Lagos: Federal Ministry of Justice.
Polak, O. (1961) The Criminality of Women, New York: Barnes.
Rotimi, A. (1984) “Perspectives on the Armed Robbery Offence in Nigeria”, in: Indian Journal of Criminology, vol. 12, No. 2.
Tamuno. T. (1985) “The Responsibility for Crime Control in Nigeria”, IBADAN: Nigerian Institute of Social and Economic Research.
Nigerian National Paper (1990) Report for the Eighth United Nations Congress on the Prevention of Crime and the Treatment of Offenders, held at Havana, Cuba, August 27-September. 7, 1990, Lagos, Nigeria: Government of the Federal Republic of Nigeria.
United Nations Social Defence Research Institute (1990) Juvenile Social Maladjustment and Human Rights in the Context of Urban Development, Publication No. 22, Case Study No. 3, Lagos, Nigeria. (Rome Frateili Palombi Editori, October, 1984).
World Demographic Estimates and Projections 1950-2025, New York: United Nations, Serial No. ST/ESA/SER.R/79.

Crime and Control in Comparative Perspectives: The Case of India

R.S. Shrivastava

1 Introductory Remarks

There is some justification to the view that the developing nations have to encounter the same crime problems as the developed world because of the growing 'internationalization' of technological, economic, social, and cultural life. This internationalization of aspects of development and change also extends, to some degree, to the growing international dimensions of crime. Terrorism, international drug trafficking, and organized crimes are illustrative of the emerging global patterns of criminality. No country today is an 'island' unaffected by the diverse ramifications of international criminality. There is also a further argument that when the modernization process reaches a certain stage at which the economic security and social wellbeing of a majority of the population is assured, the patterns of crime begin to change from crimes typical of poverty to crimes typical of the affluent society.

The assessment of the relationship between crime and development can be made only with reference to the specific, and sometimes unique, social and cultural context. The meaning of specific conditions such as poverty is determined for people within their social and cultural context. Tradition, social institutions and cultural values are crucial variables in determining the containment or growth of crime in a modernizing society. Patterns of crime and antisocial behaviour require an analysis of the context in which 'system-specific' variables determine the outcome in differing social-cultural contexts (Teune 1990, pp. 54 -55). The fact remains that there is a paucity of crime data for most developing countries (Owomero 1987). In most developing countries, including India, inadequate attention has been paid to the evolution of criminality that has accompanied social change and development. Rather, the preoccupation has been with the wider questions of social, economic, and political transformation. Moreover, the legal and judicial systems of most developing countries are a legacy of the colonial period. They have not been modified to reflect the requirements of the changing situation.

2 Crime Trends and Crime Patterns

2.1 Official Crime Statistics

One of the most crucial and controversial problems is the assessment of a country's total crime problem using its statistics of officially registered crimes. This is one area in which there is always a vast gap between reality and appearance. The best source of Indian crime statistics is the published annual report entitled, 'Crime in India'. It is published by the National Crime Records Bureau of the Ministry of Home Affairs, Government of India. Although it provides valuable information about crime situation in India, it suffers from some limitations. There is always some time lag involved in collecting, compiling and presenting crime statistics at the national level. At the time of writing this paper, the latest available publication was 'Crime in India – 1986' published in June, 1989. Various law enforcement agencies handle different types of law violations. The NCRB publication pertains only to crimes handled by police departments of various states of India. There are some agencies of law enforcement, other than the police which handle some very vital types of socio-economic violations. Unfortunately, the annual report, "Crime in India", does not truly reflect the total dimension of the Indian crime problem because crime statistics from these agencies are not included in it and they are not available elsewhere in a compiled form.

The reporting system used by police agencies has several drawbacks. Therefore, the crime statistics furnished by these agencies also do not represent the Indian crime scene. A few of the shortcomings will be pointed out to enable us to better assess the Indian crime picture using the data of crimes registered by the police agencies. One of the most prevalent tendencies among police departments is to minimise or conceal crimes for a variety of reasons. Crime figures are fudged, largely because police efficiency is judged on the basis of crime statistics. In order to save themselves from criticism from the government, the political parties and the mass media, statistics are deliberately distorted to reduce crime rates. Police fail to register crimes. Adding to this the number of unknown cases or unreported crimes, there is much that is not known about the Indian crime problem. In India, such serious offences as rape are sometimes not reported to the police due to the serious social stigma attached to victims in this traditional society. For many other crime categories as well, at least fifty per cent of the crimes are either not reported or are unknown to the police. Citizens fail to report crimes to the police because they lack faith in or fear the police, judicial proceedings are long and cumbersome, they fear reprisals from criminals, they are situated a long distances from police stations, particularly in rural areas, and the costs in terms of time and money are significant.

Keeping these drawbacks in mind let us now try to quickly assess the total dimensions of Indian crime as represented in "Crime in India – 1986". These statistics provide only the most general picture of crime in India.

2.2 Crime in India: Trends and Patterns

One salient characteristic of India is its rapid population growth. It could be expected that population growth would be accompanied by a proportionate growth in crime as well. But the striking feature of the Indian crime scene is that the crime rate has, by and large, outstripped the rate of population growth. Table 1 indicates the rate of growth of crime (Cognizable crime under I.P.C.), the growth of population and rate of crime per one lakh[1] of population during the decade 1976 – 1986.

The period from 1976 to 1986 had witnessed political changes with far-reaching consequences for the economy, polity and society. Some of these changes are reflected in the fluctuating crime scene as well. The picture may be clear if we look at the trends in some important forms of crime. According to 'Crime in India – 1986', some of the important forms of crime showed a marked increase in 1986 over that recorded in 1976. The data for the following offenses[2] reflect the dramatic growth in rape (104.3), counterfeiting (90.2), murder (63.6), culpable homicide not amounting to murder (62.3), robbery (24.6) and cheating (15.3). Some forms of crime also showed a decline during the same period[3]. These were: burglary (23.5), criminal breach of trust (19.6), theft (11.4) and dacoity (4.3). The above figures indicate that such violent crimes as rape, murder, culpable homicide not amounting to murder, and kidnapping and abduction have been rising in recent years in India, while crimes against property like burglary, robbery, dacoity and theft have declined. The increase in violent crimes reflects the increasing complexity and changing dynamics of interpersonal and intergroup relationships. Some violent crimes like murder, and some of those which are accompanied by violence, such as dacoity, have social, structural and historical factors as their base. They result from a sub-culture of violence that has become established as a means of resolving various disputes and differences in interpersonal

1 One lakh = 1,00,000
2 Percentage of increase shown in brackets
3 Percentage of decrease shown in brackets

Table 1: Incidence of Cognizable Crime Under The Indian Penal Code and Population in India from 1976 to 1986

Year	Estimated mid-year population in millions	Total Cognizable crime under the Indian Penal Code	Rate of Crime per one lakh of Population[a]
1976	613.3	10,93,897	178.4
1977	625.8	12,67,004	302.5
1978	638.4	13,44,968	210.7
1979	651.0	13,36,168	205.2
1980	663.6	13,68,529	206.2
1981	690.1	13,85,757	200.8
1982	705.2	13,53,904	192.0
1993	720.4	13,49,866	187.4
1984	735.6	13,58,660	184.7
1985	750.9	13,84,731	184.4
1986	766.1	14,05,835	183.5
Percentage change in 1986 over 1976	+24.9	+28.5	+2.9

Source: Crime in India - 1986, National Crime Records Bureau Ministry of Home Affairs, Government of India, p. 1.
Notes:
a) One lakh = 1,00,000

relationships. It is not surprising that the highest number of cases of murder were reported from states like Uttar Pradesh, Bihar, Madhya Pradesh and Maharashtra, which have a few pockets where crimes of violence, an organised mafia and intercaste conflicts have had a long tradition. While the declining trend in the conventional crimes against property such as burglary and theft should be taken with a grain of salt, it should be remembered that these conventional crimes, – 'crimes of poverty' if you like –, are being outnumbered by those known as 'economic crimes'. These economic crimes are a consequence of industrialization, urbanization and other processes of change and development. The recent emergence of such crimes in Indian society requires an extended analysis of the factors leading to their rise. There has been an upward trend in crimes of counterfeiting involving coins and currency, cheating and criminal breach of trust. While the crimes of counterfeiting showed a sharp increase of 56.9 per cent in 1986 over the previous five year's

Table 2: Cases reported under Local and Special Laws during 1982 to 1986

Crime head	1982	1983	1984	1985	1986	Percentage change in 1986 over 1985
Arms Act	60,690	64,413	59,205	61,987	56,954	- 8.1
Narcotic Drugs and Psychotropic Substances Act	14,590	14,356	14,440	14,277	13,253	- 7.2
Gambling Act	2,01,630	1,89,863	1,76,829	1,79,419	1,63,097	- 9.1
Excise Act	1,12,243	1,13,338	1,07,967	1,06,163	95,011	- 10.5
Prohibition Act	3,56,334	3,88,224	3,65,526	3,56,840	3,65,300	+ 2.4
Explosives & Explosive Substances Act	3,071	3,477	2,905	3,373	3,205	- 5.0
Immoral Traffic (Prevention) Act	15,890	15,325	14,209	14,815	14,403	- 2.8
Motor Vehicles Act	10,84,506	9,98,067	11,37,539	11,92,537	11,73,061	- 1.6
Prevention of Corruption Act	278	328	723	503	204	- 59.4
Customs Act	137	149	102	84	158	+ 88.1
Indian Railways Act	41,039	48,655	36,749	32,478	37,460	+ 15.3
Other Offences	10,79,660	10,84,868	10,00,614	11,34,005	10,62,548	- 6.3
Total of all cognizable crimes under Local & Special Laws	29,70,068	29,21,063	29,16,808	30,96,481	29,84,654	- 3.6

Source: Crime in India - 1986, NCRB.

average, cheating indicated an increase of 18.7 per cent during the same period. The increase in these crimes alone reflects a proliferation of industrial and commercial activities.

Several offences are defined under local and special laws whose incidence and enforcement differ from state to state. This category includes such offences as the Arms Act, Narcotic Drugs and Psychotropic Substances Act, Gambling Act, Excise Act, Prohibition Act, Explosives Act, Immoral Traffic (Prevention) Act, Motor Vehicles Act, Prevention of Corruption Act, Customs Act and Indian Railways Act. Table 2 presents cases under these Acts during 1982 – 1986.

In India the crimes committed in the category of local and special laws are twice as numerous as the crimes committed under the category of

Indian Penal Code. However, it should be mentioned that the apparent declining trends of these offences (as indicated in table 2) may be deceptive. The figures given in table 2 represent cases registered exclusively by State Police agencies. But there are other agencies which also deal with the same types of violations. If their figures are added, the number of such cases would be much higher. The number of newly emergent crimes (such as the white collar and economic offences), handled by specialised agencies, is much higher than the conventional crimes which fall under the jurisdiction of the Indian Penal Code and are the responsibility of state police agencies.

2.2.1 Juvenile Delinquency

The level and form of juvenile delinquency reflect more faithfully than adult crime, the changes in Indian social structure, cultural values, and shifts in standards of discipline and civilized behaviour. There is much less juvenile delinquency in India than in most western industrialised countries including the United States. In a comparative study of crime and delinquency rates in India and the United States, Sandhu (1987, p.10) found that in 1978 juvenile offenders contributed only 3.3 per cent of all crimes committed under Indian Penal Code. In the same year, America juveniles under age 18 committed 21.4 per cent of all violent crimes, and 45.5 per cent of the property crimes. Though delinquency may be a comparatively 'minor' problem in India, more recent figures show that it has risen steadily. Its rate of growth is greater than that of general criminality. Table 3 provides data showing the proportion of criminality attributed to juveniles and its rate of growth.

Juveniles are represented more significantly in crimes governed by local and special laws than by those under the Indian Penal Code. For example, total juvenile crime cases under I.P.C. were 49,317 in 1985 and 55,887 in 1986. In contrast, the total number of juvenile cases under local and special laws were 76,492 in 1985 and 78,743 in 1986. This shows that they are much more likely to be violators of such special laws as the Gambling Act, Prohibition Act, and the Motor Vehicle Act. The figures for arrested juveniles reveal that during the years 1976-1980, more than 80.0 per cent of them were in the 16 to 21 year age group. Female representation in juvenile crime varied from a low of 4.6 in 1981 to 7.7 in 1984. This shows that the proportion of female involvement in juvenile delinquency is much less than in developed industrialized countries where it may represent as much as one third of total juvenile delinquency. A typical Indian juvenile delinquent handled by law enforcement officials would be an adolescent male of Hindu religion who is illiterate or with only primary schooling. He would also be a first offender of 16 to 21 years of age from a low income

Table 3: Total Cognizable Crime Under IPC, Juvenile Crime Under IPC, Proportion of Juvenile Crime To Total Crime And Volume of Juvenile Crime per one Lakh of Population

Year	Population in millions (Estimated mid-year)	Total cognizable crime cases under IPC	Total juvenile crime cases under IPC	% of juvenile crime to total cognizable crime.	Volume of juvenile crime per lakh of population
1979	613.3	10,93,897	37,015	3.4	6.0
1980	663.6	13,68,529	55,129	4.0	8.3
1981	690.1	13,85,757	61,019	4.4	8.8
1982	705.2	13,53,904	59,345	4.4	8.4
1983	720.4	13,49,866	55,473	4.1	7.7
1984	735.6	13,58,660	42,803	3.2	5.8
1985	750.9	13,84,731	49,317	3.6	6.6
1986	766.1	14,05,835	55,887	4.0	7.3

Source: Crime in India - 1986, NCRB

group (a familial income below Rs.150/- or $10 per month). This prototype offender commits the so-called 'conventional' crimes and delinquent acts that make up the official crime picture. Despite the limitations of the official data, it is safe to conclude that the general trend in India is one of consistently rising rates of crime and delinquency.

2.2.2 Socio-Economic Crimes

The previous discussion has focused on only one dimension of the Indian crime problem. The other dimension is the emergent forms of criminality that are a consequence of the process of development and social, economic and political change. Unlike conventional crimes, they are not separated from the larger society but are inseparably intertwined with the legitimate social processes and institutions. This category includes some of the biggest and most pervasive crimes which do not figure in our crime statistics. These myriad crimes go under the rubric of 'economic' crimes and include such widespread and pervasive offences as tax evasion, violation of import-export regulations, infringement of currency control measures, black marketeering, hoarding, profiteering, and adulteration. These crimes and their perpetrators have acquired a high degree of acceptability, and even respectability. Several of these crimes are the result of increased industrial and economic activity as well as emergent social and political processes in India. The enormity of the problem has recently evoked serious concern. The Indian Law Commission studied these offences to find out measures to tackle the problem. In its 47th Report, the Commission defined social offences as those adversely affecting the health and material wellbeing of the community. Economic offences are those which effect the economy of the country, not merely the property or possessions of any individual victim. This is clearly an acknowledgement of the fact that crime patterns are moving away from the direct victimization of individuals towards offenses where those injured or damaged are 'anonymous' victims or collectivities. This new dimension of criminality reflects some of the characteristic features of a developing society. Economic development strategies involve a massive input of funds into an economy which has been characterised by scarcities, scarce resources and a vast gap between rising aspirations of individuals and collectivities and the opportunities for their realisation. In a state that regulates and oversees competitive bidding for permits and licences, there are numerous possibilities for manipulation, cheating, misappropriations, and various other forms of fraudulent banking and financial transactions. Shortages lead to such economic offences as black marketeering, hoarding, adulteration and misrepresentation. An enormous amount of money goes into the black market as a result of illegal transactions and corruption of the legal and administrative apparatus. The link between processes of development and the emerging forms of criminality is quite complex and requires an extended analysis. The graph of crime in India helps illustrate the complex correlations that exist and may explain these complex interrelations better than the conclusions derived from any aggregate data.

3 The Indian Scene: An Analysis

The current Indian scene is dominated by a raging controversy about what is sometimes called the criminalisation of society. Criminal and deviant patterns have infiltrated normal institutions and the interlocking of politics, economy, and crime has led to 'patterned evasions' (Schur 1969 p.194). Many sectors of society are alienated from the dominant and professed social norms. Our political ideology and social framework were inherited from the ideals of the National Movement of the pre-independence era. They synthesised western and traditional Indian values in what is known as the Gandhi-Nehru vision. The Gandhian vision gave specific importance to means-ends relationships based on certain moral values. In the socio-economic realm, Gandhi's vision emphasised grassroot efforts to improve the conditions of masses steeped in poverty, illiteracy and squalor. Instead of symbols of gross affluence and conspicuous consumption he emphasised sharing of community resources for the mass welfare. Nehru's vision was geared to, and dominated by, a certain 'pragmatic idealism' (Rathore 1989) which was a departure from Gandhi in some significant ways. While recognizing the importance of means as visualised by Gandhi, Nehru put more emphasis on the final goal – the establishment of a modern, secular, humanistic Indian society which would be founded by harnessing the latest science and technology. This culminated in the adoption of the Constitution based on the values of democracy, socialism and secularism. However, there has been a wide gap between these professed ideals and actual practice. This has led to wide ranging social unrest, violence and crime both at the individual and collective levels (Srivastava 1987, p.83). The increasing criminalisation of society, rampant corruption, and violence are reflections of a severe moral crisis confronting contemporary Indian society. The moral predicament has been brought about by a rapid erosion of morality in public life, a decline in ethical standards among both individuals and collectivities and disintegration of traditional social institutions under the impact of modernisation (Bidwai 1988, pp. 60-61). A new set of values centered around consumerism, and conspicuous consumption has taken root. These values and life styles are propagated mainly by those newly rich in rural and urban areas who have benefitted most significantly from the economic development and enhanced social mobility since Independence. Their new found wealth, often acquired by illegitimate means, and the absence of appropriate cultural values have resulted in a declining emphasis on the values of austerity, simplicity and savings. This newly rich middle class emphasises means over ends, opportunism and corruption, with limited controls over their behaviour. As in the industrial-economic sphere, the 'brokers and agents' in Indian politics have had a field day, personally benefitting economically, politically and socially. Because elections are expensive, politicians depend on funds raised from their allies in the business world. Licences, permits and quotas are doled out on the basis of state patronage, therefore businessmen become willing partners in the careers of their political allies. Over the years this spoils system based on mutual give and take has become well entrenched. Political corruption, election funds and black money are convenient allies of each other. As this process of collusion between big business and politics has advanced, the businessmen have gradually developed sufficient skills to manipulate the levers of political power for their own benefit. They are aware of the dependence of politicians on them for funds; they have discovered several loopholes in the system. They have learned about the many weaknesses of individual politicians so that they are almost in a position to manipulate or even blackmail them to their advantage.

4 Crime and Punishment: An Indian Perspective

The fact that crime and delinquency have been increasing is a fact acknowledged by many observers of the Indian crime scene. While the trends in traditional crime are better reflected in official statistics and show a persistent upward trend, the category of emerging social and economic crimes is poorly recorded and reflected in official statistics. But it is gradually overshadowing traditional crime both in its magnitude and impact. There has been a realization that the conventional approaches will not meet the growing challenges or yield the desired results. Only fundamental changes in the political and economic structure can contain the alarming trend in criminality related to the abuse of political and economic power. Since Independence there has been much discussion of the need to streamline the existing criminal justice system comprised of police, prosecution, the judiciary and the correctional system to enable it to cope with this new world of crimes. There has, however, been little actual change. With limited available resources, the problems of transforming a traditional, inequitable society into a modern democratic one has prevented policy makers from devoting sufficient time and attention to the criminal justice sector. There have been commissions and committees at the government level which have provided excellent recommendations on means to reform the existing legal, police, judicial and correctional systems. But most of their recommendations have had little chance of implementation. Criminal law solutions have been sought to solve economic and social challenges. Crime and other related social problems have been sought to be solved by social legislations. But the enforcement of these new legislations leaves much to be desired. At the same time there has been no concerted effort to streamline or eliminate some obsolescent and unjust laws which have become irrelevant in the current changing situation. Some of the ciminal laws are more than a century old and were formulated during the colonial rule under circumstances that are not relevant to the present. For example, only in 1973 the almost one hundred year old criminal procedure code underwent some modifications but these revisions, however, did not change the outmoded police or judicial process. On the other hand, some excellent traditional institutions of social control have declined under the impact of the 'modernization' process. Traditional India had very effective institutions at the village level known as Panchayat (village council). Furthermore, village courts used to serve as effective bodies of social control and agencies for dispensing justice at the local level. At a time when many countries are conducting experiments to enhance people's participation in the criminal justice system, India's ancient institutions of community participation are struggling for revival.

4.1 Penal Options

The Indian penal laws include both 'soft' and 'hard' options. Generally speaking, the approach towards juvenile and female offenders is 'softer' than for adult male criminals. Punitive strategies dominate because of a lack of facilities, resources, trained personnel as well as the persistence of conventional attitudes. The prime example is the legislation relating to juvenile delinquency. Despite the provisions in the very progressive Juvenile Justice Act of 1986, thousands of children were lodged in jails along with hardened criminals instead of being housed in reform schools as foreseen by the Juvenile Justice Act 1986. The Act came into force in 1987 but the Supreme Court had to pass an order to all state governments as late as May 1989 to establish 'within two months' the appropriate number and types of mandated juvenile institutions and to appoint the requisite number of probation officers. What this underlines is that despite legislated criminal justice reforms, little has been done in practice.

4.2 Female Offenders and Victims

The plight of female offenders is much worse as they are often subjected to various kinds of harassment, and even molestation. Instances of 'custodial rape' are not uncommon in India. It is for this reason that the Indian Law Commission in its 135th report on 'women in custody' suggested several changes in legal procedures to eliminate harassment of women in custody and to protect their rights. In the conservative Indian social system with its biased norms applying only to women, it becomes very difficult for a woman to report the offences of rape or molestation and pursue her case through the long and tortuous legal procedures. The law was changed and since 1983 the burden of proof has been shifted to the accused; he has to prove his innocence. The punishment for rape has also been enhanced and now ranges from a minimum seven years to life imprisonment. There is even stricter punishment for custodial rape – a rape committed by government officials entrusted with the woman's care. Increasing awareness among women of their rights and conscious efforts on the part of women's organisations have led to the enactment of several pieces of legislation to curb various traditional 'crimes against women'. Among these new laws are the Anti-Dowry Act, the Anti-Sati Act, the various laws to prevent teasing and molestation, and to prevent misuse of women's body in commercial obscene advertisements. Various strategies have been formulated to combat various forms of violence against women. These include strict execution of laws relating to crimes against women, effective cooperation between various women's organisations, voluntary agencies and the legal agencies, and creation of women police units.

4.3 Crime and Social Injustice

Apart from women, there are some other weaker sections in Indian society which have remained oppressed through centuries due to the rigid caste system. The Indian Constitution also recognizes such sectors of society as Scheduled Castes and Tribes. Centuries of indefensible repression continue unabated. Crimes of caste is a special category requiring state intervention and legal measures. The Untouchability Prevention Act and the Protection of Civil Rights Act 1955 failed to check the crimes against Scheduled Castes and Tribes. According to the 28th Report of the Commissioner for Scheduled Castes and Tribes (1989), the number of cases of murder and rape of Scheduled Castes and Tribes persons rose steadily from 1981 to 1986 (Indian Express May 5, 1990). The increase in such cases necessitated the enactment of the Scheduled Castes and Scheduled Tribes, Prevention of Atrocities Act of 1989, with more draconian measures containing such special provisions as the establishment of special courts to provide legal redress for this most oppressed group. The aim of the Act was laudable. Past experience with a similar Act, Anti-Untouchability legislation, suggests that after the Act became more punitive in 1976 the conviction rate fell. It declined from 27.8 per cent to 17.1 per cent in 1979 to 19.5 per cent in 1986. This suggests that when judges are faced with draconian penalties, they prefer to acquit or at least to apply more stringent rules of evidence in order to convict. In any case, the new legislation of 1989 is a reflection of both the magnitude of victimization of the traditionally downtrodden sections of Indian society as well as the current societal values and attitudes.

The alliance between the state power structure and the privileged strata of society (often acting through mafia power) has meant that the state machinery itself has been geared to safeguarding each other's mutual interests (Dube 1989, p. 8). In any situation of conflict between the privileged and the weaker sectors of society, the state machinery invariably comes to the rescue of the tormentors. The state has built up a criminal apparatus to commit or tolerate politically motivated violence and crime in society. The state is a mute witness or an active collaborator to many of the crimes committed against members of the Scheduled Castes and Tribes. Despite the professed ideal of removing longstanding discrimination suffered by a vast number of people, the disadvantaged have found little or nominal improvement in their intolerable humiliation and suppression.

The affirmative measures (Policy of reverse discrimination) have failed to make a real dent into the core of the problem (Shrivastava 1988, p. 179). As far as crimes against 'Harijans' are concerned, the practice of Untouchability was abolished by the Indian Constitution and was made a punishable offence in 1955. Despite this the state has failed to stem the growing crime, violence and atrocities against members of Scheduled Castes and Tribes. The very fact that new legislation had to be enacted (The Scheduled Castes and the Scheduled Tribes, Prevention of Atrocities Act, 1989, enforced on 30 January, 1990) with an unprecedented list of offences and punishments for atrocities against these castes shows that forty years of freedom have meant little for these sectors of society. The list of offences codified in this legislation illustrate the crimes commonly committed against members of these groups. They include: wrongful dispossession from a house or land, bonded labour, preventing an eligible person from voting, rape (including gang rape and custodial rape), parading a person publicly in the nude, assaulting or violating the modesty of a woman, instituting a false or malicious suit or other legal proceedings against an Scheduled Caste or Scheduled Tribe member, or subjecting a person or forcing him to eat or drink an obnoxious or inedible substance, or dumping excreta in his premises. Even the state machinery commits crimes against these groups as indicated by the fact that this new legislation provides specific penalties for public servants. The Act also mandates capital punishment for any person who intentionally gives false evidence which results in the execution of a member of these groups.

The fact of the matter is that criminal victimization takes place not only against the traditionally weaker sectors of society but also against the 'neo-poor' sections whose ranks have been swelling largely due to the distorted and uneven development of the economy. It is ironic that those who need the maximum protection of law receive the least of it: "As all governments represent the strong and profess to protect the weak, the state of the weaker sections of society has a direct and symbiotic relationship with the theory and administrative processes of criminal justice" (Sharma 1981, p. 196). This, in effect, signals a breakdown of the rule of law. The implication of this is that the rule of law is eroded to the extent that the politically and economically resourceful criminal gets away without suffering of any kind for his misdeeds. Apart from the immunity he may receive from his political allies, the various loopholes in law and legal processes come to his rescue. Charges against him may be filed but no further action is taken, deliberately or otherwise. He may be released on bail and get an opportunity to terrorise witnesses and complainants or destroy evidence. He may 'bargain' for a 'friendly' investigation and prosecution by bribing the police and other agents. The Indian judicial process is known for such legendary delays that the criminal can rest assured that nothing will happen to him for a long time, or even during his life time!

4.4 Capital Punishment

This brings us to another burning issue of contemporary penology, the death penalty and its status in India. Prior to 1956, the death penalty was routinely meted out. Moreover, the courts had to state the reasons for not awarding death sentence for offences punishable with death. By a 1955 amendment, the imposition of the death sentence was left to the discretion of courts. But they were provided no guidance. The question of its abolition was frequently raised both in and outside parliament. Through successive court decisions, the status of capital punishment has changed in India although it has not been abolished. The constitutionality of section 302 of the I.P.C., concerning imposition of the death penalty, was challenged on grounds that it provided unguided and unfettered discretion which violated the equality clause. After a significant Supreme Court ruling, it is now normal to award life imprisonment in cases of murder. In only the 'rarest of rare cases', the courts may award death sentence. This may be done only after recording 'extenuating reasons' for such sentence. According to 1988 statistical information furnished by the Attorney-General of India, only 30 persons had been hanged out of a total of 85,000 murder cases brought to trial during a five year period (Nariman 1989). Another ruling of the Supreme Court in a 1983 case laid down a principle: if a person under sentence of death is made to wait for a period exceeding two years for his execution- it is a violation of his right to speedy justice, and such delay would be grounds for substituting the death sentence by life imprisonment. Yet another Court ruling struck down the mandatory provision of a death sentence (Section 303) for murders committed by a life convict. The court found this provision unconstitutional in as much as it condemned the life convicts as a 'dangerous class'. This was an assumption, which in the court's opinion, was not supported by scientific data. Thus, the fate of the death sentence in India hangs in balance between the abolitionist and anti-abolitionist forces. On the other hand, some forms of crime like terrorism, smuggling and illicit trafficking in drugs have aroused serious concern and evoked demands for stiffer penalties including death. For example, the Narcotic Drugs and Psychotropic Substances Act of 1985 and the Prevention of Illicit Traffic in Narcotic Drugs Act of 1988 provide for death penalty for second or subsequent conviction for quantities above the minimum prescribed by law.

4.5 Challenge of Economic Crimes

Many have suggested a new strategy to deal with the 'economic offences' like tax evasion, adulteration, profiteering, generation of black money and similar criminality. As has been mentioned before, these offences affect the country's economy, the health and material welfare of the whole community, rather than the wealth and welfare of an individual victim. These crimes violate the Constitutional mandate given to the State to ensure that the operation of the economic system does not result in the concentration of wealth or means of production in a way that is detrimental to the common good. In a 1985 study conducted by the National Institute of Public Finance and Policy, it was found that in 1983-1984 there was approximately Rs. 37, 000 crores, or nearly a fifth of GNP in the black market. It constituted about 75 per cent of taxable income on which no taxes were paid. The report also listed the factors contributing to black money: high rates of taxation, unrealistic rules and complexity of controls, political and electoral contributions, inflation, steady decline in moral standards, corrupt tax administration, weak deterrence as well as other factors. Among the well known methods of generating black money were: under-invoicing, suppression of receipts, exaggeration of expenses and other forms of tax evasion. Black money is generally used in acquiring real estate, valuable ornaments, 'benami' transactions, exchange violations, and conspicuous consumption. It is in this context that the Indian Law Commission in its 47th report recommended that the substantive as well as procedural law relating to these crimes should depart from that applicable to ordinary crimes. Among some of these departures, it suggested shifting the burden of proof to the accused, enhancing the maximum penalties to reflect the social disapproval of these crimes, restricting judicial discretion and mandating minimum punishments, establishing special courts to deal speedily and effectively with these crimes, and using special provisions like preventive detention in certain cases. For certain offences, like smuggling and drug trafficking, preventive detention for more than three months is already being enforced.

Special drives are sometimes launched to cleanse the business and corporate world of its inherent corruption (India Today, Aug., 1989).

There is always a severe reaction from the corporate world. It is claimed by the corporate lobby that this 'raid-Raj' would adversely affect the industrial growth of the country. But over 90 per cent of the industrialists have violated one or another law because of what they claim are 'unrealistic policies'and stiff rules and regulations. They also complain that the corporate sector has been 'painted black' by undue and widespread publicity in the mass media concerning raids on and arrests of businessmen. They argued that this advance publicity prejudiced the general public and the persons affected would stand unjustifiably condemned. This situation symbolizes the changing social concerns, the shifts in legal policies, and the resistance met in dealing with the economic offenders.

4.6 Corporate Criminal Responsibility

There is a changing opinion about legal and judicial opinion about criminal responsibility for corporate crime. There has been a sharp debate in the Supreme Court about the criminal liability of the multinational Union Carbide, in whose Bhopal Plant one of the 'greatest industrial disasters of the world' occurred in December. As a result of this accident hundreds of persons were killed and thousands were blinded or left physically handicapped. As part of a compromise, the company has been granted immunity from all criminal liabilities. The case has been reopened in the Supreme Court. The judgement would have far-reaching implications for Indian jurisprudence relating to corporate criminal responsibility. Meanwhile, in another case of gas leaks involving an Indian industrial giant -the Shri Ram Food and Fertiliser Industries- the Supreme Court rejected their plea to exempt them from personal liability. The court held that the top men of the company can be excused only in case of sabotage or circumstances beyond human control. Otherwise, imposition of personal liability would ensure proper maintenance of safety devices which would considerably reduce, if not eliminate risk to the workmen and the surrounding community. The court further observed that, "if the contention of Shri Ram is that there is no risk, there is no reason why the officers should hesitate to give an undertaking to the courts that in case of death or injury they would be personally responsible". The new thinking in the judiciary is reflected in yet another case (Krishna Gopal Vs. State of M.P. 1986) decided by the Madhya Pradesh High Court. The judgement reads: "A vagrant commiting a petty theft is punished for years of imprisonment while a billion dollar price fixing executive comfortably escapes the consequences of his environmental crimes. Society is shocked when a single murder takes place, but air, water and atmospheric pollution is read merely as news without the slightest perturbance till people take ill, go blind, or die in distress on account of pollutants, that too resulting in the filling of pockets of a few".

5 Policing Society

The increased strength of the police is a good indicator of the growing dimensions of crime and the escalating societal reaction. In India, routine crime prevention and detection duties are assigned to civil police. According to the 'Crime in India' report, the total police strength in 1986 was 10,32,312. There were 31.4 policemen per hundred square kilometer area and 13.5 policemen per ten thousand population. A developing and complex society like India has been facing varied problems of internal security, civil disorders, and social tensions and unrest. In order to cope with these emerging problems special police forces have been raised from time to time, almost as an ad hoc and reactive measure. These special police and paramilitary forces have a total strength of more than 3.7 lakh. Although each force has been assigned a specific role, they sometimes get mixed up. These special police and paramilitary forces handle such varied problems as counterinsurgency, the maintenance of law and order when state or civil police prove incapable, the control of riots and mass violence which erupt frequently on caste, communal, linguistic and regional issues. They also protect central government establishments, railway property, serve in relief and rescue operations in times of natural crises, deal with terrorism which has now acquired alarming proportions in some parts of India, and provide police controls on the long international borders with neighbouring countries. Furthermore, they perform civil defence duties, and provide industrial security and protect VIPs. These diverse police functions reflect the broad range of problems occuring in Indian Society which necessitate new police forces and law enforcement agencies.

6 Conclusion

The previous analysis has shown that the criminalization of various sectors of society has occured because of certain social, economic and political changes. This is not to suggest that the normal social, political and legal processes have been overtaken by criminal processes. In fact, the anticriminal processes do contain them but the circumstances which could help in this containment are fast receding. The normal institutions -social, political, legal- need to be strengthened to stem the corruption. However, positive trends are not absent. Indian society has shown resilience in the face of difficult challenges. The neo-rich class values have not taken deep roots. People's awareness of the challenges, their desire for constructive reforms, and the processes of reconciliation do provide hope for containing, and even reversing the trend toward the criminalization of society. There is a hope for regeneration through those grassroot movements and social activists which are scattered throughout the length and breadth of India. The state itself has to take the lead in mobilizing for social action. It has to remove the crime and conflict producing potential of uneven development. It has to put legislative, judicial and media institutions back on track and restore their credibility and legitimacy.

References

Bidwai, P. (1988) "Acquisitive Hedonism", in: The Times of India Magazine, Nov.-Dec. 1988, pp. 60-62.

Dube, S.C. (1989) "Reflections on Rural Transformation: The Indian Context", Silver Jubilee Lecture, Department of Sociology, University of Jodhpur, March 8.

Indian Express (1990) "Reform the System", Editorial, May 5.

India Today (1989) "Crime, Money and Politics", New Delhi: August 31, pp. 22 – 29.

Nariman, F.S. (1989) "Shall we hang the death penalty", in: Indian Express Magazine, Jan. 22, p. 1.

National Crime Records Bureau (NCRB)(1986) Crime in India, New Delhi: Ministry of Home Affairs, Government of India.

Owomero, Basil O. (1987) "Crime Rates and Development in Africa: Empirical Analysis of Data from Nigeria, Kenya, and Tanzania", in: Indian Journal of Criminology, vol. 15, No. 2, p. 107-120.

Rathore, L.S. (1989) "Political Culture of India's Ruling Class", Presidential Address, Rajasthan Political Science Conference, Bhilwara, December, 4-5, p. 3.

Schur, E.M. (1969) Our Criminal Society, Englewood Cliffs, N.J.: Prentice Hall.

Srivastava, S.S. (1987) "Towards a Rational Criminology in Indian Context", Indian Journal of Criminology, vol, 15, July, p. 83.

Shrivastava, R.S. (1988) "Justice Model and Social Conflicts in Contemporary India", in: The Journal of Sociological Studies, vol 7, pp. 174-185.

Sharma P.D. (1981) Police, Polity and People in India, New Delhi: Uppal Publishing House.

Sandhu, Harjit S. (1987) “Low rates of delinquency and crimes in India: A case for strong social controls. “in: Indian Journal of Criminology, vol. 15, No. 1, pp. 9-16.

Teune, Henry (1990) “Comparing Countries: Lessons Learned” in: Comparative Methodology: Theory and Practice in International Social Research, Else Oyen ed., London: Sage

Part III
Crime and Control in Socialist Nations

Delinquency and the Development of Penal Sanctions in the German Democratic Republic (GDR)

Lothar Reuter

1 The Dynamics of Crime and Control

As available comparative analyses show, the GDR is a country with a relatively low level of delinquency. In 1987, 114,815 criminal offences were recorded in the territory of the GDR. The crime rate[1] 690 recorded offences per 100,000 population. The number of prosecuted offenders was 88,781, or a rate of 651 convicted offenders per 100,000.

These figures were taken from official statistics and it is, therefore, obvious that they do not reflect the true scale of the existing crime rate and need not be discussed in detail. The dark figures of delinquency, especially those concerning offences against property, have to be guessed at, as they are statistically immeasurable. If we analyze the official statistics, with all their inherent inaccuracies, a quite clear picture of long term trends in the level and dynamics of registered crime emerges, one in which there is a generally low level of crime commission. This situation is real and there is a high level of personal security for citizens. I would like to reject any suggestion that the criminal statistics of the GDR are manipulated to achieve propaganda effects. Our society is indeed not threatened by the alarming phenomenon of "delinquency" and there is no need to fear a snowballing crime rate .

The present level of delinquency is the result of a long, often contradictory process of social development. Social relationships have changed fundamentally and a social order has been created in which crime is becoming more and more alien. The decline in the crime rate is obviously linked with changes in social relations. We see evidence to affirm our Marxist belief in the social determinism of delinquency and the necessity for fighting crime at its true social roots. Having said this, there are extraordinarily complex social phenomena affecting crime commission. Consequently, delinquency and its development can not be explained uni-dimensionally. Thus, explaining the level and development of delin-

1 i.e. offenders per 100,000 inhabitants=rate

Table 1: Development of Criminal Offences[a]

Average of the years	Total	per 100,000 inhabitants
1946-1948 (3 years)	472,295	2,536
1950-1959 (10 years)	157,466	878
1960-1969 (10 years)	132,741	776
1970-1979 (10 years)	124,802	739
1980-1985 (6 years)	121,152	726
1980-1987 (8 years)	119,062	714

Notes:
a) Table1 was compiled by the author on the basis of th facts from section XXIV (dealing with the administration of justice) of the Statistical Yearbooks of the German Democratic Republic. Concerning 1987 see "Statistical Yearbook of the GDR 1988", Berlin 1988, p.395.

quency in the GDR only as a phenomenon of “Social Control” would be an unjustified simplification of the real problems and societal contradictions. Yet, we should not underestimate the impact that “Social Control” has on crime prevention in a socialist society. Conversely, the freeing of “Private” limitations and the release of social, democratic energies also creates new conditions. With this background, I would like to provide a statistical overview of the GDR crime rate over time.

In 1986, crime reached its lowest level since the founding of the GDR in 1949. At that time there were a reported 110,768 offences and a rate of 666 crimes per 100,000 population. An increase in 1987, possibly attributable to an extensive amnesty implemented in that year, did not alter fundamentally the long term trend towards a diminution of crime (see table 1).[2] The yearly fluctuations in the crime rate are a consequence of the anarchic character of delinquency. The statistical data are also affected by the execution of criminal policy. Amnesties always affect the crime rate and the amnesty of 1987 also affected the criminal statistics for 1988. Temporary rises in the crime rate are no reason for concern[3].

---

2 Table 1 was compiled by the author on the basis of the facts from section XXIV (dealing with the administration of justice) of the Statistical Yearbooks of the German Democratic Republic. Concerning 1987 see “Statistical Yearbook of the GDR 1988”, Berlin 1988, p. 395

3 The statistical recording of registrated cases was realized until 1963 according to the finally decisions given by the investigating authorities, with which the suspicious criminal offence was established. Subsequent decisions made by a public prosecutor or courts, which did not prove the suspicion, were not taken into account. Since 1st January 1964 the statistical recording of criminal cases

The altogether positive development in delinquency is, however, no reason for self-satisfaction and a diminution in the fight against crime. Without a doubt, crime in the GDR is still a mass social phenomenon which has negative effects on the society and the individual. These include the loss of personal security, considerable material damage and loss of confidence. The regressive trend in the crime rate is slowing down, one could speak of a flattening out of the crime rate curve. Further progress in stemming delinquency can in the end, probably only be achieved by progress in the social-economical field. The penal sanctions which form part of the criminal justice system are only one link in the chain of the entire societal complex of crime prevention. The effect of specific crime prevention measures are extremely difficult to isolate and even more difficult to guage. However, their basic task is to support the efforts of society in general in repressing and preventing delinquency. Penal sanctions not only punish offenders but also are intended to overcome the social reasons causing crime and assist in the social integration of offenders.

2 The Structural Problem of Criminality

It is of fundamental importance to understand the structural problem of criminality in order to analyze the level and development of crime in our country and the criminal prosecution strategies developed to deal with it. Changes in social conditions have affected the content of crime and have led to the decline in delinquency. The following data shows the structure

---

has been carried out at the time of the legal trial conclusion uniformly. That includes: the sentences by public courts; the hand-over of criminal cases to social courts; the decision to revoke maesures of criminal responsibility and temporary suspension of the proceedings (because the identity of the guilty person has not been found out or he is absent or because a transference of the case or an extradition of the accused/defendant to another state took place). The statistical recording is being carried out by respective public authorities, which (court, public prosecutor or investigating committee) make the decisions which conclude the trial. The statistics of criminal offences is being kept in the system of the public prosecutor uniformly. Concerning the theoretical basis of the criminal statistics in the GDR see H. Harrland (1963), Die Bedeutung der Kriminalitätsstatistik für die Leitung des Kampfes gegen die Kriminalität, ihre Folgen, ihre Organisation und ihre Arbeitsweise, PhD, Halle-Wittenberg, and H. Harrland et al. (1968) Kriminalstatistik (Leitfaden), Berlin.

of criminal offences during the last three years in the GDR, arranged in selected groups of punishable acts (total number of punishable acts).[4]

In 1987, 75.87% of all registered offences occurred in these few offence categories. Between 50 and 60% of all offences are crimes against property.

In a comparative study of the changes in delinquency, there is no point in including the immediate post-war crime data but this would clearly show the dramatic changes in crime rates. The following data clearly shows the main developments since the 1950's in crime against socialist property, a category of crime with particular legal-political relevance. Much crime against socialist property was committed in the GDR in the 1950's. It had a special meaning because much of it was aimed at the social-economical foundations of the new order. This criminality, however, was never as numerous as the offences committed against the personal property of citizens. In the early period of social development, repressive points of view concerning the use of criminal law against such offences predominated. Subsequently, after the socialist system became more secure, the criminal justice system adopted a policy that differentiated according to the seriousness of these offences. At this time, minor property offences were decriminalized (offences causing damage less than approximately 50 M were decriminalized). The vast majority of these offences have always been punished by sentences not requiring imprisonment. The principle of stake here is that all material gain realized by these offences should be lost. Justifiably, very little understanding is shown either in the legal or political arena to those offenders who commit offences such as speculation that result in shortages of essential goods needed by the population. This behaviour contravenes the moral concepts of the honest working citizens in our country.

Since the 1950's, offences against the national economy have undergone great changes. In 1958, 11,545 such offences were registered, but in 1987 there were only 782 cases. (see table 2).

The changeover to a new management system, the consolidation of socialist economy and the limitation and on private capitalistic activities led to a decriminalization of many offences against the economy. Because of the steps taken in 1961 to protect the GDR border, black marketeering and speculation from the west to east and east to west could no longer be committed. By forming agricultural production co-operatives, new conditions arose concerning the trade of farm products. The abolition of the system of compulsory delivery, against which many criminal acts had been aimed, eliminated the motive for these offences. Today we mainly have to deal with criminal acts which have caused serious damage such as shipping

4 See "Aus der DDR Kriminalstatistik 1987", in: Neue Justiz, vol.7, p. 285.

Table 2: Selected Offences [a]

	1985	1986	1987
Premeditated homicide	137	112	136
Wilful bodily harm	10,132	9,842	10,304
Rape	571	518	563
Intimidation and abuse for sexual acts	462	402	377
Sexual abuse of children	965	914	1,084
Sexual abuse of juveniles	148	136	156
Robbery and blackmail	758	768	781
Larceny of socialist property	20,885	20,290	20,504
Fraud/Fraudulent breach of trust to the detriment of socialist property	6,546	6,643	6,508
Crimes against national economy	601	590	782
Larceny of personal/private property	30,153	29,838	30,260
Fraud/Fraudulent breach of trust to the detriment of personal and private property	1,004	912	931
Arson	338	298	315
Negligent incendiarism	479	480	497
Causing a serious traffic accident	3,220	3,126	3,181
Endangering road safety through drunken driving	2,574	2,508	2,574
Unauthorized use of vehicles	4,786	4,301	4,320
Unauthorized possession of arms and explosives	337	275	294
Resisting a public officer in execution of his duties	1,098	1,045	981
Hooliganism	1,853	1,874	1,996
Acting as accessary after fact/ receiving of stolen goods	2,666	2,610	2,198
Forgery of documents	1,034	977	899

a) Source: "Aus der DDR Kriminalstatistik 1987", in Neue Justiz, 1988, 7, p. 285

Table 2 (continued): Proportionate calculations result in the following picture for 1987:

Offences	**Proportionate %**
(1) **Offences against property**	50.7
(2) **Assault cases**	10.0
(3) **Traffic offences**	8.8
(4) **Resisting public officers/Hooliganism**	2.6
(5) **Aiding and abetting/receiving stolen goods**	1.9
(6) **Sexual offences**	1.8

and air accidents, other accidents and fires caused by negligence. Today penal sanctions are intended primarily to protect the of economical discipline whereas in the 1950's and 1960's, their primary purpose was to defend the principals of the socialist economic system, especially in the planned economy.

Offences against national and public order always held and still hold special importance for the GDR. These offences which concern relations between the two German states are inseparably connected with the problems of guaranteeing security and stability. They have an explosive political nature. These criminal acts have greatly influenced the political and social climate in the country which helps explain the complexity of the legal-political procedures used against such offences. Legal-political guidelines have emerged which result in the strict treatment of violators of public order. Troublemakers and violent criminals are severely punished. Offenders can not count on tolerance from the state, if they commit acts which intentionally or aggressively undermine its authority or if they disrupt public order by leading anti-social lives.

Commission patterns for offences against life and health have shown very little change over the past 30 years. The rate of premeditated homicide cases has remained relatively constant and at a very low level. The fact that the courts in the GDR have not imposed the death-penalty for murder since the mid-1970's has had no decernable influence on the development of these crimes in the 1980's. Cases of premeditated bodily harm as well as premeditated homicide cases are mainly crimes committed spontaneously in certain conflictual situations. Cases of premeditated bodily harm are on the whole not serious offences. Almost half of the offenders are handled by social courts, but cases of particular brutality and ruthlessness are punished severely. Over the last 30 years the number of sexual offences has fallen considerably. In 1958 a total of 10,026 sexual offences were registered, but only 2,180 were reported in 1987.

While sexual crimes against children are as a rule punished severely today, other sexual crimes are treated with greater tolerance and some are not punished at all.

Two remarks should follow:

Firstly, certain crimes which are serious crime problems in other countries do not exist or have only minimal importance in the GDR. It is a fact that there is no addictive drug criminality in the GDR. Criminal violations of the addictive drug laws, a total of 40 to 50 per year, are almost always committed by aliens. In its pursuit of these criminal acts, the GDR adheres to the appropriate international obligations. No doubt, the declining criminal addictive drug problem is a significant advantage for the GDR. White-collar crime is also non-existent in the GDR. Furthermore, at this point in time, the GDR is not confronted with the problems of

Table 3: Offender Development

Year	**Offender**	**Per 100,000 of the criminally responsible population**
1980	99,881	729
1981	95,929	699
1982	92,447	675
1983	94,482	689
1984	93,504	683
1985	85,292	624
1986	82,753	606
1987	88,781	651

international terrorism. These crimes, linked with certain legal-political processes, do not have relevance for the GDR.

Secondly, new problems have developed in the GDR which have required criminalization, (eg. violations of the laws concerning environmental protection), or have prompted discussion about the necessity for criminalization, (eg. violations of the laws concerning computerized data). Here too, the GDR follows international trends.

First of all, an analysis of the impact of the justuce system reveals that the GDR, in comparison with other countries, has a relatively high percentage of solved cases, varying between 80 to 90%. We understand this to be an indispensable requirement for ensuring legal responsibility for everyone, regardless of their social position. To achieve these results requires a highly efficient system of criminal prosecutions. In my view, one cannot philosophise about the sense and purpose of penal sanctions if every second offender has the statistical chance of evading punishment.

The following summary shows certain trends in the development of the offender population in the 1980's.

An offender is defined as: Someone who was legally sentenced by a national court whose case was decided in a social court or was not considered to be criminally accountable.

Two groups of offenders are subject to special penal sanctions. These are recidivist and juvenile offenders. At first, there was a favourable trend in the number of recidivist offenders as the following statistical data[5] from the 1960's shows:

Whereas the proportion of offenders held answerable to the social

5 See H. Harrland (1968) "Zur Entwicklung der Kriminalität in der DDR", in: Neue Justiz, vol. 13, p. 393.

Table 4: Recidivist Offenders[a]

Year	Pre-convicted offenders		Offenders answerable to social courts		Together	
	Total	%	Total	%	Total	%
1964	18,433	20.0	2,127	2.3	20,560	22.3
1965	14,811	17.9	1,867	2.2	16,678	20.1
1966	15,457	17.9	1,663	1.8	17,120	18.8
1967	15,195	16.6	1,412	1.5	16,607	18.1
1968	14,281	17.5	1,400	1.5	15,681	19.2

Notes:
(a) Source: H. Harrland, Zur Entwicklung der Kriminalität in der DDR, in Neue Justiz, 1968, 13, p. 393

courts has remained unchanged, the proportion of previously convicted offenders has risen sharply, and at present, accounts for approximately one-third of all offenders. The proportion of recidivists has risen very quickly because of complicated problems facing the GDR. The necessary social integration of such offenders cannot be attained with the growing severity of penal sanctions. Those who see the causes of recidivism solely in the special maliciousness of offenders, ask for tougher measures. In contrast, those who ask about the social reasons behind the repeated criminality endeavour to eradicate the conditions. At present there is a new approach towards rehabilitating recidivists. The requirement that recidivist be subjected to harsher sentences will be eased to create better chances for the social reintegration of offenders.

In contrast to the situation with recidivist, there have been positive developments in trends concerning the offence rates of juvenile offenders. In the 1970's, approximately every fifth offender was a juvenile. The number of juvenile offenders has decreased sharply; they now account for only 15% of all cases. Only about every second juvenile offender is now sentenced by a court which also shows the relatively tolerant attitude towards crimes committed by juveniles. On the other hand, the last few years has shown an increasing intolerance of juvenile offenders who are stigmatised as problem children. Unreasonable strictness is often applied to these offenders.

3 Control Strategies

What I have spoken about so far, in my opinion, shows that delinquency and penal sanctions are inevitably connected. The appearance of certain types of crime -in our country at least- has caused a specific pattern of reaction. But obviously, criminality does not explain these patterns adequately. The political and moral systems values, developed during the GDR's history, have determined the application of penal sanctions.

On the other hand, penal sanctions themselves have undergone important changes. These changes have supplanted the penal sanctions and the sanctioning system of the 19th century (the Penal Code of the German Reich of 1871 which stayed in force in the GDR until 1968). The 19th century system influenced the first decades of GDR penal policy but it only provided for prison and penitentiary sentences. It did not deal with the increasingly complex crime which could be served by sentences not requiring imprisonment.

During the 1950's short prison sentences were already being substituted by probation although this was not the original intent of the law. It was not until the 1960's that a real change took place in penal policy. Conditional convictions have only been part of legal practice since 1958. This sanction grew ever more important. In the years 1961 to 1963, the system of penal sanctions was entirely revamped. The first penal code (still in force after four amendments) of the GDR was enacted in 1968. This code reflected socio-economic developments of our country including far reaching changes in social relations and moral concepts. In 1960/61 the socialist conditions of production appeared. The new penal sanctions permitted the reeducation of offenders through collective education at their workplace and in their residential environment. Such a system does not function automatically but requires close links between the criminal justice and the people. Today the direct participation of the public (not only through the traditional co-operation by means of jury service) in the criminal justice system has become an integral characteristic of our criminal justice system. It is also an indispensable part of the system of penal sanctions. This change in punishments was the result of a long evolutionary process and the resistance of many had to be overcome. An ideal state of affairs was not, however, created as the "Socialization" of criminal justice, of course, depends on the attainment of real democracy in a socialist society. It requires the active, conscious participation of all citizens.

Table 5.: Penal Sanctions In The Years 1964 and 1965 [a]

	1964	1965
Imprisonment sentences	18.6%	20.3%
Sentences without imprisonment	41.6%	37.5%
Hand-overs to Social Courts	32.4%	36.2%
Not sentenced	7.4%	6.0%

Notes:
100 = all offenders
(a) Source: H. Harrland, Zur Entwicklung der Kriminalität und einigen Problemen ihrer Bekämpfung, in Neue Justiz, 1966, 20, p.617

Table 6: Penal sanctions from 1961 to 1965

Year	Hand-overs to social courts	Sentences without imprisonment	Sentences with imprisonment
1961	13,5%	39.4%	47.1%
1962	28.1%	40.2%	31.7%
1963	30.7%	40.6%	28.7%
1964	35.0%	44.8%	20.2%
1965	38.5%	39.8%	20.7%

Notes:
100 = convicted offenders plus hand-overs (not including unsentenced cases)

In the 60's, a criminal legislation regulating the response to crime changed significantly and this remains the basic pattern up to the present.[6]

In my opinion, table 6 shows the changes clearly. Penal policy tries to limit the use of imprisonment to the shortest possible term. But grave forms of criminality still exist, it would be illusionary to demand a complete abolition of imprisonment. The protection of society and its citizens from serious crime by means of imprisonment is based on our concepts of humanism. But imprisonment itself must evolve and promote productive work, the only way a meaningful life can be realised.

In relation to the given questions, I would like to limit my analysis to the following few problems.

1. An important change in sanctioning practices is provided by the assignment of criminal cases to social courts (so called conflict committees in factories and facilities, and arbitration panels in the residential areas and co-operatives). The handing over of minor cases has occurred

6 See H. Harrland (1966) "Zur Entwicklung der Kriminalität und einigen Problememen ihrer Bekämpfung", in: Neue Justiz, vol. 20, p. 617.

Table 7: Hand-Overs To Social Courts From 1961 to 1965
(Calculated in handed over offenders; 100 = all convicted offenders plus handed over offenders).

Year	Hand-overs/Total Number	Hand-overs in %
1961	7,698	13.5
1962	24,261	28.1
1963	23,385	30.7
1964	27,888	35.0
1965	28,050	38.5

gradually since this procedure was first introduced at the beginning of the 1960's. It rapidly gained legal-political importance. Penal jurisdiction expanded into the social arena, a fact that was recognized constitutionally and institutionally.

Its development in the 1960's is shown by the following statistical picture:

This development led to a significant decline in the proportion of offenders convicted by state-run courts. The consequence of this trend was a clear mitigation of the penal reaction towards criminal offences. Significant decriminalization occurred through changes in penal legislation in 1968. This led to a decline in the percentage of cases handed over to social courts in the 1970's, especially those concerning minor offences against property. A further fall occurred in the 1980's. Often the preferred sanction was a fine imposed by the state-run courts because this seemed most appropriate for the crime committed. In 1982, the maximum fine was increased to 500 M, a change that was very quickly accepted. The following table[7] should clarify this development:

At present, approximately every fourth criminal case is handed over to the jurisdiction of the social courts. With certain criminal offences and groups of criminal offences, the average is much higher. This is explained first and foremost by variations in the seriousness of the offence. The following table should illustrate this for the years 1986 and 1987:

The extensive use of the social courts should not be viewed as excessive leniency. Because individuals are being prosecuted outside the traditional criminal justice system, this does not mean that they are avoiding prosecution. Rather, they are being subjected to a sustained form of public education. The social courts have proved effective in dealing with less serious offenders. One indication of their effectiveness is the extremely low rate of recidivism for offenders sentenced by these courts. It is almost

7 The information given in tables 8 and 9 has been calculated on the basis of the Statistical Yearbook of the GDR.

Table 8: Hand-Overs To Social Courts 1970 to 1986

Year	Hand-Overs/Totals	Hand-Overs in %
1970-74	24,018	27.5
1975-79	21,693	25.3
1980-84	20,617	22.6
1985	21,773	26.8
1986	20,651	26.3

Notes:
100 = Convicted offenders plus hand-overs

Table 9: Rate in percent of cases handed over, in selected crimes.

	Criminal Offences	1986	1987
1	Forgery of documents	73.6	75.5
2	Premeditated assault	44.4	43.7
3	Breach of the obligation to educate children	44.4	42.1
4	Acting as an accessary, receiving of stolen goods	34.9	37.8
5	Larceny of socialist property	36.4	35.6
6	Larceny of personal and private property	36.0	34.7

Notes:
100 = Convicted offenders plus hand-overs.

impossible to overestimate the work of the social courts in criminal matters. These courts are effective because their democratically elected members show an untiring commitment to a high level of order and discipline.

2. The change in sanctioning practices is related to the expanded use of sentences not requiring imprisonment. Probation is increasingly being used as a penal sanction. Fines have played only a secondary role both before and after the enactment of the 1968 Penal legislation. Their status was clearly enhanced by the High Court in 1979 but they have not displaced the heavy reliance on probation. The sanction imposed is determined by the particular elements of each case. The main advantage of sentencing convicted offenders to probation is that the burden is placed on the offenders ties to the community. These obligations also serve as a public control on the behaviour of the offender (e.g. through the obligation of regularly reporting to his/her work team about their fulfillment of probationary duties). The sentence is thus stripped of its anonymity. In suitable cases, offenders are supported by teams and individuals who take on the responsibility of guarantor. This is done by non-professionals

Table 10: Number of Judicially Certified Guarantors.

Year	Guarantors
1970 - 1979	4,971
1980 - 1984	5,782
1986	5,597
1987	4,877

because the GDR has no professional social workers to deal with offenders. Experience with these judicially certified guarantors has proven successful in reintegrating offenders. But much depends on the commitment of the citizens involved and the willingness of convicts to fulfill their respective obligations.

3. A serious problem with the existing justice system is that it does not take the victim into consideration. GDR legislation in 1968 tried to link victim compensation directly to penal sanction. This is most evident in the practices of social courts that as an educative measure impose obligations concerning compensation for loss or injury. In the case of probationary sentences, the state courts are expected to require compensation when the offence caused material damage. This obligation is part of the terms of probation and does not affect any compensation claims that may be made under civil or industrial law. The legislature has debated whether penal sanctions should be abolished in favor of sentences involving compensation. Many have advocated such a perspective.

4. The abolition of the death-penalty in 1987 is one of the most noteworthy changes in the system of penal sanctions .[8] The death penalty was last imposed in the 1970's, but it's abolition precludes its application in the future. The GDR never saw the death-penalty as a permanent sanction but a fact of its history. For example, in the postwar period, the death-penalty was a necessary sanction to punish those who had committed serious war crimes and crimes against humanity during the Second World War. By abolishing the death-penalty, the GDR naturally responded to worldwide demands for its abolition.

To close, I would like to summarize a few of the main ideas: The development in our country, affirms the assumption that socialist conditions gradually eliminate the social causes of criminality. A long and contradictory process has achieved a long-term decline in the crime rate. A new moral perspective on punishment has facilitated the introduction of new penalties. The core of these penal sanctions are the community social re-educational influences on the offender, probation and victim compensa-

---

8 See E. Buchholz (1987) “Abschaffung der Todesstrafe in der DDR”, in: Neue Justiz, vol. 10, pp. 398ff.

tion as a form of punishment. Social control, assistance and reintegration as well as the "normalization" of the relations between the victim and the offender are objectives of the penal sanctions. Penal sanctions have moved in the direction towards more leniency, but not towards more clemency. Sanctions have reflected the differences among offences, reserving a repressive penal policy.[9] In this respect the GDR remains open to the experiences of other nations.

9 In this connection the above mentioned extensive amnesty, which the State Council of the GDR decided on 17th July 1987 is to be referred to once more. It had an extraordinary legal-political effect. As a result of the amnesty, 24,621 sentenced people who had had to face imprisonment were released from the execution of their sentences, in 2,741 cases the given prison sentences were not enforced. The criminal procedure was stopped for 1,753 cases concerning persons who had been on remand. In 311 cases the sentence of life imprisonment was reduced to 15 years imprisonment (see the interview with the Chief State Counsel of the GDR published in the periodical Neue Justiz, 1988, p. 63). The amnesty did not effect offenders who had been sentenced for murder and spionage as well as to persons who had been called to account for Nazi- and war crimes or for crimes against humanity, only. The releases from imprisonment resulting from the amnesty led to a radical reduction in the number of prisoners. Concerning the view of comparing legal systems, see H. Roggemann (1987) "Amnestie in beiden deutschen Staaten", in: Recht in Ost und West, vol.5, pp. 281ff.

Crime Control and Crime Policy in Hungary

Katalin Gönczöl

1 Introductory Thoughts

Hungary's large prison population indicates that Hungarian criminal policy is considerably more punitive than the European norm. The number of prisoners per 100.000 inhabitants is four to five times greater than that found in the most civilized countries of Europe. In 1988 the total number of prisoners in Hungary was 20,821 which represented 196.0 prisoners per 100,000 inhabitants. In Europe, Turkey and the United Kingdom have the highest rates of imprisonment but their prison populations are 50% less than Hungary's. The reason for this unfavourable comparison is to be found in sentencing practices because a comparison of pre-trial detention shows Hungary in a relatively favourable light.[1]

The relatively frequent imposition of custodial sentences cannot be explained in terms of the stucture of delinquency or of the number of increasingly dangerous criminals. Law and order today are essentially healthier than, for example, in Italy, Spain or the United Kingdom. Indications of organised crime – particularly of organised international crime – are barely noticeable. International drug traffic only passes through Hungary and although the modern, mainly metropolitan forms of violent crime have already appeared, the majority of the prison population does not consist of the perpetrators of such crimes.

It could, of course, be argued that the nature of Hungarian crime and the struggle against it are influenced by historic traditions and that, although international comparisons may be informative, they are never authoritative. However, the actual codification and application of sentencing policy involves a choice of values which themselves originate in the political system. From the European standpoint and from the standpoint of achieving legal statehood, a civilized and humane criminal policy is as important an institution as social insurance or the freedom of the press.

In this paper I shall not attempt to assess the extent to which the prison-centred outlook of Hungarian criminal policy is the consequence of a monolithic power stucture. I have written about this elsewhere (Gönczöl

---

1 Pre-trial detention in Hungary applied to only 13,6% of all prisoners in 1988. There are countries where this reaches almost 70%.

1989). I shall, rather, search for an explanation in prevailing legal policy and developing legal practice, from which the broad forms of custodial punishment originated. My suggestions for reform rely heavily on aspects of modern European legal development. However, throughout I strive to bear in mind that nothing can be automatically transplanted from the legal system of one country into that of another. Nothing in this area has universal validity; there is no perfect solution. Attempts to influence the moral judgments of broad strata of the population and the sanctions applied to them, must take account of the customs and values of the society which have evolved over time. When developing new solutions one has to take into consideration the prevailing levels of tolerance and social cohesion which reflect those norms and the values of a society which are generally accepted as authoritative and binding.

2 Hungarian Criminal Policy in the 1980s

In the Penal Code, introduced in 1979, non-custodial forms of punishment increased to a significant extent. In addition, rules appeared which were aimed at the limitation of custodial forms of punishment or were directly intended to reduce the prison population. According to the prevailing Penal Code, the sanctions, which previously could be exclusively applied as supplementary punishments within the sphere of less serious criminal acts, could now instead be imposed independently as principal punishments (e.g. prohibition against practising a profession; or a ban from driving). Correctional work remained one of the principal punishments. The 1984 amendment to the Penal Code which introduced aggravated correctional work can only be seen as a step backwards. If it had been widely applied, the number of those subjected to imprisonment would have increased since, in addition to the obligation to work at a designated place, the 1984 amendment also stipulated residence at a specified place of accomodation. In 1987, the scale of penal sanctions was widened again with the introduction of community work. Regulations which might be independently implemented, occasionally explicitly in place of imprisonment, also increased. For example, this could have resulted from the introduction of probation for adult delinquents. Theoretically, during probation there is an opportunity for social integration: the Penal Code introduced supervision for persons on probation. In such cases, the court could also specify behavioural conditions, the adherence to which is promoted and supervised by probation officers. Prison sentences of not longer than two years could be suspended, those who were given suspended sentences were placed on supervision. Theoretically, this could have increased the sphere of social control where the aims of punishment will be achieved even without imprisonment. The provision of social support and supervision by the probation officer was intended to further both special and general prevention. With regard to this, the suspended sentence was also extended to recidivists.

The aim of reducing the prison population was explicitly expressed in an amendment which reduced maximum penalties and increased the minimum period of imprisonment from 30 days to three months. The same aim resulted in legislation extending the range of criminal acts by such alternatives to imprisonment such as correctional work or a fine. The wide-scale implementation of parole also resulted in the reduction of the prison population, although the prevailing Penal Code excludes multiple recidivists from this provision.

Notwithstanding the two amendments referred to above, the system of sanctions has, broadly speaking, been in existence since 1979. The most conspicuous fact is that quite contrary to the intention of the legislature, the proportion of enforceable prison sentences did not decrease, but remained unchanged. The various forms of non-custodial punishment were not applied with sufficient frequency by the courts (see table 1). In fact, they hardly made any use of the new form of punishment, namely the imposition of supplementary punishment as a principal punishment. It was used in less than half a percent of cases. The proportion of fines also decreased markedly, while in 1977 46.1% of all the principal punishments were fines, between 1984 and 1988 this fell to an average of 37%. The frequency of suspended prison sentences did not change and, while probation increased, this was not significant.

This unintended outcome was caused by the simultaneous effect of various factors. Most important were adverse developments in the structure of crime; an increase in the incidence of serious crime and an increase in recidivism. A fall in detection rates was another factor. As a result, the courts were compelled to consider several crimes at one hearing.

The fact that the proportion of custodial sentences did not decrease was also due to the law itself. Certain acts such as slander, formerly punishable by a fine, were decriminalised. This led to a reduction in the incidence of fines but it also contributed to the more frequent application of custodial sentences and the implementation of more rigorous sanctions against recidivists.

More detailed scrutiny of sentencing outcomes supports the above conclusions (see table 2). In 1988, only 16% of delinquents sentenced to imprisonment were first time offenders,: 21,8% were persons with a record who were not recidivists, while the remaining 62.2% were recidivists, multiple recidivists or special recidivists. One should also take into

Table 1: Punishments and Measures in Hungary 1984-1988

Year	**1984**		**1985**		**1986**		**1987**		**1988**	
Genre of Principal Punishment	**Figure**	**%**	**Figure**	**%**	**Figure**	**%**	**Figure**	**%**	**Figure**	**%**
Death Sentence	1	-	2	-	1	-	5	-	3	-
Prison punishment enforcable	16,004	26.39	15,975	27.34	16,200	25.71	15,783	23.57	13.851	21.00
Prison punishment suspended	13,074	21.55	12,818	21.94	14,035	22.15	13,479	20.13	10,754	16.30
Aggravated correctional work	-	-	357	0.61	920	1.45	822	1.23	820	1.24
Correctional work	2,777	4.58	2,478	4.24	2,407	3.80	2,319	3.46	2,312	3.51
Fine	21,079	34.76	19,575	33.50	21,891	34.55	25,770	38.49	25,735	39.02
Independent measures[(a)]	7,424	12.25	6,998	11.98	7,538	11.90	8,463	12.64	12,155	18.44
Independent supplementary punishment	281	0.47	227	0.39	276	0.44	313	0.48	323	0.49
Total	60,640	100.0	58,430	100.0	63,358	100.0	66,959	100.0	65,953	100.0

Source: Information on criminal investigation, 1988. Budapest, 1989 p. 87
(a) Independent measures: court admonition, probation, forced treatment, detoxication cure with work therapy, reform school, confiscation.

consideration that in the 1980s the proportions of first time offenders decreased annually, even if not significantly (Pateva 1987; Tavassy and Pateva 1988). These two factors suggest that the rise in the number of recidivists who committed further crimes contributed significantly to the overall level of custodial sentences. However, it is not clear that criminal careers of recidivists do, in fact, consist of particularly dangerous crimes. This is confirmed by the fact that 50.7% of special recidivists and 59.0% of multiple recidivists were sentenced to less than one year's imprisonment, while a further 23.3% of special recidivists and almost 11.0% of multiple recidivists were given non-custodial sentences.

Because more than 62.0% of custodial sentences (in 1988 this meant 8,081 persons) were for less than one year, Table 2 also indicates that the use of non-custodial punishments could be expanded. A fair number of cases- can be found where the imposition of a prison sentence could have been avoided.

The preceding paragraph also shows that there are conceptual obstacles to the development of a more differentiated criminal justice system than the present one. Particularly where the aim of punishment is special prevention, sentencing requires consideration not only of the severity of the criminal act but also of the personality of the offender, his circumstances and motives for his offence (Gönczöl 1980, p. 710). Experience seems to confirm that the sentencing authorities did not pay sufficient attention to all these factors, although this has been expected of them for quite some time. Directive Number 12 of the Supreme Court dated 1977, concerning the evaluation of aggravating and mitigating circumstances, placed a duty upon the courts: in the interest of a unified sentencing procedure, it called for: "The examination of the circumstances promoting the perpetration of crime – and the examination of the personality in an appropriate framework – as of outstanding importance in the imposition of punishment, without which differentiated imposition of punishment cannot be ensured. The personality of the offender always has to be examined in the assessment of the act. To this end, it is absolutely necessary that the investigating authority should strive in a more determined manner for the thorough assessment of the circumstances which can be evaluated from the point of view of the imposition of the punishment".

In the past decade, I have frequently drawn attention to the fact that the investigation and evaluation of personal circumstances are preconditions for the imposition and execution of every just punishment. From this viewpoint, criminal procedure creates a complex unity: information collected in the various stages of the procedure ought to serve not only as the basis of the next stage, but ought to also serve the aims of punishment. Thus, during the investigative process, it is necessary to gather not only

Table 2: Validly sentenced adult offenders according to the extent of principal punishment 1988

		Prison Punishment				Correctional Work				
	To be implemented									
Sentenced Offenders	Total	Death sentence	Total	from this under one year	Suspended	Aggravated correctional work	designated work place	community work	Fine	Independently applied supplementary punishment and measure
with a clean record	37,953 63,5%	-	2,081 5.5%	832	6,797 18.0%	224 0.6%	1023 2.7%	13 0.003%	20,787 54.8%	7,028 18.4%
punished persons not qualified as recidivists	11,784 19.7%	-	2,833 24.0%	1,854	2,994 25.4%	276 2.4%	727 6.3%	25 0.002%	3,943 33.5%	986 8.4%
recidivists	1,602 2.7%	1	867 54.2%	635	18 1.1%	46 2.8%	161 10.0%	3 0.2%	395 24.7%	111 6.9%
special recidivists	2,833 4.7%	1	2,172 76.7%	1,437	5 0.2%	88 3.1%	105 3.9%	1	344 12.1%	117 4.1%
multiple recidivists	5,634 9.4%	1	5,015 89.0%	3,323	-	171 3.0%	63 1.1%	-	355 6.3%	29 0.5%
Total	59,806 100,0%		12,968	8,081	9,814	805	2,079	42	25,824	8,271

Source: Statistical report of the Ministry of Justice about 1988

those facts which facilitate sentencing, but also those which further the aims of punishment. For example, educational programmes associated with specific deterrence clearly require the collection of specific data. At the same time, those responsible for the implementation of the punishment cannot disregard the danger of the act to society. Those charged with executing the punishment cannot say that they will only deal with the criminal's personality because the question of the extent of culpability has already been considered at the sentencing stage. For the concept of culpability can be regarded as an indication of a tendency to commit dangerous acts. Thus the available information can be utilised in the controversial re-integrational programme. The same principles ought to guide judges in the prison as well as probation officers. They have to start out from the factors set out in the sentence, even if their activity takes place at the end of the implementation of the prison sentence. They have to compare the results obtained from the prison sentence with these and then to evaluate all former information. They have to assess which measures are necessary in the given case to obtain social integration (Gönczöl 1980; 1987; 1989).

It is not the courts and other elements of the criminal justice system which can be held responsible for the failure to achieve the aims set out in the Penal Code. It has again been found that the law itself, however progressive, is not able to break through existing legal conventions. Results can only be obtained through structural changes. The controllers of the criminal justice system cannot change the objective and subjective conditions necessary for its execution by means of declarations published from above, criticising existing legal practice. The number of criminal cases in the past ten years has increased to an extent that exceeds the capacity of the system to sentence rationally. At the trial, courts will never be able to fully take into account the personal circumstances of the offender. The investigating authorities, partly because of their conventional role in the judicial process and partly because of the increasing number of cases, cannot satisfy this requirement. If they impose a sentence, without knowing the most significant part of an offender's personal circumstances, then the sanction cannot be adjusted according to the complex sentencing requirements. As a result, the likelihood of any possible favourable effect of the sentence will further decrease and the aim of special prevention will, at best, be achieved by chance.

The expressed aims of criminal policy cannot be achieved because of the previously discussed problems involved in imposing punishments, but also because the penal system is dysfunctional. The aims stipulated in the law concerning prison sentences are unattainable if there is only one qualified instructor for every 80-150 convicted persons.

The successful achievement of non-custodial forms of punishment and the social integration of those who have served time or have been released from other forms of detention, is the responsibility of the professional probation service. This system also handles tasks linked with the implementation of punishment. The full-time probation service for juveniles was set up twenty years ago, while that for adults has a history of over ten years. The probation service for those given suspended prison sentences, those allowed on probation or released from custody, consists of hardly more than 100 probation officers for adults and 300 professional specialists, mostly university graduates for juveniles. Among the latter, each probation officer deals with 180-260 cases every year. Since 1976, the number of probation officers for adults has increased fourfold, while the number of cases increased ten-fold (Wenner 1988). Probation officers specialising in juvenile cases, operating within the Child and Juvenile Protection Institutes, and probation officers dealing with adults in the county courts are already unable to handle their caseloads.

It has long been my conviction that the reform of the probation service is a necessary condition for the more frequent implementation of forms of non-custodial punishment and for the improved selection for probation of those offenders at present sentenced to imprisonment. It is for this reason that I initiated a project in the Ministry of Justice, identifying the main operational conditions of the present system. In the concluding study summarising the research results, Mária Dér, a professional probation officer, characterised the probation service in the following manner: "An organisation set up to prosecute the probationer, which demands and threatens, then punishes on the basis of behavioural rules and believes that it thereby satisfies its preventive task: with its almost ridiculous, narrow-minded system of requirements, it only alienates and gives rise to further deviance" (Dér 1989, p. 142).

Even if I regard this statement as somewhat exaggerated and do not relate it to the work of individual probation officers, but to the operation of the organisation, I must agree with the general stance. Research results clearly illustrate that today the probation service operates primarily as an organisation for punishment, serving the authorities. It is repressive in character, although when it was set up the task of providing social support was finely balanced with those of social control and crime prevention.

The role conflict and dysfunction which are present in the organisation of the probation service, conceal the failure to acquire sufficient information throughout the criminal process. Because of the lack of knowledge concerning an offender's personal circumstances or because of the rigidity of the law, the courts passed probation orders in cases when this was not appropriate from the standpoint of social integration. In most cases, the period of probation and the stipulation of behavioural rules are not adjusted to the individual requirements of the convicted person. Where probation lasts longer than is necessary, the relationship between the probation officer and the convicted person becomes formal. Rules of behaviour which fail to take into account the individual character of the offender cannot be respected. Its enforcement is unreasonable, but it is an obligation laid down in the provision of law. The lack of information affects the effectiveness of the probation officers. Approximately two-thirds of prison instructors' reports do not contain information about the offenders' qualifications, work courses attended in the prison, the quality of the work carried out, their work attainment or their health (Kevezsi 1989). In the absence of information, it is impossible for them to obtain a job even if there is a considerable shortage in the labour market.

Placing the probation service within an institutional system is controversial and the procedural position of the probation officer is poor. Probation officers for juveniles operate within the child care network, their sphere of authority differing in different regions, and occasionally in different towns. Sometimes they only carry out protective, child care assignments, at other times they take on family care cases. Although both tasks require social workers, it is doubtful whether, given their very different nature, they can be carried out by staff with identical training. The probation officers' work is hindered by the fact that the competent public guardianship authority is bureaucratically wedged between the courts and their own activity. It is mostly because of this that in 12% of cases there is a delay of 4-6 months in allocating the case. The resulting lack of contact with the offender can be a direct cause of recidivism (Dér p. 7). The investigation also showed that adult probation officers did not become integrated into the judicial system, their prestige was low and their salary was not commensurate with their qualifications.

The efficacy of both juvenile and adult probation and the reliability of sentencing are endangered by the fact that it is exceptional for the probation officers' opinion to be asked for by the court. The information and knowledge accumulated by probation officers concerning specific cases could well be utilised either in the decision about the future of the probation order or in deciding how to deal with a subsequent offence. Under the existing legal rules, probation officers' competence is limited to positively influencing the living conditions of offenders.

The de facto role of the probation service, as an agent of social control, has become apparent primarily due to changed social circumstances. The social and educational circumstances of offenders have deteriorated. Compared to the 1970s, the proportion of unskilled persons in the population has increased; that is, persons living in straitened circumstances with no permanent job (Gönczöl 1988). The solution of their problems of reintegration into the community provides probation officers with a very difficult task. It is particularly alarming that, in comparison with the 1970s, there is a considerable deterioration in the economic and environmental factors which determine offenders' living conditions.

With the movement towards a market economy, companies no longer have an interest in maintaining full employment. It is largely due to this that those who have served time or have been released from various institutions were not able to find employment as they were under the old conditions. In this situation, it has become impossible for increasing numbers of discharged offenders to find accomodation. The earlier social policy linked with the economy, has not been replaced either by the state administration or the traditional system of social service organisations. According to our data, gathered in the summer of 1989, 87% of probation officers were unable to find work for their charges within three months and 50% of them indicated complete deadlock in finding accommodation within their administrative region (Dér 1989, p.80). An increasing number of persons are released from prison with resources to provide at most a few days subsistence. Their support is the responsibility of local councils. The increasing demand for assistance, the small amount of money available for distribution and the bureaucratic nature of council support drives the discharged offenders into an uncertain existence. Furthermore, without a permanent home, they cannot even appeal for support (Wenner 1988). It is obvious that the probation officers are almost completely reduced to providing social services and support. They are constrained by their bureaucratic organisation and therefore, make concessions to the formal requirements. Their activity is, therefore, dominated by the authoritative enforcement elements and paper work.

Their situation is aggravated as their professional qualifications are inappropriate to adjust to the new circumstances. In the main they are teachers by qualification. Previously, they could acquire the most important knowledge through self-education. But today it is vitally important for them to have some knowledge of society and sociology. In order for probation officers to extend their own sphere of activity and achieve new skills necessary to represent the interests of their clients, they also need to acquire a considerable amount of legal knowledge including penal, adminstrative law, civil, criminal, labour, social insurance and family law.

The courts have some, albeit not very detailed, information about the operation of the probation service, and the basic problems expounded above. If the courts adhered to the Penal Code, and followed the intentions of those who control legal implementation, they would impose probation, suspended prison sentences with a probation order and parole, as well as combined probation, more frequently. But they would be proceeding in an irresponsible manner. Given awareness of the actual danger of recidivism, they would be turning loose a mass of offenders onto the strugging probation service and, moreoever, onto society. This would include the offenders who are presently, even if only for a short time, in prison, or in secure custody.

We have thus come full circle. Without comprehensive reforms the prison population in Hungary cannot be significantly reduced. In 1989, the political reform movements facilitated the reduction of the prison population. With the suspension of preventive detention, with the granting of a limited amnesty, with the release of conscripted conscientious objectors and vagrants, the total prison population decreased by 870. In a single stroke, these measures put an end to basic anomalies linked with civil rights. Every further improvement requires complex co-ordination primarily in the criminal and socio-political spheres. Significant results cannot be expected merely by amending the law or by issuing legal directives.

3 Possible Reforms

When advocating comprehensive domestic reforms, a stand must first be taken on the much discussed question of the primacy of the act or of the offender. On several occasions, I have expressed the opinion that the basis of criminal responsibility must be the act which is dangerous to society, and that punishment must be adjusted accordingly. This standpoint excludes the possibility of a personality-based conception of punishment (Gönczöl 1989). On the other hand, I agree with András Szabó (1987) and accept the necessity for the individualisation of punishment as such, in order to correct inequalities created by formal legal equality. I do not fully agree with the view, recently represented by Károly Bárd (1987, p. 206), according to which criminal procedure can only be built on formal legal equality, since the trial is not the place to reveal social inequalities and even less to eliminate them. Bárd (pp. 221-222) is correct when he says that criminal jurisdiction is not due to, and therefore cannot undertake, the elimination of social injustices and inequalities. Furthermore, it is not the task of the criminal justice system to take on the role of institutions charged with the socialisation of the individual or to remedy their failures. Its task is rather to impose punishment for the comission, thereby acting as a rational and deterrent force against the offender. If the punishment is to have deterrent force, this also depends on the extent to which the persons to be punished evaluate their situation in light of the punishment. Hacker (1924, p. 42) wrote 75 years ago: "This is why we see so frequently – that the deterrent force of punishment is less among members of the lower social classes; they lose less during the implementation and execution of the punishment".

If, during the criminal procedure, no light is cast on the individual circumstances of the offender, then the sentence may be very just from the standpoint of formal equality, but unreasonable from the standpoint of the person concerned. Alternatively, it may be more detrimental than intended and therefore unjust. For example, a fine unpaid because of social circumstances, which is then changed into a prison sentence, means graver legal consequences than a fine of the same sum in another case, which only involves giving up a small proportion of an individual's income. A similar injustice would result if prison sentences were to be imposed only and exclusively by reference to the act, for they would not have the same consequences for different categories of offenders. For some, prison is a haven, for others a stopping point on the road to becoming a social outcast. Both situations should be avoided unless, for the protection of society, deprivation of freedom is unavoidable. In some cases, punishment can accomplish its aim through the imposition of a probation order, a ban on driving, a ban on engaging in one's profession, or a suspended prison sentence of a longer period combined with victim reparations, or with a subsidiary punishment of a fine. Which sentence is sufficient and just in a particular case can only be decided in light of the offender's circumstances. It is, therefore, essential to discover personal characteristics and to view them as elements of the case. This permits the individualisation of punishment which is a task of the criminal justice system. If one can accept this in principle, then it must be made obligatory for those who participate in the criminal justice system to expose these characteristics and to ensure that the knowledge is used in the sentencing process.

However, it is already quite clear that the information currently available to probation officers should be better utilised in sentencing than it is at present. The broad-scale application of non-custodial punishment is inconceivable without the acquisition of a pre-sentence report. To this end, the constitutional position of professional probation officers needs to be altered, they must be regarded as authorities assisting the court. The organisation of the probation service must be integrated into the criminal justice system but not into the sentencing process. The institutionalisation of individualisation in connection with non-custodial punishments makes it absolutely necessary that the promise of the offender, his word of honour and his agreement with the court be incorporated in the Hungarian criminal justice system. Csaba Kabodi (1989) wrote: "If criminal law can base special procedures on the confession of the offender, I do not see that the promise of the culprit to the judge should be risky from any point of view. After all, if he undertakes to commit a crime, then he cannot be stopped from committing his offence, nor from disposing of his own future: whether he feels himself able to engage in community work or not, or rather chooses to serve a prison sentence".

A similar declaration would be necessary to undergo certain treatment or attend school. The requirement that one obtain the offender's word of honour indicates that he is not only the object, but also the subject of criminal procedure, and is responsible for his own future.

If we take the necessity for reducing the prison population seriously, and we cannot really do anything else. Then we must develop the necessary infrastructure for a wider application of non-custodial punishments than exist at the present time. Hostels for the homeless should be set up, as well as institutions providing employment for the unemployed. At present, such institutions are mostly absent from the Hungarian institutional system. The most obvious and simple solution would be for institutions intended for the direct prevention of recidivism to be developed within the penal system. However, this is a trap. The limits of the competence of penal power must be taken into consideration. An institution cannot be a realistic alternative to prison if it is within the penal system. Even though it is operated by the probation service and described as an accommodation for the homeless, it can always develop sooner or later into a place for secure custody. They are realistic options in areas where temporary half-way houses receive offenders and newly released persons in such a way that the probation officer co-operates with the social worker employed at the temporary accommodation. Consequently, non--custodial forms of punishment developed for offenders, who require social or other types of assistance, must be linked to the existing, albeit inadequate, social, health, educational and cultural institutions. Criminal policy can demand the development of institutions to satisfy special needs, but by itself, within its own framework it cannot accomplish the tasks which other organisations have failed to perform.

However, the above does not exempt the probation service from self development. The introduction and implementation of new types of non-custodial disposals cannot be achieved without a considerable increase in the number of probation officers, mainly for adults. As I have indicated, completion of their qualifications could be similar to those of social workers armed with legal knowledge, because their work assignment can only be imagined within a criminal justice sytem. The probation service responsible for juveniles and that responsible for adults, should be integrated while preserving their distinct competence. It is possible that the integrated service should be directed by the judge in the prison, their roles are intertwined and their efficiency in handling individual cases would be increased with co-operation.

After having resolved these conceptual and structural dilemmas it is possible to embark on reform and codify the law. However, this process would take several years, because the introduction of these innovations would require lengthy preparation. To achieve these new ideas on the probation service, can only be accomplished together with the development of the organisation itself. The scope of community service should be considered. Short-term imprisonment can be seen in a new light (Szük 1987). Probation service and suspended prison sentences, which nowadays seem to merge in practice, should be clearly differentiated. Suspended prison sentences should possibly be increased to two or three years (Nagy 1986). Our commitments in international agreements make the termination of forced labour a necessity (Kabódi pp. 12-13).

These sketchy recommendations are summary in character but they show that the implementation of reforms aimed at the reduction of the prison population is not merely an administrative and judicial task. A multi-year interdepartmental reform commission should, therefore, be established in which judges, prosecutors, police and probation officers, together with representatives of social and educational administration, researchers, prepare a definite plan that pays considerable attention to emerging social processes. They should formulate their recommendations in light of practical experience, regularly backed up by research.

It must be said that even after the commencement of carefully prepared work and gradually accomplished reform, the prison population will not decrease significantly in the immediate future. It is to be expected that the structure of crime will continue to develop in an adverse manner. The amount of dangerous and organised crime will increase. The established patterns of crime allow us to conclude that the presence of groups alienated from society and living in the periphery, may increase in the long-term. The effect of institutional systems of crime prevention -social measures, educational reform and help rendered by spontaneous organisations- will, at best, be felt only in the coming decades. Crime may be halted only at a later date because of the increased cohesion of society attributable to the democratic reforms. The present government will either build further prisons or through reforms will contribute to the growth of modern civilisation.

References

Bárd, Károly (1987) Difficulties in the division of the punitative power, Budapest.

Dér, Mária (1989) The Probation service, Manuscript, Budapest.

Gönczöl, Katalin (1980) "The evaluation of personal circumstances during the application of the new Penal Code" in: Magyar Jog, vol.8.

Gönczöl, Katalin (1987) Typology of the recidivists, Budapest.

Gönczöl, Katalin (1987) Crime and Socio-policy, Budapest.
Gönczöl, Katalin (1988) Economy-crime-criminal policy, Valóság.
Gönczöl, Katalin (1989) Limits of the punitative power – its socio-political possibilities, Thesis Manuscript, Budapest.
Hacker, Ervin (1924) Introduction to the philosophy of the criminal law. Offprint from the 1923/1924. Almanach of the Miskolc Academy of Law, Pécs.
Kevezsi, Klára (1989) The forms of noncustodial punishment and the place, and role of the probation service in the Hungarian legal system and legal practice, Manuscript, Budapest.
Kabódi, Csaba (1989) Noncustodial Punishments and human rights with particular consideration to the obligations resulting from our international agreements, Manuscript, Budapest.
Nagy, Ferenc (1986) "About the overburdenness of the prisons", in: Belügyi Szemle, 12.
Pateva, Antal (1987) "Would this really be the solution?", in: Belügyi Szemle, 4, pp. 76-78.
Szabó, András (1987) "The criminal law of the reform, the reform of criminal law, in: Kriminológiai Közlemények, No. 26-27.
Szük, Lásló (1987) Short-term prison sentences, Publ. Jur. et. Pol. Miskolc.
Tavassy, Tibor and Antal Pateva (1988) "After-care for those released from prison sentence", in: Criminological and Criminalistic Studies, No. 25, Budapest, pp. 208-253.
Vabrik, Lásló (1989) The social adjustment of minors released from corrective institutions and prisons, Belügyi Szemle, No. 10.
Wenner, Margit (1988) "The situation of professional probation officers and their work in the structure of the court", in: Magyar Jog, No. 2.

Documents

1) Directive No. 12 of the Supreme Court about the evaluation of the aggravating and mitigating circumstances in order to unify the practice of punishment. Bírósági Határozatok, 1977, February, p. 81.
2) No. V punitive authoritative ruling of the Supreme Court about suspended prison sentences and the period of probation. Bírósági Határozatok 1979, July, pp. 501-505.
3) No. 14 Directive of the Supreme Court about the evaluation of recidivism. Bírósági Határozatok, 1979, July, pp. 482-483.
4) Report on the sentencing practice of the independently implemented supplementary punishment instead of the principal punishment and the probation order. "Judicial Directorate of the Ministry of Justice 13.110/1982. (III.1) Manuscript.

5) Report on the investigation of the foundedness and edition of decisions in criminal cases. Judicial Directorate 31.106/1987. (III.1) Manuscript.
6) The main characteristics of the implementation of the legal consequence following prison sentence between 1985-1989. Manuscript, Budapest, 1989.

Crime and Control in China

He Bingsong

1 The Basic Situation of Crime After the Foundation of the People's Republic of China

The situation of crime after the founding of New China may be discussed in four periods.

1.1 1949 – 1956

In this seven-year period, China completed the socialist transformation of the ownership of the means of production. Table 1 indicates the dynamics of crime in this period. The fundamental characteristics of crime in this period were as follows:

1. Crime decreased significantly after the foundation of the People's Republic of China. Social order was reestablished after dramatic steps by the government. In these few years, China cleaned up many of its bandits and hooligans. It eliminated influences of underworld gangs and secret societies. The government also cleared away narcotics, prostitution,

Table 1: The Statistics of the Reported and Solved Criminal Cases in China from 1950 to 1956 (Not Including Economic Cases) in the Population

Year	Population (10,000 is a unit)	Number of Cases	Number of Cases Solved	Incidence of Cases Solved (%)	Incidence of criminal cases (for every 10,000 population)
1950	55,196	513,461	361,477	70.4	9.3
1951	56,300	332,741	258,207	77.6	5.9
1952	57,482	243,003	162,326	66.8	4.2
1953	58,796	292,308	130,077	44.5	5.0
1954	60,266	392,226	260,048	66.3	6.5
1955	61,465	325,829	192,565	59.1	5.3
1956	62,828	180,075	119,210	66.2	2.9

gambling, and other repulsive social crimes. As a consequence of these measures, the incidence of crime declined after 1956.

2. In the early period, counterrevolutionary crimes accounted for the majority of criminal cases. Between 1949 and 1953, the counterrevolutionary offenders made up 70 percent of the total number of people arrested. The significant resistance of the overthrown exploiting class precipitated a strong governmental reaction, thereby contributing to a significant share of total crime.

3. Larceny, arson, rape, murder, and robbery were the predominant nonpolitical offenses. For example, 139,826 larceny cases made up 77.5 percent of the total criminal cases, the less numerous were the other reported crimes in 1956 – 6,361 rape cases, 6,192 murder cases, 5,544 arson cases, and 1,129 robbery cases.

4. The majority of the economic crimes were committed by the capitalists who evaded or refused to pay taxes, engaged in speculation, stealing, deceiving and snatching of public property, and bribery. Some economic crimes were also committed by state officials, their offenses included improperly taking public property or accepting bribes.

5. Most of the offenders were the surviving dregs of the old society and the counterrevolutionaries. After 1956, the conditions began to change. The proportional contribution of workers, peasants, and state officials to the total offender population increased to 79.1 percent.

6. At this time, juveniles accounted for only 20 percent of the offender population.

1.2 1957 – 1965

During this period, China began to construct a more total socialist society. The crime data from this period are contained in table 2. Its primary features are as follows:

1. The incidence of crime obviously dropped. The incidence of cases was only 3.9 per 10,000 every year. In some rural areas, no cases occurred in successive years. During this time the social order and the general mood of society were good due to the founding of New China. Even from 1959 to 1961, when the Chinese economic situation became difficult and the living standard in China fell, the incidence of crime only rose slightly, an increase attributed to a rise in the number of larceny cases. The level of public security was still good.

2. The counterrevolutionary cases decreased significantly, but their number was still notable. The most frequent ordinary criminal offense was larceny. Murder, rape, robbery, arson, and other serious criminal offenses also contributed a significant proportion.

Table 2: The Statistics of the Registered and Solved Criminal Cases in China from 1957 to 1965 (Not Including Economic Cases) in the Population

Year	Population (10,000 is a unit)	Number of Cases	Number of Cases Solved	Incidence of Cases Solved (%)	Incidence of criminal cases (for every 10,000 population)
1957	64,653	298,031	211,304	70.9	4.6
1958	65,994	211,068	197,771	93.7	3.2
1959	67,207	210,025	204,774	97.5	3.1
1960	66,207	222,734	201,574	90.5	4.4
1961	65,859	421,934	330,796	78.4	6.4
1962	67,295	324,639	240,882	74.2	4.8
1963	69,172	251,226	199,473	79.4	3.6
1964	70,499	251,352	167,514	77.8	3.1
1965	72,538	216,125	142,378	65.9	3.0

3. Juvenile delinquency began to rise accounting for 30 percent of the total criminal offenses, and this percentage was larger in the big and medium-sized cities. For example, in Beijing, Shanghai, Tietsin and three other big cities, juvenile delinquents accounted for 38 percent of the total offenders in 1965.

4. The incidence of crime in the big and medium-sized cities was higher than that of the rural areas and it was higher in the coastal areas than in the interior.

1.3 1966 – 1976

In this period, owing to the long-term and over-all "left" erroneous line and the sabotage carried out by the Lin Biao and Jian Qing counterrevolutionary groups, the Chinese national economy suffered heavy losses. The people of China fell into civil strife. The legal system and the social order were sabotaged. The offenders reacted violently. Commission rates for murder, rape, hooliganism, theft, robbery and other violent crimes reached significant proportions. From 1966 to 1972, the work of the judicial organs was thrown into confusion. Statistics could not be compiled and this affected the compilation of criminal statistics. The limited data of this period, 1972 through 1976, is summarized in table 3.

Table 3: The Statistics of the Reported and Solved Criminal Cases in China by the Public Security Organs from 1972 to 1976 (Not Including Economic Cases)

Year	Population (10,000 is a unit)	Number of Cases	Number of Cases Solved	Incidence of Cases Solved (%)	Incidence of criminal cases (for every 10,000 population)
1972	86,727	402,573	218,228	54.2	4.6
1973	88,761	535,820	340,641	63.6	6.0
1974	90,409	516,419	337,322	65.3	5.7
1975	91,970	475,432	327,345	68.9	5.2
1976	93,261	488,813	317,258	64.9	5.2

Notes:
Owing to the special historical condition, these figures do not reflect the real situation of crime.

1.4 1977 – 1989

In this period, a new socialist perspective was introduced. It sought to modernize China and opened up the society. The incidence of crime during this period is summarized in table 4. The main characteristics of crime in this period were as follows:

1. The criminal offenses were becoming more serious day by day; violent criminal offenses became more pronounced. The average incidence of crime during this period was 6.3 for every ten thousand, much higher than the rate (i.e., 3.9 for every ten thousand) recorded during the second period. Besides the period of the Great Cultural Revolution, crime rates were at their highest during this time period. The crime rate increased, especially in the last two years when it rose at an even more rapid rate. According to the incomplete statistical data, in 1989 the number of criminal cases exceeded a million and were estimated at more than a million and several hundred thousands. The most notable increase in criminality occurred among the most serious offenses. According to the statistical data, the number of the serious criminal cases in the entire country was 50,000 in 1980, 67,000 in 1981, 64,000 in 1982, 80,000 in 1985, 97,000 in 1986, 123,000 in 1987, 205,000 in 1988, and 366,000 in 1989, increasing by 500 percent over 1982. Among all categories of criminality, serious theft, murder, intentional injury, rape, robbery, explosion and other violent offenses were the most frequent.

Examining the nature of the serious offender population yields the following data for arrests approved by the procurators. In 1989, throughout the country, 70,882 serious thieves were arrested, an increase of 82.9

Table 4: The Statistics of the Reported and Solved Criminal Cases in China by the Public Security Organs in the whole Country from 1977 to 1988 (Not Including Economic Cases)

Year	Population (10,000 is a unit)	Number of Cases	Number of Cases Solved	Incidence of Cases Solved (%)	Incidence of criminal cases (for every 10,000 population)
1977	94,524	548,415	400,132	73.0	5.8
1978	95,809	535,698	385,782	72.0	5.6
1979	97,092	636,222	439,696	69.1	6.6
1980	98,256	757,104	538,425	71.1	7.7
1981	99,622	890,281	650,874	73.1	8.9
1982	101,117	748,476	579,039	77.4	7.4
1983	102,071	610,478	431,292	70.6	6.0
1984	103,051	514,369	395,735	76.0	5.0
1985	104,231	542,005	427,009	78.8	5.2
1986	105,214	547,115	433,315	79.2	5.2
1987	105,636	570,439	463,766	81.3	5.4
1988	109,614	827,706	626,573	75.7	7.5

percent over 1988. The number of murderers arrested was 13,743, a 14-percent increase. The number of persons charged with injury to another was 27,727, a 10.5-percent increase, and the number of offenders who set off explosives was 580, an increase of 34.9 percent. Furthermore, the number of arrested rapists was 32,820, a 9-percent increase. Their crimes were dangerous and caused serious loss to the state or loss of life and property. According to the statistical data, in 1989, criminal offenses caused death to 23,000 victims and loss of property estimated at three thousand million yuan.

2. The number of youthful offenders increased rapidly and offenders tended to be younger and more violent. According to the statistical data, crime by youths made up 60.2 percent of total crime in 1983, 63.3 percent in 1984, 71.4 percent in 1985, 72.4 percent in 1986, and 74.3 percent in 1987. In 1989, the courts in China convicted 293,435 juvenile delinquents, an increase of 36.4 percent over 1988. Each year the age of juvenile delinquents became younger and younger. Juvenile delinquents under 18 years of age accounted for 29.8 percent of all criminals in China in 1982, 26 percent in 1983, 32.3 percent in 1984, 43.4 percent in 1985, and 30.8 percent in 1986.

Juvenile delinquency was characterized by use of violence. According to the statistical data, the juvenile delinquents comprised 41.16 percent of murderers, robbers, and rapists in China in 1985, and 41.01 percent of the total number in 1986. The number of juvenile delinquents committing violent offenses increased, especially among those between the ages of 14 and 18. Between 1985 and 1986, the number of murders, robberies, arson, explosions, forcible rape, and other violent offenses committed by juveniles age 14 to 18 doubled.

3. The number of fleeing criminals has increased over the years. Attempts to wipe out criminal gangs were unsuccessful and they developed quickly. According to the statistical data, the number of fleeing criminals captured throughout the country increased annually. In 1985, a 9.67-percent increase was recorded over the previous year. In 1986, the equivalent figure was 10.7 percent; in 1987 it was 20.5 percent, at which time it reached a total of 55,880. The number held constant in 1988.

Criminal gangs have been a serious component of the Chinese crime problem. In the campaign to strike severe blows at these criminal offenders, more than 197,000 criminal gangs of various types were wiped out. Moreover, more than 70,000 members of these gangs were arrested and most of those arrested were convicted. After the campaign, criminal gangs arose again. In 1987, 3,600 criminal gangs were captured throughout the country with a total membership of 138,000 which represents a 20 percent increase over 1986 in both the criminal gangs and their members. In 1989, the criminal gangs captured in China increased by 70.9 percent over 1988 and their membership increased by 65.4 percent. These gangs carried out serious criminal activities such as larceny, robbery, deception, smuggling, selling narcotics, selling guns, kidnapping, and selling of women, etc. Many of these crimes were committed in succession. Hence, they caused heavy damage to the society. Some criminal gangs colluded with secret societies while others were evolving into secret societies. The criminal gangs have become the most serious and outstanding problem of the present criminal justice system.

4. The various economic offenses were more serious in this period than in any other period. See table 5.

In recent years, economic offenses have increased. According to the statistical data, in 1989 the courts at different levels accepted and heard 76,758 cases of serious economic offenses such as corruption, taking bribes, speculation, smuggling, deception, evading taxes and refusing to pay taxes, etc. These offenses increased by 39 percent over 1988. In 1989, the courts convicted 105,818 economic offenders, an increase of 41 percent over 1988. The most prominent economic offenses were corruption and bribery.

From 1982 through 1988, 218,000 cases of economic crime were filed and investigated. This total included 127,000 corruption cases and 31,000

Table 5: The Number of Registered and Investigated Economic Cases Accepted and Heard by the Procuratocy in 1979-1988

Year	**1979**	**1980**	**1981**	**1982**	**1983**	**1984**	**1985**	**1986**	**1987**	**1988**
Number of Cases Considered	784	15,964	45,247	60,129	44,428	43,000	52,729	81,591	59,405	66,300
Number of Registered and Solved Cases	806	10,031	16,934	33,000	23,516	22,000	28,000	49,557	30,965	31,200

cases of bribery. These two offense categories numbered 160,000, making up 73.4 percent of all economic cases.

In 1989, all the procurators in China accepted 116,763 corruption and bribery cases and filed and investigated 58,926 corruption and bribery cases. This represented an increase of 160 percent and 180 percent, respectively, over 1988. In 1988, the filed and investigated corruption and bribery cases concerning more than ten thousand yuan numbered 2,943. Cases involving more than 100,000 to 200,000 yuan totaled 122 whereas cases involving 500,000 to 1,000,000 yuan numbered only 22. Only 15 cases concerned more than 1,000,000 yuan. The largest sum amounted to 3,240,000 yuan. In 1989, the filed and investigated cases of corruption and taking bribes valued at more than 10,000 yuan amounted to 13,057, an increase of 340 percent over 1988.

5. In recent years, a significant increase was noted in two offense categories: state officials accused of abusing their offices and of violating the law and of infringing upon the rights of citizens. According to the statistical data, in 1988 12,000 cases were filed and investigated in these two categories, an increase of 10.2 percent over 1988. In 1989, these cases totaled 15,298, an increase of 27.4 percent over 1988.

6. Ugly social phenomena such as kidnapping and selling persons, spreading obscene articles, engaging in prostitution and visiting prostitutes, drug taking and trafficking in narcotics, etc., were prohibited, but could not be wiped out. These crimes spread quickly. The crimes of kidnapping and selling persons began to increase in 1985. In 1986, 1,258 cases of kidnapping and selling persons were filed by all the public security organs in China. This represented a 160 percent increase over 1985. In 1989, 11,086 offenders were arrested for kidnapping and selling persons in China, several times the total for 1986.

The activities of engaging in prostitution and visiting prostitutes has spread quickly in recent years. From 1987 to 1988, the number of people arrested for engaging in prostitution and visiting prostitutes totaled 118,9000, an increase of 130 percent over the 51,000 people arrested between 1984 and 1985.

Gambling also spread very quickly. In 1987, 173,000 gambling cases were discovered and dealt with in China. In 1988, these cases totaled 215,000, a 24.8 percent increase. In the four months from October 1989 to February 1990, 155,000 gambling cases were discovered and dealt with by the authorities. This was only 10 percent less than the total number of gambling cases discovered and dealt with in the entire year of 1987.

The crimes of making, dealing in and spreading obscene articles were struck at for many years, but their growth could not be checked. Such activities became the "yellow scourge" in reality as well as in name. In 1989, a campaign of wiping out obscene articles was launched throughout the country. According to the incomplete statistical data, 30,000,000 volumes of banned books and periodicals and 40,000 tapes and video tapes were seized and more than 1,800 offenders were investigated and dealt with within two months.

Although the scourge of opium was wiped out in China in 1953, the activities of using and trafficking in narcotics has gained ground in recent years. Taking advantage of a Chinese open door policy, some international narcotics traffickers smuggled in collusion with criminal elements in China, transported narcotics through China to other countries. In 1989, the Chinese public security organs tracked down 547 cases of narcotics trafficking, an increase of 100 percent over 1988. They seized 169 kilograms of opium and 488 kilograms of heroin and arrested 749 Chinese and foreign offenders who dealt in narcotics. In the beginning of 1990, China tracked down a big case of drug trafficking and arrested 10 traffickers in Burma, Hong Kong and Macao, seizing 221.3 kilograms of heroin and assets of 1,600,000 yuan. At the same time, drug use became more serious. For example, more than ten thousand drug addicts were identified in De-Hong-Zhou, Yunnan Province.

7. The number of counterrevolutionary cases decreased, but their seriousness increased. According to the incomplete statistical figures, from the end of 1983 to the end of 1987, the counterrevolutionary cases which were heard by the courts in China numbered only 4,756 amounting to only 0.28 percent of all criminal cases during this period. In 1987, the number of counter-revolutionary cases declined to only 271, making up 0.09 percent of the total criminal cases for the year. The harmfulness of their activities, however, could not be underestimated. Reactionary forces in neighboring and other foreign countries continuously sent agents to China to carry out sabotage and subversion. In 1989, the counter-revolutionary riot in Beijing is indicative of their harmfulness.

The simultaneous changes in the economics, politics, culture, and morality of society were reflected in the changing characteristics of criminality. There are historical and external causes for Chinese crime, but the deepest roots of crime lie in the innate conditions of material and cultural life of the socialist society. A contradiction exists between production relations and productive forces as well as between the superstructure and economic base. It runs counter to the basic standpoint of historical materialism that the cause of crime is not intrinsic to a socialist society and is a consequence of a historical legacy.

Since the Third Plenary Session of the Eleventh Central Committee of the Communist Party of China, crime has increased in quantity and diversity. These changes reflect the profound political, economic, cultural, and moral changes caused by the reform and open door policy of China. The politico-economic structure of China and its ideology and the superstructure of China are in a state of change. The entire social structure is relatively unstable. The control of the government over society has weakened. Hence, in this stage of reform, the increase in crime is inevitable and can not be halted.

I do not agree with the theory of synchronism which prevails in criminological circles. It affirms that the increase in crime in China will synchronize with the development of economics. This standpoint is incomplete for two reasons: first, the development of economics is not the sole cause of the noted increase in crime because the crime increase is also determined by politics, cultural, and moral changes accompanying reforms. Second, the development of economics and the productive forces plays not only a negative role in arousing crime, but also an active role in controlling crime. The decreasing and withering away of crime are, in the final analysis, conditioned by the development of the productive forces.

I believe that the increase of crime is inevitable in this reform period, but it does not mean that the growth will continue unabated. When the reform period concludes, the socialist system will be improved. The new politico-economic structure created as a result of the reforms will be in a relatively stable state for a period of considerable time. To a great extent, the decadent ideologies of feudalism and capitalism will be overcome. The socialist ideology will occupy a stable, dominant position. The socialist productive forces and the national economy will develop. The living standard and the quality of life will also rise. In this historical stage, crime will decrease. In the light of the future historical development of the whole human society, the well-directed productive forces and economic prosperity will inevitably lead to a highly developed civilization. The law of the development of history determines that under these conditions crime will gradually decrease and eventually be eliminated.

2 Prevention and Control of Crime in China

In any society, fluctuations in crime rates depend on the result of the interaction of factors promoting and controlling crime. When the former is stronger than the latter, the incidence will rise; when the reverse occurs, it will drop. Therefore, the main point of preventing and controlling crime is to weaken the factors promoting crime and to strengthen factors controlling crime.

Crime is the comprehensive reflection of various negative factors of a society. There are political, economic, cultural, moral and many social reasons contributing to the occurrence of crime. Therefore, China has adopted a policy of comprehensive management for preventing and controlling crime. The leadership of the Communist Party of China mobilizes the whole society to fight crime. The masses work with the special organs to conduct a coordinated policy based on attacking and preventing crime. The policy uses political, economic, legal, cultural, educational, administrative, and other means to eliminate the factors and conditions which contribute to crime commission. The object of this policy is to control, prevent, and decrease crime and to reform most offenders.

Since the founding of New China, the prevention and control of crime has been successful. For forty years, the average incidence of crime has been only 5.9 crimes for every ten thousand. Higher rates of crime were noted in 1950 and 1981 when 9.3 crimes 8.9 crimes for every ten thousand were recorded respectively in those years. As compared with crime rates of other countries, the incidence of crime in China is comparatively low. For example, in the United States it was 503.1 for every ten thousand to 595 for every ten thousand in the eighties. In West Germany, it was 291.4 for every ten thousand in 1983 and 675.5 for every ten thousand in 1984. In the Soviet Union, it was about 65 for every ten thousand in recent years. The different incidence of crime in these countries is a result of political, economic, cultural, and moral differences, as well as the differential impact of crime prevention and control strategies. China's experience in preventing and controlling crime can be summarized as follows: A focused legal policy that strikes at serious criminal activity is the core of a comprehensive crime policy.

Only by directly striking at the criminals can we effectively end the sabotage carried out by criminal offenders. Such action also deters those planning to commit crimes and causes criminals to surrender. By mobilizing the masses and supporting them in the struggle with criminal offenders, we can control crime more effectively. If criminal acts are not combatted with sufficient severity, criminal offenders will be encouraged to commit crime. Their criminality will be more blatant, and the masses' enthusiasm for the struggle against crime will be diminished. The incidence of crime will, consequently, rise significantly. This insight has been proven by both the positive and the negative experiences of China's fight with crime over the last forty years. For instance, in the primary period of the founding of New China, the counterrevolutionary activities were rampant. In 1950, the incidence of that crime amounted to 9.3 for every ten thousand. One of the main reasons was that the government did not severely strike at the counterrevolutionaries. It made the mistake of leniency towards criminal offenders. In 1978, there was again a rapid rise criminal cases. The incidence of crime rose from 5.6 to 8.9 cases for every ten thousand citizens. The main cause was that the fight against offenders was not severe enough. On the contrary, when the struggle against crime intensified throughout the country, the offenders were restrained and the incidence of crime dropped. This indicates that the increase in crime may at least be halted. For example, after the government cracked down on serious criminal activities in 1983, more than 120,000 criminals surrendered themselves. Mass citizen cooperation resulted in information on several thousand criminals and more than 1,700,000 tips to aid in solving cases. The incidence of crime dropped from 7.4 to 5 for every ten thousand and continued at that lower level in successive years. The people gained a sense of security. They claimed, "the country is prosperous and the people live in peace."

Of course, the control of criminal offenders requires a feasible policy. China always adopts a criminal policy that combines punishment with leniency towards certain categories of criminal offenders. The concrete policy analyses the different types of criminals and differentiates among offenders. It deals severely with the minority and attempts to educate the majority. It tries to mobilize the masses to isolate criminals. This proves to be the most effective strategy to prevent crime and decrease criminality. The criminal offenders are always given different treatments. Severe punishment is inflicted on the following criminals: any criminal whose criminal act is serious and causes serious harm, any leader of a criminal group, any criminal who commits a serious crime and causes heavy damage under aggravating circumstances, and any criminal who refuses to repent and continues to do evil. Lenient treatment is given to the following groups of criminals: any criminal whose criminal act is comparatively minor and whose harmfulness is not major, any criminal who surrenders himself and performs meritorious services, and the ordinary members of a criminal group. A consistent policy of striking hard at the most serious and incorrigible criminals and winning over and educating the majority needs to be maintained. Illustrative of this policy is the action of the Supreme People's Court and the Supreme People's Procuracy on August 15, 1989, which announced that "Any Offender Who Commits Corruption, Bribery, Speculation or Other Crime Shall Surrender Himself and Confess By the Prescribed Time." The Notice prescribed that any criminal who surrendered himself and confessed or performed meritorious services might be treated leniently, punished lightly, receive a reduced sentence or even be exempted from criminal punishment. As a result, within the prescribed time 36,711 criminals surrendered and the masses provided 133,765 tips. The impact of the criminal policy and its validity are indicated by these statistics. Chinese crime policy is based on the belief that mercy to the criminals means cruelty to the people. As a result of this doctrine, it does not consider the circumstances of a crime or the trends in criminality in different periods. Nor does it analyse the concrete situation of a criminal. Experience has shown that deviation from this doctrine connives and encourages the sabotage of criminals and causes serious damage to the interests of the state and the people.

2.1 Reforming and Rehabilitating Criminals Through Labor

Improvement of the reform process is an important element in the comprehensive management of the crime problem.

The success of society's efforts to reform criminals determines not only the incidence of new crime, but also the total incidence of crime. Criminals who have not been reformed and are released, corrode the society and corrupt social values. They lure, abet and even organize others to commit crime. Therefore, China has consistently devoted attention to the reform of criminals and has formulated principles and policy in order to achieve effective results.

Since the founding of New China, incarcerated offenders have reformed criminals and become law-abiding citizens after their release. Hence, the incidence of new crime in China is comparatively low. For example, the incidence of recidivism within three years after release was 10.47 percent in 1982, 6.16 percent in 1983 and 6.76 in 1984. The number of repeat offenders as compared with the total number of criminals is also small. According to the statistics of the public security organs, the proportion was 2.14 percent in 1982, 2.48 percent in 1983, 2.9 percent in 1984, 3.07 percent in 1985 3.19 percent in 1986, 3.07 percent in 1987. The success in reforming criminals in China is a factor contributing to the low incidence of crime.

There are two basic methods for reforming criminals in China. One is through institutions such as prisons where individuals are reformed through labor. The second are work locations where individuals are reformed through labor among members of their collective. The majority of the offenders are sentenced to the former. The second type applies to all criminals who are put in society to be reformed by the masses. They are organized by the public security organs and operate at enterprises and institutions. Offenders who are sentenced to supervision, release on parole, or whose sentence is suspended, are subject to this penalty within the community.

For the criminals being reformed in the reform-through-labor institutions, China adopts a policy of "reform first, production second". At these institutions, they integrate productive labor with political, cultural and technical education. The principle of socialist humanism is applied to the criminals. This policy helps promote the reform of criminals.

Anyone who commits a minor illegal act and is not subject to criminal punishment, is subject to an administrative measure of compulsory education and rehabilitation through labor. Those subject to this sanction are offenders who live in big or medium-sized cities or those who have fled from rural areas to cities, railway lines, factories and mines and committed crimes there. The committee of management of rehabilitation leads the work of rehabilitation through labor. The term of rehabilitation through labor is from one to three years and may be prolonged for one year if necessary. During the term, the offender receiving rehabilitation through labor shall, under severe management, receive political, cultural and technical education, take part in productive labor organized by the place of rehabilitation and may receive suitable payment. Since 1956, China's policy of work of rehabilitation through labor has educated and saved the lives of tens of thousands of people who took a wrong step in life. Turning these offenders into law-abiding citizens has assumed an important role in the prevention and control of crime.

2.2 The Prevention of Law Violation and Crime Commission is a Central Component of the Crime Control Strategy

The prevention of crime requires a reduction in the negative factors inducing crime, as well as the deterrence of crime commission. It is a positive, active, and most fundamental measure to control crime. It is more important than the two other links previously discussed, i.e., striking at and reforming. In the light of our experience, it is especially necessary to pay attention to the following problems:

1. In order to prevent crime, we must think strategically. We must develop and utilize political, economical, legal, cultural, educational and administrative measures to resolve the important crime problems.

As previously stated, the deepest roots of crime are the contradictions that exist in society. Therefore, the fundamental method of preventing and controlling crime is to execute social reforms and push social development forward. The criminal problem in a given period is a reflection of the society's weaknesses or its negative factors. Through social reform, these weaknesses can be eliminated or conquered so as to prevent and control crime. For instance, corruption and bribery are important criminal problems which affect the overall social situation. These problems occur because of shortcomings in the political-economic structure of China. Particularly relevant are the lack of a supervisory mechanism to oversee the political authority and the imperfections of the democratic and legal system. Therefore, the problem of corruption and bribery should be placed in the general context of the overall reform of the political structure and the expectation of honest performance of official duties.

Only by carrying out a comprehensive strategy by means of political, economic, legal, and cultural measures can we effectively prevent and even wipe out crimes such as bribery of officials and the pursuit of private gain by officials. For instance, at the end of 1989, the struggle to eliminate six crimes (i.e., prostitution and visiting prostitutes; making, dealing in and spreading obscene articles; kidnapping and selling women and children; private growing, smoking, trafficking and transporting of narcotics; assembling people to gamble; and gaining money by cheating with the help of superstition) was enacted throughout the country. These six offenses are also an important component of the crime problem. Only by a general reform strategy and the development of a cultured civilization and legal system can such crimes be prevented and reduced.

2. The policy integrates the work of special organs and the masses to prevent crime. To promote this objective, the following measures are taken:

a. Strengthen the work of the committes of public order and guard to enhance public order and organize a forcible network to control crime. Early in 1951, the committees of public order and public guard, mass autonomous organizations, were established in the urban and rural areas. Through these committees, the Party and the governments mobilize the masses to maintain public order. Such committees now total 800,000; their membership is approximately 9,000,000. Such committees can be found in all organizations, enterprises, and institutions in urban and rural areas. Under the leadership of local governments and public security organs, these committees organize the masses to maintain social order, prevent crime and struggle with illegal acts and accidents endangering the public order. In addition, organizations of joint defence consisting of about 2,000,000 people have been established throughout the country. They include guard teams at factories and villages. They constitute a necessary auxiliary force to help the public security organs maintain public order. As the economy developed, the following organizations were established: specialized public order organizations in the streets, busy sections of towns, fairs and markets; professional public order organizations of various trade outlets, such as hotels, taxis, etc.; and public order organizations of individual traders. Thus, a well-developed and varied public order system existed at many levels and a comprehensive network to curb crime was established. To mobilize and organize the masses to defend the socialist revolution and the process of socialist construction, it is necessary to maintain a stable social order, prevent, control, and strike at law violations and crime commission. The mass joint defence organizations play an important role in educating and saving juneniles from delinquency.

b. To control crime, it is essential to establish mass mediation organizations, strengthen mediation work, decrease quarrels, and prevent crime commission caused by the intensification of conflicts. Many crimes, such serious violent offenses such as murder, explosion and arson, often occur because people's quarrels are not settled reasonably. In some districts, the quarrels result in 80 percent of murder cases. The importance of mediation work is obvious.

In order to strengthen mediation work, the people's mediation committees were established in the beginning of the 1950's. Under the leadership of the government and the people's courts, the people's mediation committee mediates people's quarrels, strengthens people's unity, and educates the masses for the socialist morality. At present, there are 980,000 people's mediation committees and 6,200,000 mediators in China. They can be found in streets, factories, mines and the rural areas. They mediate more than 6,000,000 quarrels every year. Thus, they prevent the intensification of conflicts, curb crime and maintain public order. According to the incomplete statistics, between 1981 and 1986 the mediation committees in China prevented 367,000 deaths which might have occurred through 1985 and prevented 73,132 such cases in 1986.

2.3 Organizing the Masses to Help and Educate the Juvenile Delinquents

So-called social help and education rely on the mass force and the support of every circle; ie the society helps and educates the young people who perform light illegal acts but when applicable, criminal penalty or administrative sanctions are not or who are released after serving their sentences or after receiving rehabilitation through labor to conquer evil thought and habit and to resolve their living, dwelling, learning, employment, marriage and other actual problems. This measure creates a good social environment for them and prevents them from committing crime again. The method is varied and different according to the different object, e.g., heart-to-heart talk, learning in class, visiting, tourism, competitions, physical training, etc. In recent years, many factories, enterprises, schools and rural areas have established various social help and educational organizations. They have educated and saved a large number of misguided young people, making them beneficial to the society. These organizations have made great contributions to the society.

3 Strengthening the Construction of Spiritual Civilization, Educating the People for Political Thought, Morality and Legal System, Enhancing the People's Quality and Cultivating the Good Moral Look of the Society

Everybody knows that crime is closely related with social consciousness (including individual and colonial). In the past ten years, the cause of the increase in crime is that the construction of the spiritual civilization has been lost. The free flood of the backward and outworn thought and culture corrode the socialist morality and the mood of society. In 1983, Deng Xiao-peng pointed out, "Many things account for the occurrence of the various negative phenomena of social, evil trends, criminal activities and the anti-socialist hostilities of some people at present. Of course, all of them cannot be attributed to the confusion of the ideological line. But the effect caused by the confusion of the ideological line cannot be underestimated." Therefore, to strengthen the construction of the spiritual civilization and to increase and eliminate the outworn social consciousness are the important ways of preventing and controlling crime. Thus, it is necessary to educate the people for political thought, socialist morality and socialist legal system in various ways and various types. In 1985, China began to spread legal knowledge among the people. It is a very good way of educating the people for legal knowledge. Among the seven hundred fifty million people who should learn legal knowledge, five hundred million people have learned legal knowledge. By the end of 1990, the task of the spreading of legal knowledge will be completed. The people who have learned legal knowledge have strengthened their sense of abiding and enforcing law. The work of spreading legal knowledge plays an important role in preventing and controlling crime.

In the face of the rising of the incidence of crime, some hold that the increase in crime is the cost which must be paid by any country in the course of the development of economy and therefore, it is impossible to control crime. This pessimistic view is undesirable. The rising of the incidence of crime in China does not mean that China is unable to control crime. Only by adopting the correct criminal policy and vigorous measures to control crime, conquering the shortcomings in the respect of politics, economics, culture and morality, and decreasing and wiping out the negative factors and influences, can we prevent and control the vicious rising crime and maintain a relatively low level to its rising. In respect of the control of crime, any pessimistic view and idea of inertia are useless.

Part IV
The Interpretative Turn: A Second Look

Power, Individualism and the Sanctity of Human Life: Development of Criminality and Punishment in Four Cultures

Hans Haferkamp
Hyacinthe Ellis

1 Development of Criminality and Punishment in Four Cultures

Criminality in Western Europe (W.-Europe), the U.S.A., Japan and Jamaica has evolved along very different lines over the last 25 years. In the countries which represent W.-Europe in this essay, namely the Federal Republic of Germany, England and Wales and France, a large increase in criminality, measured in offence rates, can be seen from police crime statistics. In the U.S.A., looking at officially registered crime, we find a similar increase. In contrast to this, we find that in Japan, criminality is on the decrease, even in the major cities. In Jamaica, an exponent of developing countries, criminality increased slowly in two waves from the year of independence in 1962 to 1967 and from 1973 to 1979. In 1984 the rate was not very different from that in 1978. Detailed research shows slight oscillation in all four cultural areas, which does not, however, change the overall trends.

The evolution of rates for total crimes reported to the police contrast with the development in rates for special offences. An analysis shows that in Jamaica the rates for serious offences against persons are high, and that they increased substantially during the time considered. While the rate for murder and manslaughter decreased in Japan from 2,8 in 1960 to 1,4 in 1980 and also in France from 5,9 (1960) to 3,9 (1980), it increased over the same period from 2,2 to 4,4 in the Federal Republic of Germany (FRG), from 1,1 to 1,6 in England and Wales, and from 5,1 to 10,0 in the U.S.A.(Dörmann 1984, p.415). But the highest rates for murder and manslaughter are to be found in Jamaica. The rates for robbery increased in the U.S.A. in the 10 year period from 180,7 (1972) to 250,6 (1981). But in Jamaica they rose from 135 to 210.[1]

In contrast, the rates for robbery in W.-Europe and Japan are comparatively low. Analyzing property crimes (burglary, breaking and entering and theft) we find high and increasing crime rates in the U.S.A. and W.-Europe, moderate rates in Jamaica, and stable or decreasing rates in Japan.

Given the results of research on the 'dark figure' of crime, it can be stated that the offence rates are certainly wrong. In reality, the spread of criminality in the U.S.A. and W.-Europe, in Japan, and Jamaica even more so, is larger than official crime figures show. Jamaica even more so, is larger than official crime figures show. Nevertheless, research shows that offence rates describe the general trend reliably; criminality in W.-Europe and the U.S.A. has increased in general. Whereas in Jamaica rates for serious crimes against persons have risen considerably[2] and in Japan, rates have decreased slightly or at least remained stable. These developments cannot be explained by changes in the population structure, for example by the percentage increase of 20-29 year-olds, the age-group, which commits the most crimes.

If we look at the development of penal law and its application in the FRG we arrive at the conclusion that the "Zug zur Milde" (trend towards mitigation) proposed by Franz Exner in 1931 for the German Reich is valid for the development of criminal legislation. It applies in the FRG today, in spite of certain movements in the opposite direction which, however, do not deny the overall trend (Haferkamp 1984). Mitigation in defining offences is not all that obvious, but it is especially and immediately visible in sanctions. The mitigation in sentences is evident in the abolition of the death penalty and prisons involving hard labour, the decrease in short-term prison sentences and the rise in probationary sentences and fines. Conflicting examples such as an increase in the density of police and other examples of social control, the few new criminal offences and the even fewer instances of harsher penalisation are mere deviations from the "trend towards mitigation".

In England and Wales, we can see a tendency towards mitigation, albeit not quite as strong as in the FRG. A few offences have been decriminalised, among the most notable is male homosexuality. In 1965 in

---

1 All Jamaican data from: National Planning Agency: Economic and Social Survey. Every year forthcoming

2 In the case of Jamaica dark-figure research is lacking. But all experts on crime development in Jamaica agree, that the dark-figure in all Jamaican statistics – for example also for unemployment statistics – is for reasons of lacking systematic data collection very high. This is especially true for crime statistics.

England and Wales, the death penalty was to all intents and purposes, struck off the list of penal sanctions. At present it is only applicable in the case of high treason, and even then, if at all, only in time of war. A change in the application of the penal code is conspicuous in other sorts of crime. We can observe a trend away from prison sentences (Lewis 1984, p. 5).[3] Finally the development of penalisation and social control in France is also marked by a tendency towards mitigation, but this is by far the weakest, compared to England and Wales and the FRG.

The tendency to mitigation in the U.S.A. is not one of constant progress but a strongly oscillating one. Criminal legislation and the application of the penal code moved from a high level of control in 1972 to one of considerable mitigation only to return steadily to a tightening-up of sanctions. The development of punishment in the U.S.A. shows more oscillation around a long-term trend. At the moment there is a tightening-up in criminal law, especially in its application. Outward signs of this continuous movement away from mitigation, also ascertainable in the long-term in the U.S.A., are 1. the reintroduction of the death penalty, 2. the rise in the number of prison inmates, 3. the introduction of strictly controlled neoclassical punishment, and 4. new penalisation of behavioural patterns. Of these, the reintroduction of the death penalty stands out, if we recall that of all the large western democracies only the U.S.A. still proclaims and executes the death sentence.

In contrast to the tendency towards mitigation in W.-Europe and the oscillating movement towards more control in the U.S.A., Japan is a country where stability of social control is the main feature. In 1974 some new criminal acts were written into the criminal legislation. The death penalty is handed out but rarely carried out. In accordance with the Japanese penal code, a high proportion of sentences imposed consist of incarceration (Nakayama 1981, p. 139). The strength of social control also becomes clear if we call to mind the size and operation of the various institutions of social control. The density of police presence in Japan is greater than in W.-Europe or the U.S.A. On the other hand there are signs of mitigation in progress, but they are so few and far between as not to affect the picture of stable social control.

A contrasting situation existed in Jamaica, a country whose penal legislation is modeled on that of Great Britain, in the period 1962-1985. In spite of some mitigations, there has been stable control. Moreover, since 1974 there has been a general tendency to tightening-up of sanctions. A very striking point was the Gun Court Act of 1974 which contains more serious sanctions and restrictive criminal procedures in offences where

3 This is true until 1984. This changed very much under Thatcher and there was dramatic growth in the prison population.

guns are used (Ellis 1983). In the 23 years following Jamaican independence, the death penalty was imposed more frequently and the figures of those executed increased. In the Spring of 1985, 166 murder convicts were on death row.[4] This is more than 7 death row inmates per 100,000 inhabitants, a rate that is more than ten times higher that of the U.S.A. with 1,400 murder convicts on death row, (and 249 million inhabitants). On the other hand, there was a marked decrease in the number and the rates of persons sentenced to prison in the period from 1970 to 1982. In contrast, the number and rates of prison inmates increased from 2.082 or 126 per 100,000 in 1962 to 3.355 or 150 per 100,000 in 1982. The police force also increased, consistent with the trend in W.-Europe.

In summary, we find that only in independent Jamaica did sanctions increase in the post-1974 period. In contrast, we have a trend towards mitigation in W.-Europe. The development of punishment in the U.S.A. and Japan lies between the described tendencies in Jamaica and W.-Europe – Japan for reasons of its stable control and the U.S.A. due to a strongly oscillating process.

2 Structural Properties of Modernity: The Levelling-Out of Power, Individualisation and the Sanctity of Life

How can we explain the differing development of criminality and punishment in the four cultures? Three of the processes of change in the course of modernity have, in varying degrees, developed differently. They are the three trends which typify the development of modernity:

- a trend of levelling-out of power;
- a trend to individualism;
- a trend of valuation of the sanctity of life.

2.1 Trend to the Levelling-Out of Power

Increasing rationalism in all areas of activity leads to a growth in achievement. It leads to improved results in the organization of work, administration, socialisation, and the establishment of a sense of purpose in life. But a precondition for these results is that the leaders at the top

4 See The Star, April 9th 1985, p.1

and those who undertake the work, have a willingness and capability for achievement and are successful in their tasks. For all the actors concerned, both above and below, there is often one unconsidered consequence of achievement -he who achieves becomes more important. As a consequence he is heeded and his suggestions, whishes and needs become influential. This is valid in many ways. At the top: anybody who can lead already has influence. Employers and party leaders, the initiators of social movements, church leaders, they all create areas of action where people can achieve. Those at the bottom of the pyramid of authority become indispensable in modern societies because large organisations are predicated on the division of labour. The central thesis is that those responsible for achievement had differing positions of authority. In modern societies, in the areas of industry, politics, public administration, and education the importance of achievement at the top grew less and less. At the same time, the relevance of achievement from below grew continually (Elias 1978, pp. 147-149).[5] A loss of influence and power at the top go hand in hand with a diminution in the level of achievement because those in power no longer achieve enough to demand obedience from those below. When the actors at the grass roots gain more power, they demand more participation. We see a varied demand for participation in modern societies which the political institutions cannot accommodate. At the top, claims to authority are being relinquished, but below, power and the wish to participate are increasing. Protest crops up more and more, even going so far as to be criminal, when the masses' desire for self-realisation leads to conflicts. This is certainly not to say that freedom of action leads regularly to criminality. Actors can also react quite differently to this situation. But if those involved believe themselves to be strong enough to achieve much coveted aims by by-passing norms, then as a result of calculation they may resort to criminal action.

In the face of growing protest and rising criminality, the leaders, by reason of their loss of power, react with policies of mitigation and the waiving of sanctions. This is a fact, in spite of all protests to the contrary, and in spite of all warnings of perceived repressive tendencies of the state that have been expressed by radical criminologists.

These trends have developed to varying degrees in the four cultures.

---

5 N. Elias' theses concerning the socialisation of the monopolisation of power. in: 1978, p. 147ff

2.1.1 The New Concept of Achievement in Key Industries, the Rise in Criminality and Mitigation of Punishment in W.-Europe

There is much evidence in W.-Europe societies that management at the top is declining importance. There is widespread discussion of the lack of initiative, the absence of leadership qualities and the narrow-mindedness and indecisiveness of employers and politicians at the top. There is no visible difference among the FRG, England and Wales and France. On the other hand, the achievements of the actors below are becoming more and more important in key industries. In the FRG, in the automobile, machine and chemical industries we can see a growing appreciation of qualifications and professional expertise. If the employer wants to modernise, then he has to offer his workforce something! That is why the workforce and its representatives demand a high price for their co-operation in the process of modernisation (Kern and Schumann 1984, p. 16). The strong position of the employees in the firm not only affects the political sphere but also has consequences for the private sphere and actions not visible to the public eye. The acquisition of enhanced power leads to a growth in freedom of action but this also leads to more conflicts in W.-European societies between the actors who make use of freedom of action and those who expect conformity. Actors who have gained power and exert it, engage in manoeuvres to increase their sphere of action. Conformity is not as compelling as before, deviance is on the increase.

The development of punishment can be explained by this visible loss of authority. When authority declines, the ability to sanction also decreases and mitigation occurs. The few cases where control is growing in W.-Europe point to attempts to defend authority. This applies only to a limited number of criminal laws and also to the spreading of social control. "The development of police forces and their expansion and re-organisation can be explained by major political instability and social unrest within the society" (Heiland 1984, p. 25). The development of criminality and punishment in W.-Europe can thus be explained by the sociology of authority.

2.1.2 The Regaining of Power and the Tightening of the Penal Law in the U.S.A.

Well-known characteristics of the U.S.A are the lack of a labor party and the lack of class consciousness. These result in a one of the world's lowest levels of participation (about 20%) in trade unions. A further structural characteristic is the relatively low level of political participation, despite a level of educational attainment superior to that of most other countries (Stack 1984, p. 230). The limited extent of political participation is reflected in the low percentage of voters at the elections (40 – 45% of the population), and minimal participation of poor people. Political participation is kept low by a two-party system where two parties do not differ very much, in contrast to the situation in Great Britain. In such a situation, political apathy is likely to be high. Another characteristic of the U.S.A. is the long standing racial problem which has not undergone any radical change in the last 30 years. Other important developments have taken place against this backdrop.

During the presidencies of Kennedy and Johnson, from 1960 to 1968, a policy of promoting participation was pursued strongly at the top and expressed most meaningfully in Johnson's concept of the "great society". At the grass roots this policy was accompanied by social unrest due, especially, to lasting racial discrimination in everyday life and the development of slums in parts of the cities. These features contradicted the president's declared aims. Moreover, this was a time of experimenting with new and sometimes deviant lifestyles. After 1968, a change of policy occurred when Nixon tried to regain power. After a typical delay of approximately four years, his policies took effect in the laws and budget. (The reason for this lag was that the previous administration had established policy and funding authorizations which were not immediately changeable). A further stabilisation of authority by Reagan succeeded due to economic recovery and the strengthening of America's military position. This change of policy also had a marked effect on everyday life.

Equally conspicuous is a growth in hierarchies in other areas. In the education system the principle of bringing children up under stricter discipline is more popular today in the U.S.A than in W.-European societies. If we take a look at the economic sector, we come across an equally marked hierarchy. In the key firms there is a very rigid pecking order and strict control of internal career advancement (Baron and Bielby 1984, p. 454). The emphasis on achievement in American industry is so pronounced, that there has only been a small decline in the importance of those at the top. In fact, since 1970 there has been a noted stabilisation of authority in industrial firms.

Examining the relationship between the development of authority structures and the development of criminality, we see that the surrendering of political authority that occurred through 1968 was accompanied by a constant rise in criminality. But criminality rose even in the following years when the power base of the leaders was improving. Only in a single year in Nixon's term, 1972, and a single year under Carter, 1977, did the Total Crime Index and the Property Crime Index fall. The change at the top of the authority pyramid did not have the expected effect on criminality. For this reason the development of criminality in the U.S.A cannot be explained by processes of change in authority.

In spite of rising criminality, in the 1960's and the beginning of the 1970's there were a series of libertarian decisions by the American Supreme Court (Cole 1981, p. 28), a result of the fact that the Liberals were in power in Washington. "Crime got easier, in part because punishment was milder. The rewards and status of hard work diminished" (Samuelson 1984, p.60). A sweeping change in the policy of punishment appeared after the Nixon administration began to win back power. War was declared on crime with the result that the number of those sentenced to prison rose, and the number of prison inmates increased since 1972. Both developments slackened off slightly under Carter, but still the numbers showed a rising tendency. "During the past 10 years the war on crime has become one of the major domestic policy efforts" (Cole, p. 28). Sanctions became more severe with later changes in the leading political ideology and with the growth of popular conservatism. The reintroduction of the death penalty should also be understood as an expression of the reassumption of power.

The U.S.A was going through a development which shows that it is not possible to engineer large jumps in social development consciously. Societies move like snails (Günter Grass). Kennedy and Johnson wanted the U.S.A to leap forward to more humanity and more equality. But the outcome was an artificial creation, the -"Great Society"-; which had no foundation in U.S society then, and would not have today either. It had to collapse if individual freedom was not to be laid low. From this viewpoint, the development of punishment in the U.S.A might be explained by an analysis of trends in power relations.

2.1.3 Defence of Authority, Stable Penal Law and Controlled Criminality in Japan

Japanese society is generally noted for its rigidly structured hierarchies. Within social groups one can see the almost unlimited operation of the seniority principle (Kühne and Miyazawa 1979, p. 99). Japan's economy was more or less destroyed, as a result of the war. The main condition for its reconstruction was the creation of an efficient industry and workable policies. A similar situation existed in the FRG and other W.-European societies after 1945. Japan's success in creating efficient industrial and political sub-systems was due to the strong position of the industrialists and politicians. Whereas the leaders of industry and politics in the FRG and the other W.-European countries could not maintain this position, in Japan it has been possible right up to the present day. In industry the many firms and businesses are organised in one hierarchy. We find the gigantic corporation at the top, and a number of small firms are sub-contractors, just as in the U.S.A. In general the 'better performance' of the

Japanese economy" (Tokunaga 1984, p. 25) is evident although even Japan did not remain untouched by the depression of the early 1980s.

There is also the commonly held opinion that the firms register a high level of achievement, at the top too, in contrast to W.-Europe. This is a long-term trend and is not just recently evident as in the U.S.A. All observers agree that the leaders of firms in Japan show an extraordinary degree of initiative in the search for new products and production methods (Tokunaga, p. XVI). They feel and accept responsibility for production to a greater extent than is found in W.-Europe or the U.S.A. At the same time, the "Great Old Ones" at the top of the firms cultivate the ethos of the patriarch. On the one hand they are able to demand obedience from below successfully, but they also have a large range of protective obligations towards those below. The authority relationships in Japan are marked by strong reciprocity of obedience and protection. In this way, Japanese firms, meaning its leadership, provide services for the workforce that W.-Europeans and North Americans find unbelievable. They share many of the social services found in W.-Europe, but there is also a system of extra services which encompasses extraordinary privileges, including membership of expensive clubs, and a wide range of leisure activities offered free or at bargain price. The leadership even takes pains to help employees with private problems. A serious work ethos, a commitment to work with the utmost care, a readiness to work overtime at any time, and a feeling of personal responsibility for the firm, are all conspicuous within the workforce (Kühne and Miyazawa, p. 95). Internally, there are also distinct ranks of workers and employees. There are also employment contracts for life. Because of these existing power relationships in the firm, there is far less participation than in W.-Europe. Unions exist but they are bound to the firms. "This fact undoubtedly has a profound influence on the behaviour and consciousness of trade unionists, who are mostly regular employees of big firms" (Tokunaga, p.IX). Their attitude is one of great cooperation.

In the education system teacher-pupil relationships are marked by obedience. "Obedience in Japan takes the form of total submission. Any criticism of or opposition to authority tends to be seen as heroism" (Nakane 1970, p. 103). In schools, the emphasis on achievement is pronounced. Admission exams are talked of in terms of "examination hell" or "examination war". The existence of hierarchies also affects the elementary school life. This is still – or especially – evident in speech patterns. Miyazawa informs us that, the greater the difference in hierarchical rank, the less one is allowed to articulate one's own will in discussion (Kühne and Miyazawa, p. 99).

It would not be an overstatement to suggest that criminal action is limited by the existing power structure. Metaphorically speaking, Japanese dependents are so enmeshed in hierarchical leadership structures and by a system of social control, that the road to criminality is blocked off. The slight criminality, compared to that of W.-Europe, is the result of the well developed system of primary and informal social control in Japanese society. In conclusion, the stable authority relationships in Japan appear to provide the explanation for the consistently low level of criminality in that society.

2.1.4 Civil Rights, Regaining Power and Increasing of Punishment in Jamaica

Jamaica become a sovereign state in 1962 after more than three hundred years of colonial domination by Britain. The transfer of authority from imperalist powers to local cadres was marked by a long period of social and political discontent. An incipient struggle ensued during which time the emergent middle class became a politically conscious force.

Agitation for constitutional reforms resulted in the formation of two major political parties: the Jamaican Labour Party (more social democratic and liberal in the European And North American sense) and the Peoples National Party (more socialist in the European sense). Over the years since Independence, the parties have held office alternately, attesting to not only the power but also the volatility of the masses. Jamaicans are serious about their rights to political participation. Turnout at the polls ranges between 70% and 80% except on two occasions (1967, 1972) when only 57% of registered voters exercised their rights. These occasions were marked by unprecedented political violence. The election year, 1967, was the beginning of a very violent era in Jamaica. Handguns were introduced and used indiscriminately to intimidate real or suspected political rivals. Gun violence has continued up to present time (minimised in the elections of 1989) but the earlier intimidating features and effects of political rivalry have subsequently diminished to a certain extent.

Independence in Jamaica was a milestone in the long search for full rights of citizenship, for social justice, and for a re-distribution of economic and political power. It heralded the questioning of norms, ideals and values. It was a time of political consciousness-raising and expectations were high. The reality is, however, that the poverty and social backwardness of the masses as a result of colonialism have persisted. There is a high level of clientelism (Stone 1983). Political favours are traded for continued support of a political incumbent.

The failure of both parties to assess the basic social and economic needs of the masses is attributable in a very general sense, to their adopted ideological positions. The Jamaica Labour Party, essentially conservative in political character is primarily supportive of the business and commercial sectors. Not entirely indifferent to mass needs, the party interprets development and progress in the narrow context of modernization. It itself creates greater material expectations on the part of the masses, a greater demand on government to fulfil these expectations, greater frustration when expectations are not met. Responses may be in the form of collective action or an increase in individual criminal behaviour. The latter has been the Jamaican experience.

The Peoples' National Party, from a neo-socialist position, tried to redress the unjustices against the deprived masses through the institutionalization of social welfare programmes designed to provide physical, social and psychological improvement in daily living. Such well-intentioned programmes are often far beyond the resources of Jamaica whose fragile economy is, from time to time, aggravated by the emigration of substantial numbers of middle and upper class entrepreneurs in the business and commercial sectors in search of greater prosperity.

In independent Jamaica, there was a loss of political authority because of the inability of the leadership to meet the economic needs of the masses. Criminality rose as the masses chose alternative, illegitimate and deviant routes to fulfill their needs.

During the decades of the 1960's and 1970's criminal deviance -especially violent crimes against the person- was met with strong sanctions and stepped-up police activities. The police were given free reign with the gun to discipline law-breakers. The gun court legislation authorised the indefinite detention of gun-wielders and their associates. On occassion, the army was enlisted to assist in crime-fighting. All this might be interpreted as the response of authorities to declining or lost state power. From here we might conclude that there is definitely a link between authority structure and crime -that a weak authority-structure will be associated with strong sanctions against criminal behaviour. On the other hand, we observe that during the 1970's there also were strong tendencies towards mitigation. The gun court legislation was amended to remove repressive penalties. The parole system was introduced and criminal justice procedures were reformed to keep young offenders (17-24 year-olds) out of prison. We also note a decline in rates of police activity (crimes cleared-up), conviction and imprisonment over time. This occured without change in the ever weak political authority. The level of crime, especially violent crime against the person, remains high.

The situation in Jamaica does not really compare with W.-Europe or the U.S.A. and is very different from that which obtains in Japan. Jamaica stands in sharp contrast to W.-Europe whose tendency oscillates depending on the incumbent political authority. In Jamaica, progressive sanctions – especially the abolition of capital punishment. In independent

Jamaica, political leaders operate from a position of economic powerlessness in the wake of increasing demands for social transformation.

2.2 The Trend to Individualisation

Many sociologists in W.-Europe and the U.S.A. see general universal tendencies towards the strengthening of mass culture and the loss of individuality. This swing from sociology to cultural criticism is a thoroughly noteworthy tradition with a list of strong adherents (Weber 1958, p.231). If we take an unprejudiced look at the development of modernity, then Toennies' (1912) pair of concepts "Gemeinschaft und Gesellschaft" which are otherwise considered obsolete, seem to be enlightening. According to this notion, instead of stronger ties in social units with modernity, we can expect more individuality because modernity is marked by a strong orientation towards individuality. A collective orientation would be expected from the traditional "Gemeinschaften".

If we establish a connection between the growth in achievement and influence of those subject to authority, then we might argue that individualism might also lead to lessened cooperation, dependence and conformity and to enhanced freedom of action. The latter might be expressed in the predominance of 'individual' and 'deviant' acts which are criminal. Conversely, the greater collective orientation of Gemeinschaften might promote conformity and, therefore, less deviance.

No doubt in W.-Europe, the U.S.A., Japan and Jamaica there are many noticeable aspects which Toennies describes as typical of "Gesellschaft". These cultures, however are essentially different regarding their representations of collective and individual orientation.

2.2.1 Competitive Individualism and the Rise in Criminality in W.-Europe, the U.S.A. and Jamaica

Observers agree that individualism is far less widespread in W.-Europe than in the U.S.A. But, as we have seen, the existing individualism in W.-Europe is central to an explanation of the development of criminality in that area.

Let us take a look at social control and the effects of the surviving collective orientation. The processes of mitigation described in the introduction lead without any doubt to a further weakening of social control and a further decrease in collective orientation. Therefore, they encourage the occurence of individual and not sub-culturally bound criminality. In conclusion, we find that the moderate individualism of W.-Europe leads to an intermediate result.

There is no question that the U.S.A., as Tocqueville already noticed in 1833, is distinguished by a very conspicuous "competitive individualism" (1956). Merton has convincingly demonstrated its importance for property crime as an expression of innovation (Merton 1957, p. 141). On the other hand, general social control through family, business and neighbourhood is very poorly developed. As we indicated earlier, the U.S.A. places an inordinate value on specialised control by law and order agencies in the fight against crime. Conservatives place their faith in the effects of punishment. They want to solve the problem of rising crime by deterrence. They try to control action with the formal mechanism of punishment. Punishment has a notably weaker effect on individualistic persons, than the impact of informal controls on individuals who are collectively orientated. The result is that extreme competitive individualism in the U.S.A. leads to higher criminality. Any attempt to solve the problem of rising criminality with strict formal social control is, therefore, futile.

2.2.2 The Group and Conformity in Japan

All sections of Japanese society are completely rationalised. At the same time independent freedom is very limited. Individualisation was and is a consequence of the 'Protestant Ethic', an ethic absent from Japanese society. There are not functional equivalents (Bendix and Roth 1971, pp. 192ff) because "in eastern religions and philosophies (...) the individual person in his uniqueness and independence is quite unknown or is judged negatively. Of the four main religions and pilosophies of Japanese history, Buddhism, Shinto, Taoism and Confucianism, not one emphasises the individual with his own soul-life, as is the custom in Christianity" (Kühne and Miyazawa, p. 91f). The ideal of self-realisation is unknown to the Japanese.

Three groups in particular should be stressed. Foremost, the business family with the boss at the top. Then there is the family clan organised according to the principle of seniority and is strictly hierarchical. The third important group is the neighbourhood founded on the traditional union of neighbours in closely-knit living conditions. This ebitomizes the total control of individuals by family, business and neighbourhood. The actor is surrounded by groups which check his inclinations to deviate from established expectations. De Maistre, Bonald, even Durkheim's concept of coherent society, are well illustrated by Japanese society.

If our thesis is correct that the levelling-out of power leads to protest against existing structures, this protest may assume either social or individual form. It can express itself in social protest movements or in individual deviance. But the latter hardly comes into question for the actors of Japanese society.

Criminal action is always a form of claiming or expressing individual freedom. The actor feels himself to be free and in a certain sense he is. He wants to act freely, exempt from restrictions. It is no mere coincidence that actors who act criminally often use the word "free" in describing what they have done (Haferkamp 1975). They feel strong and powerful enough to take on conflicts. They want to behave differently, they want to break out of the norm, they want to take something away from others or injure them. Whereas criminality in Jamaica, W.-Europe and the U.S.A. is egoistic in the sense of Durkheim's suicide typology, it is obviously quite different for the actors in Japanese society. They feel a sense of group-belonging and yearn for recognition by the group. Clifford thinks that the Japanese generally only sees himself through the eyes of others (1976, p. 8). We may add this from Mead's terms. The 'I' is missing next to the 'me'. The 'I' in its contest with the 'me' first created the American and Western European personality. The authority of the 'me' exerts an unbelievable pressure to conform. Japanese actors do not want to disgrace family, friends and colleagues.

Pressure to conform publicly has increased drastically with the modernisation of Japan, the development of the mass media and the publicity given to many previously unknown practices. Tight social control combined with effective mass communication produce new reactions to behaviour patterns which do not even have to be criminal in order to be highly problematic for the actors.

In a free society with little control, the situation is quite different. There deviance is widespread and criminality is normal. "If crime is the price of freedom, then we can see that it is a price the Japanese are not willing to pay" (Clifford, p. 8). Regarding Jamaica, the U.S.A. and W.-Europe on the other hand it would seem as if it is the price that will be paid in any case.

We arrive at the following thesis: the lack of a 'Protestant Ethic' and a spirit of individualism leads to low deviance and decreasing criminality in Japan. There, groups that continue to exercise strict social control along with the existence of a powerful mass media restrain individual actions.

2.3 The Trend of Valuation of Sanctity of Human Life

With the rise of neo-marxism in social sciences, the role of ideas and values is underrated in sociology. Perhaps the only exception was the enduring discussion of the Protestant Ethic and the accompanying idea of individuality. But there are other ideas or values which influence social actions strongly. Among them are ideas about criminal and punitive actions. A central value is the sanctity of life. It is a typical idea for modernity that did not exist previously in slave and feudal societies. The lives of slaves or bondsmen depended on the economic calculations of masters or the discretion of lords. In modern society, life is an absolute value, and injuring others is a crime. In some societies even the state has no right to kill. Since slavery and bondage were not abolished in the four cultures at the same time, it is assumed that each country will present a different estimation of the sanctity of life.

2.3.1 Anti-feudal Fights and Sanctity of Life

The idea of the sanctity of life emerged very early in the old World of W.-Europe. We find a similar situation in Japan. In W.-Europe, as well as in Japan, there was a struggle between dependents and feudal princes who, during the time of absolute governments, could preside over the lives of their subordinates. A dependents' goal in the struggles was for the greater protection of their lives against murderous attacks executed by the sovereigns of their representatives. In an era of rationalism, killing people at will became more and more the exception.[6] As a consequence, the death penalty for murder was first abolished in Europe. It is handed out with great reluctance in modern Japan. We think that the low murder rates in these cultures might be a result of the internalisation of values respecting the sanctity of life.

2.3.2 Late Consequences of Slavery: Low Valuation of Human Life by Criminals and the State

Over three hundred years of chattel slavery has desensitized the Jamaican population to interpersonal violence and devalued the sanctity of human life. This is reflected not only in the level of crimes against the person but also in the types of sanctions imposed by the State. The death penalty is still issued and increasingly, criminal offenders (and sometimes suspects) are being shot to death by the police. Explanations of low valuation of human life by Jamaicans reflect a history of socio-political and psychological violence, the hallmark of Jamaica's development from slavery to independence, as well as mass socialization into subcultural strategies for survival.

6 This refers to the post-World War II period.

2.3.3 Deep South, Murder and Execution of Death Penalty

The U.S.A. presents a contrasting picture of differences in ideology, life-styles and historical evolution between the North and the South. While the North was committed to Liberalism and placed a high value on the sanctity of life for all men, the South, because of its economic dependence on slave labour, only valued the lives of Southern whites -the slave was no more than a chattel.

The history of the South shows a pattern of gross abuses of individuals, particularly in the treatment of black prisoners. This was mitigated only by the intervention of the North. Since violence begets violence, it is not surprising that there was and still is in the South, much lack of respect for human life, evidence of which is the greater use of the death penalty (Glaser and Zeigler 1972, pp. 329-332) and of incarceration, than in other parts of the country recorded for the U.S.A. as a whole.

3 Conclusions

From our analyses of the four cultures discussed we conclude that the factors contributing to the development and control of criminality are:

- The levelling-out of power in W.-Europe;
- Competitive individualism in the U.S.A.;
- Group control in Japan;
- Political inefficacy, and devaluation of human life in Jamaica.

The rise in criminality in W.-Europe is the result of growing participation and moderate competitive individualism. The dominant tendency towards mitigation is a consequent of the loss of authority in that society. In the U.S.A., the extremely well-developed competitive individualism contributes to soaring criminality and negates the effects of low political participation which is hypothesized as a check on criminality. The increased use of punishment in the U.S.A. is a result of the successful defence of authority and reassertion and maintenance of power by political and industrial leaders. In Jamaica, the rise of criminality against the person is a consequence of the ineffective and sometimes manipulative actions of independent political actors and the devaluation of the sanctity of human life due to historical processes and adverse political experiences. Since gaining independence, developments in the political economy have stimulated, rationalized and reinforced violent responses among the dispossessed, their potential preys and their anxious controllers. The intensification of punitive control in the 1970's was a response to the loss of state economic power as well as an attempt by the authorities to secure political power. The pattern of crime and control portrays a low reverence for life.

The rise in criminality in W.-Europe and the U.S.A. is an unintended and unwelcome product of highly regarded economic and political processes, namely, the increase in opportunity for legitimate political participation, and a political liberalism that fosters excessive individualism. The rise of criminality in Jamaica is more accurately attributed to limited political maneuverability and a political libertinism that mitigates unfulfilled economic expectations. These attributes tend towards greater freedom of individual action, including greater freedom to opt for deviance and criminal behaviour.

Greater political hegemony, authoritarian control and the lack of competitive individualism yield less freedom of action, greater conformity and reduced levels of crime in Japan. On the other hand, the successful defence of authority must be seen in terms of the strong feeling of solidarity – of being part of a group – among members of the Japanese society. This latter fact also leads to strict social control and further curbing of criminality.

References

Baron, J.N. and Bielby, W.T (1984)"The Organization of Work in a Segmented Economy", in: American Sociological Review, vol. 49.

Bendix R. and Roth, G. (1971) Scholarship and Partisanship: Essays on Max Weber, Berkeley, Los Angeles, London.

Clifford, W. (1976) Crime Control in Japan, Lexington.

Cole, G.F. (1981) "United States of America", in: Major Criminal Justice Systems, George F. Cole, St.J. Frankowski and M.G. Gertz eds., Beverly Hills and London.

Dörmann, Uwe (1984) "Interpolstatistik: Kein wahrer Spiegel der tatsächlichen Kriminalitätsbelastung", in: Kriminalistik, 8 – 9.

Elias, N. (1978) Über den Prozeß der Zivilisation, vol. 2, Frankfurt/M..

Ellis, H.M. (1983) "Public Policy and Societal Reaction: A Review of Social and Political Factors surrounding the Legislation against Gun Crimes in Jamaica". Paper presented at the IXth International Congress in Vienna.

Exner, F. (1931) Studien über die Strafzumessungspraxis der deutschen Gerichte, Leipzig.
Glaser, D. and M.S. Zeigler (1972) "The Use of the Death Penalty V. Outrage at Murderer", in: Readings in Criminology, P. Wickman and P. Whitten eds., pp. 329-332.
Haferkamp, H. (1975) Kriminelle Karrieren. Handlungstheorie, Teilnehmende Beobachtung und Soziologie krimineller Prozesse, Reinbek bei Hamburg.
Haferkamp, H. (1984) Change in Power and the Explanation of the Contradictions of Deviance and Conformity, Toleration and Control. Paper presented at the 1984 Annual Meeting of the Society for the Study of Social Problems in San Antonio.
Heiland, H.-G. (1984) "Economic Crises and Crime: Comparative Analysis", Manuscript for the 4th Meeting of the Select Committee of Experts on Economic Crises and Crime, Bremen, December 3rd and 4th.
Kern, H. and M. Schumann (1984) "Industriearbeit im Umbruch-Versuch einer Voraussage", in: Soziologisches Forschungsinstitut Göttingen, Mitteilungen 10/November.
Kühne, H.-H. and K. Miyazawa (1979) Kriminalität und Kriminalitätsbekämpfung in Japan, Wiesbaden.
Lewis,C. G. (1984) England and Wales – The relationship between Crime, Economic Factors and Social Control from 1951 to 1983. Manuscript for the 4th Meeting of the Select Committee of Experts on the Economic Crisis and Crime, Bremen, December 3rd and 4th.
Merton, R.K. (1957) Social Theory and Social Structure, New York.
Nakane, C. (1970) Japanese Society, London.
Nakayama, K. (1981) "Japan", in: Major Criminal Justice Systems, G.F. Cole, St. J. Frankowski and M.G. Gertz eds., Beverly Hills and London.
Samuelson, R.J. (1984) "Escaping the Poverty Trap", in: Newsweek, September 10th.
Stack, S. (1984) "Income Inequality and Property Crime. A Cross-National Analysis of Relative Deprivation Theory", in: Criminology, vol. 22.
Stone, Carl (1983) Democracy and Clientelism in Jamaica, Institute of Social and Economic Research, University of the West Indies, Jamaica.
Tocqueville, A. de (1956) Democracy in America, New York.
Tönnies, F. (1912) Gemeinschaft und Gesellschaft. Grundbegriffe der reinen Soziologie, Berlin.
Tokunaga, S. (1984) "Preface", in: Industrial Relations in Transition. The Cases of Japan and the Federal Republic of Germany, Tokunaga, S. and Bergmann, J. (eds.), Tokyo and Frankfurt.
Tokunaga, S. (1984) "The Structure of the Japanese Labour Market", in: Industrial Relations in Transition. The Cases of Japan and the Federal

Republic of Germany, Tokunaga, S. and Bergmann, J. eds., Tokyo and Frankfurt.
Weber, M. (1958) Gesammelte politische Schriften, Tübingen.

Abbreviations

AG	Amtsgericht (=County or Regional Court)
B.A.	Bachelor of Arts
BGH	Bundesgerichtshof (=Federal Court of Justice)
DISIP	Political Police in Venezuela
Dr.	Doctor
etc.	and so on
ed.	editor
eds.	editors
e.g.	for example
EGStGB	Ergänzungsgesetz zum Strafgesetzbuch (Supplement to the Penal Law)
esp.	especial(ly)
et al.	and elsewhere/other things/others
figs.	figures
FRG	Federal Republic of Germany
GDR	German Democratic Republic
GNP	Gross National Product
i.e.	that is
I.P.C.	Indian Penal Code
LG	Landgericht (= District or Local Court)
LL.D.	Doctor of Laws
M.A.	Master of Arts
MRI	Ministerio de Relaciones Anteriores
M. Sc.	Master of Science
N	Nigerian Dollar
NCRB	National Crime Records Bureau
NCS	National Crime Survey
n.d.	no date or not dated
No.	number
OCEI	Oficina Central des Estadística e Informática
OLG	Oberlandesgericht (=Higher Land or Local Court)
op. cit.	in the work cited
OSR	Opportunity Standardized Rate
p.	page
Ph.D.	Doctor of Philosophy
pp.	pages
PTJ	Judicial Police in Venezuela
Rs.	ind. Rupies
StRG	Gesetz zur Reform des Strafrechts

UCR	Uniform Crime Report
U.K.	United Kingdom
USA or U.S.	United States of America
VIP	very important person
vol.	volume
vs.	against
W.-Europe	Western Europe

Notes on Contributors

He Bingsong is a Professor of Law and Director of the Teaching and Research Section of Criminal Law of the China University of Political Science and Law. His correspondance address is China University of Political Science and Law, 41 Xue Yuan Road, Beijing, China.

Christopher Birkbeck received his Ph.D. in Criminology from the University of Wales (U.K.) in 1981. He is Assistant Professor of Sociology at the University of New Mexico and Associate Professor of Criminology at the Universidad de Los Andes, Venezuela. He is currently studying the situational aspects of crime and preparing a monograph on crime in Venezuela. His correspondance address is: The University of New Mexico, Department of Sociology, Albuquerque, NM 87131.

Hyacinthe Ellis is a Lecturer in Criminology and Social Psychology at the University of the West Indies, Department of Sociology and Social Work. She received her B.A. in Sociology & Government from University of Hull (England), her Diploma in Public & Social Administration from the Oxford University, her M.Sc. in Sociology from University of the West Indies and Ph.D. from University of Bremen. Much of her published work has been Government Reports. She has published articles on Crime and Violence. Her correspondence address is: University of the West Indies, Department of Sociology and Social Work, Mona Campus, Kingston 7, Jamaica W.I.

Katalin Gönczöl is Professor of Criminology at the Eötvös University, Budapest. She has done extensive research on violent crime in Hungary, typology of recidivists, criminal policy in practice and social reproduction of crime and has published numerous books and articles on these and other criminological topics. She is Vice-president of the Scientific Advisory Board of the International Centre of Comparative Clinical Criminology, Secretary General of the Hungarian Association of Criminology and Deputy Secretary General of the Directory Board of the International Society of Criminology. Her correspondence address is: Eötvös University, 1364 Budapest, Egyetem Tér 1-3, Hungary.

Hans Haferkamp studied Sociology, Economics, Statistics, social education and social work. Dr. in Bielefeld 1972. 1974 - 1987 Professor of Sociology at the University of Bremen. Recent main publications in criminology: Kriminelle Karrieren-Handlungstheorie, Teilnehmende Beobachtung und Soziologie krimineller Prozesse (1975); Herrschaft und

Strafrecht (1980); Soziologie der Herrschaft (1983); Wohlfahrtsstaat und seine Politik des Strafens (1990).

Hans-Günther Heiland holds a Dr. in sociology from the University of Bremen and is currently lecturer of sociology and criminology at the University of Bremen. He is author of Wohlstand und Diebstahl (1983) and Economic crisis and crime (1985) with Thierry Godefroy, Hans Haferkamp, Ragnar Hauge and Christopher Lewis. His published articles have appeared in Kriminologisches Journal, Kriminalsoziologische Bibliografie and Monatsschrift für Kriminologie und Strafrechtsreform. Correspondence address: Universität Bremen, Fachbereich 8/ Soziologie, Postfach 330 440, 2800 Bremen 33

Matti Joutsen is the Director of the European United Nations regional institute for crime prevention and control (HEUNI). He holds a LL.D. in criminal law from the University of Helsinki, where he currently holds the position of docent in criminal policy. Previously, he was a criminologist at the Finnish National Research Institute of Legal Policy, and served briefly as lower court judge. Dr. Joutsen has published many research reports, monographs and articles on juvenile delinquency, victims of crime, the structure and operation of the criminal justice system, general criminal policy and international cooperation, and on criminal law. His correspondence address is: HEUNI, POB 34, SF-00931 Helsinki

Hisao Katoh is Professor of criminal law and criminology at Keio University, Tokyo. He holds degrees from the Graduate School of Osaka and Keio University (PhD) and has been a visiting professor at the University of Munich (1984/85), University of Bremen (1987). He has received the fellowship of Alexander von Humboldt. His research interests focus on problems of criminal policy, principles of criminal procedure, penal policy and criminal sanctions. He is author of many books, reports and articles. His present principal area of research is organized crime. His correspondence address is: 15-45 Mita, 2-chome, Minato-ku, Tokyo-108, Japan

Olufunmilayo Oloruntimehin is Reader in the Department of Sociology and Anthropology, Obafemi Awolowo University Ile-Ife, Nigeria. She teaches and carries out research in Sociology, Criminology and Sociology of Law. She is author of many papers and a member of the International Sociological Association. Her correspondence adress is: Obafemi Awolowo University, Department of Sociology and Anthropology, Ile-Ife, Nigeria.

Lothar Reuter holds the Chair of Penal Law and Procedural Law at the Friedrich-Schiller-University, Jena. Among his 110 publications is Kommentare zum Strafgesetzbuch (1979), Nach der Strafe (1987) with Käupl and Strafrecht der DDR (1988). Correspondence address: Friedrich-Schiller Universität Jena, Sektion Staats- und Rechtswissenschaft, 6900 Jena, Schillerstr. 1, UHH, 23.OG.

R. S. Shrivastava is Associate Professor and Chairman at the University of Jodhpur, India, Department of Sociology. He holds a Ph.D. in sociology from the University of Jodhpur. He has published many articles on crime, imprisonment and control in India, social work and drug abuse. He is a member of the Research Committee on Deviance and Control, International Sociological Association. His correspondence adress is: University of Jodhpur, Department of Sociology, 10. Central School Scheme, Jodhpur 342 001, India.

Louise I. Shelley is Chair and Professor in the Department of Justice, Law and Society and also a professor in the School of International Service at the American University. She received her B.A. from Cornell University, her M.A. in Criminology and Ph.D. in sociology from the University of Pennsylvania. She is author of Crime and Modernization and Lawyers in Soviet Work Life as well as numerous articles and book chapters. She has received many fellowships including the Guggenheim, NEH and Fulbright. Correspondence address: The American University, Department of Justice, Law & Society, 4400 Massachusetts Avenue, N.W., Washington, D.C. 20016

Index

Bei Fragen zur Produktsicherheit wenden Sie sich bitte an:
If you have any questions regarding product safety,
please contact:

Walter de Gruyter GmbH
Genthiner Straße 13
10785 Berlin
productsafety@degruyterbrill.com